THE CHRONICLE OF THE CZECHS

Cosmas of Prague

THE CHRONICLE
OF THE CZECHS

*Translated with an introduction and notes
by Lisa Wolverton*

The Catholic University of America Press
Washington, D.C.

The paper used in this publication meets the minimum requirements of
American National Standards for Information Science—Permanence of
Paper for Printed Library Materials, ANSI Z39.48-1984.
∞

Library of Congress Cataloging-in-Publication Data
Cosmas, of Prague, 1045?–1125.
  [Chronica Boemorum. English]
  The chronicle of the Czechs / by Cosmas of Prague ; translated with
an introduction and notes by Lisa Wolverton.
      p. cm. — (Medieval texts in translation)
  Includes bibliographical references and index.
   ISBN 978-0-8132-1570-9 (pbk. : alk. paper)   1. Bohemia (Czech
Republic)—History—To 1526.   I. Wolverton, Lisa.   II. Title.
III. Series.
   DB2081.C67134 2008
   943.71′021—dc22
                                                2008032128

For Margot and Jing

CONTENTS

LIST OF MAPS, FIGURES, AND TABLES

ACKNOWLEDGMENTS

I undertook this as my "baby book" but was forced to complete it under unexpected, and frankly unjust, duress. Thus, while I still dedicate it to my girls, I owe a deep debt to the friends who came through in the crunch so selflessly. John Van Engen, indefatigable and ever generous, read the first draft of the entire translation and much else besides, even at the expense of his own work. Jonathan Lyon donated his expertise to identify the German noblemen Cosmas mentions. Rachel Koopmans's insights helped hone the Introduction, as did input from Barbara Corrado Pope and Erin Rowe. Tom Noble shepherded the volume into his series with enthusiasm and sympathy for the constraints imposed upon the project from outside. The unflinching support of my History Department colleagues in Eugene kept my spirits up. I can only hope that this volume lives up to the faith that all these kind, smart people placed in it, and in me, at a juncture critical to both.

At an earlier, more leisurely stage of the project, Tyler Fall worked up preliminary translations of many chapters and thus helped get the translation truly under way. I must also thank Jitka Sonková and the students in her Slavic folklore class at the University of Iowa; they read the first eight chapters of Book 1 in an early draft and provided helpful feedback on the translation's accessibility. The readers for the Press, especially Piotr Gorecki, offered detailed comments that were of great help to the final editorial revision. Steve McEntee produced the beautiful maps.

Many years ago now, Daniel Sheerin taught me to read Latin, coached me through Cosmas for the first time, and encouraged me to undertake a translation someday. I will be glad if he is now chuckling at Cosmas's pretensions as much as I remember him doing then.

Ian McNeely, my inseparable companion in all things, helped with the babies, the book, and everything else. To say the very least, I thank him.

MAP I. Central Europe

MAP 2. The Czech Lands

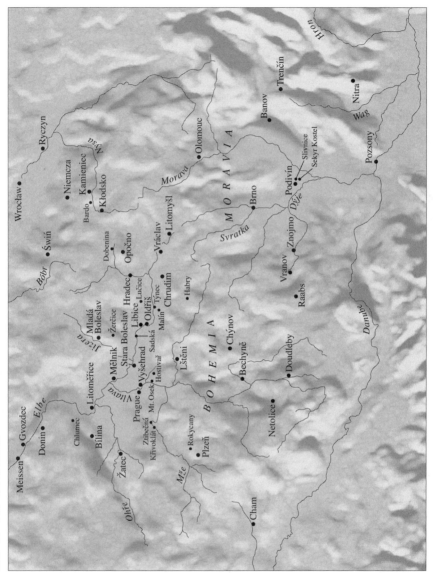

MAP 3. Central Bohemia

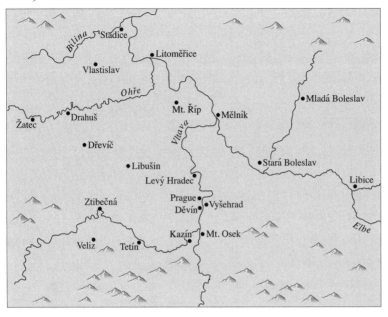

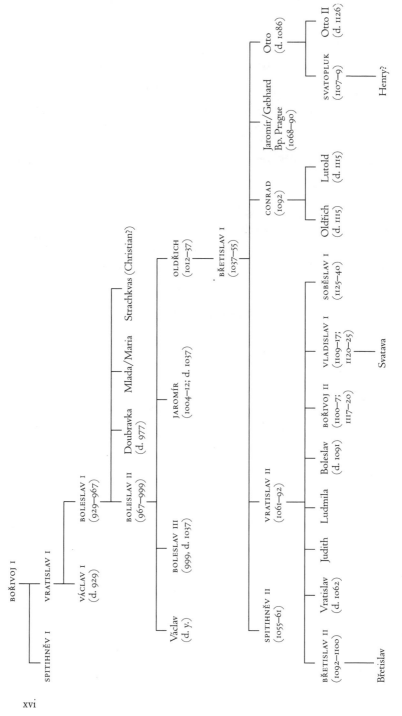

FIGURE 1. Přemyslid Genealogy (in accordance with the *Chronicle*)

BOŘIVOJ I

VRATISLAV I

SPITIHNĚV I

VÁCLAV I
(d. 929)

BOLESLAV I
(929–967)

BOLESLAV II
(967–999)

Doubravka
(d. 977)

Mlada/Maria

Strachkvas (Christian?)

Václav
(d. y.)

BOLESLAV III
(999, d. 1037)

JAROMÍR
(1004–12; d. 1037)

OLDŘICH
(1012–37)

BŘETISLAV I
(1037–55)

SPITIHNĚV II
(1055–61)

VRATISLAV II
(1061–92)

CONRAD
(1092)

Jaromír/Gebhard
Bp. Prague
(1068–90)

Otto
(d. 1086)

BŘETISLAV II
(1092–1100)

Vratislav
(d. 1062)

Judith

Ludmila

Boleslav
(d. 1091)

BOŘIVOJ II
(1100–7;
1117–20)

VLADISLAV I
(1109–17;
1120–25)

SOBĚSLAV I
(1125–40)

Oldřich
(d. 1115)

Lutold
(d. 1115)

SVATOPLUK
(1107–9)

Otto II
(d. 1126)

Břetislav

Svatava

Henry?

Note: CAPITALS indicate dukes of Bohemia, with reign dates in parentheses.

xvi

TABLE 1. Přemyslid Dukes of Bohemia

Bořivoj I	(ca. 894?)	Břetislav I	(1037–55)
Spitihněv I	(?)	Spitihněv II	(1055–61)
Vratislav I	(?)	Vratislav II	(1061–92; king after 1086)
St. Václav I	(?–929)	Conrad	(1092)
Boleslav I	(929–67)	Břetislav II	(1092–1100)
Boleslav II	(967–99)	Bořivoj II	(1100–1107; 1117–20)
Boleslav III	(999–1004)	Svatopluk	(1107–9)
Jaromír	(1004–12)	Vladislav I	(1109–17; 1120–25)
Oldřich	(1012–37)	Soběslav I	(1125–40)

TABLE 2. Bishops of Prague and Olomouc

Prague		Olomouc	
Thietmar	(973–82)		
Adalbert	(982–97)		
Thieddag	(998–1017)		
Ekkehard	(1017–23)		
Izzo	(1023–30)		
Severus	(1030–67)	John I	(?–1086)
Jaromír/Gebhard	(1068–90)	Vecel	(1086?–92?)
Cosmas	(1091–98)	Andrew I	(1092–96)
Hermann	(1099–1122)	Henry I	(?)
		Peter I	(?)
		John II	(1104–26)
Meinhard	(1122–34)	Henry Zdík	(1126–50)

INTRODUCTION

INTRODUCTION

Sometime before 1120 an elderly Czech cleric sat down to write a Latin history of his land and people. Frustrated by the civil conflicts that had dominated the previous two decades, he decided to give his contemporaries an account of their past that might inspire them to better conduct in the future. He knew this would not make him popular: "men in present times," he comments, "do nothing good themselves and so refuse to believe the good deeds they hear of others."[1] But however difficult it might be to describe the deeds of men yet living, he found that the past beyond recent memory could be impossible to recover at all. Still, Cosmas (c. 1045–1125), dean of the cathedral church in Prague, was committed to reporting the truth, so far as he was able. A man of literary erudition, considerable rhetorical skill, and a knack for storytelling, he was equally keen to demonstrate those gifts to a younger generation of local intellectuals. The work he wrote, which he himself called a *Chronica Boemorum*, or *Chronicle of the Czechs*, is pretentious and political, uneven and inspiring, capacious and markedly focused. It seeks to define the Czechs as a nation through history, compel them to think about their political culture, and urge reform, justice, and responsibility. One outcome: Cosmas would become the first Slavic historian of a Slavic people.[2]

1. 3.49.
2. The anonymous *Deeds of the Polish Princes*, written at almost the exact same time as the *Chronicle of the Czechs*, was composed by a foreign monk (probably from St.-Giles in Provence) at the court of Duke Bolesław III. *Gesta principum polonorum/Deeds of the Princes of the Poles*, trans. Paul W. Knoll and Frank Schaer (Budapest: Central European University Press, 2003).

The chronicle begins with the origins of the Czechs in a mythic age and concludes with the author's own death in October 1125. It is divided into three books of nearly equal length that together present a chronological history of the Czech Lands (Bohemia and Moravia) over more than 250 years. Cosmas mainly reports the deeds of their rulers, dukes of Bohemia drawn from a single dynasty, the Přemyslids, originating in pre-Christian times. A parallel theme explores the history of the bishopric of Prague—Cosmas's own institutional home. Although chiefly interested in political events and concerned almost exclusively with Bohemian and Moravian, rather than broader European, developments, Cosmas nevertheless includes a wide array of historical information and anecdotes. Scholars and students will find rich material here on almost every subject: saints, religious practice, Christianization, ecclesiastical institutions, miracles; social and gender relations; geography and fable; money, urban development, and political administration; battles won and lost; relations with neighboring rulers; the status of Jews and other minorities; and much more.

The Chronicle of the Czechs is also notable for its style, combining an almost arcane classicism with immediately accessible mininarratives, erudite citations with naturalistic scenes and characters, proverbial sayings both folksy and learned. Thoughtful and self-conscious about the historian's task, Cosmas was an adept Latinist, well versed in rhetoric and sophisticated literary techniques. The product of one of the best schools of his day, Liège, he exemplifies the education and literary style associated with late eleventh-century cathedral schools.[3] Cosmas interweaves biblical and Roman authorities to create a text that nevertheless stands as a genuine original, a refraction of his own distinctive voice. He treats historical sources— whether oral tales, hagiographic texts, earlier chronicles, or other lists and documents preserved at the cathedral in Prague—as the

---

3. For a useful introduction to the intellectual life of the eleventh-century cathedral schools (though it omits discussion of Cosmas or of historiography), see C. Stephen Jaeger, *Envy of Angels: Cathedral Schools and Social Ideals in Medieval Europe, 950–1200* (Philadelphia: University of Pennsylvania Press, 2000).

raw material for his own rendering of the past. Unlike many other medieval historians, Cosmas was no mere compiler, whether of literary quotations or historical data. As a consequence, *The Chronicle of the Czechs* is a lively, immensely readable story, one filled with wordplay, irony, and layered meanings.

This engaging history stands as virtually the *only* source for early Bohemia, making it the foundation for subsequent Czech history, medieval or modern.[4] All historical scholarship on eleventh- and twelfth-century Czech Lands rests heavily, if not exclusively, on the words of Cosmas. His shadow looms as large in the Czech historical tradition as Bede's does in the English.[5] His influence on Czech literary culture has also been profound and lasting: the pre-Christian myths in particular form a ubiquitous substratum of national (and nationalist) art in every medium, from opera, to murals, to "folk tales" for adults and children.[6] Whatever his original intentions, Cosmas's history would indisputably shape the consciousness of his nation for more than seven centuries. For all

4. From the first mid-twelfth-century continuations (see n. 30 below), to its fourteenth-century recasting as a vernacular poem by "Dalimil," through the birth of modern Czech history by František Palacký, through the standard turn-of-the-century survey by Václav Novotný, to my own recent work. See *Staročeská kronika tak řečeného Dalimila*, ed. Jiří Daňhelka, Karel Hádek, Bohuslav Havránek, and Naděžda Kvítová, 3 vols. (Prague: Academia, 1988); Franz Palacky, *Geschichte von Böhmen: Grösstentheils nach Urkunden und Handschriften*, vol. 1 (Prague: In Commission bei Kronberger und Říwnac, 1836); Václav Novotný, *České dějiny*, vol. 1, parts 1–2 (Prague: J. Laichter, 1912–13); Lisa Wolverton, *Hastening Toward Prague: Power and Society in the Medieval Czech Lands* (Philadelphia: University of Pennsylvania Press, 2001).

5. The only book-length studies of the chronicle are both by Dušan Třeštík: *Kosmas* (Prague: Svobodné slovo, 1966), and *Kosmova Kronika: Studie k počátkům českého dějepisectví a politického myšlení* (Prague: Academia, 1968).

6. On the transformation of Libuše through the ages, for instance, see František Graus, "Kněžna Libuše—od podstavy báje k národnímu symbolu," *Československý časopis historický* 17 (1969): 817–44. For this reason, the legends are by far the most studied aspect of Cosmas's chronicle. The scholarly literature, in both Czech and Polish, is too large to summarize here. See the most recent book by Dušan Třeštík, *Mýty kmene čechů* (Prague: Lidové Noviny, 2003), for a full bibliography. In the English-language scholarship, Patrick Geary treats them briefly in *Women at the Beginning* (Princeton: Princeton University Press, 2006), 34–42.

these reasons, *The Chronicle of the Czechs* occupies an incomparable place in the medieval history of central Europe.

The Chronicle of the Czechs

The *Chronica Boemorum* is a Latin text by a Christian cleric. Cosmas was thoroughly educated—steeped, even—in Latin: in the liturgical recitation of the Latin Bible and in the study of Latin grammar and the canonical "school-texts" of Roman antiquity. In this he was little different from contemporary authors elsewhere in Catholic Europe, all endeavoring to read, write, and work in a language other than their native tongue. Cosmas's Latin varies considerably in difficulty and in tone: occasionally laconic, more often verbose, dramatic if rarely pompous, sometimes sarcastic, ironic, or amusing. He draws heavily on his ancient favorites and the Bible in a way that stops just short of being mannered; instead, he makes their words resonate as his own. His work exhibits a unique style, a strong authorial voice, and not a few idiosyncrasies.

Book 1 is thoroughly preoccupied with origins: of the Czech people's connection to their land; of ducal rule and of the Přemyslid dynasty; of their capital at Prague; of Christianity in Bohemia, its martyrs and institutions; of good governance and bad; of foreign and domestic enmities. For Cosmas this is the distant past, murky and uncertain, an age of legend, hagiography, and half-documented history. Book 1 ends with the enthronement of Duke Břetislav I in 1037, a decade before Cosmas himself was born. There was much he simply did not, or could not, know: thus many years are left blank, and some of what he reports is garbled and confused by comparison with other non-Bohemian sources available to historians today.[7] Still, in Book 1, not only the legends at its outset but many of the scenes, speeches, and set pieces in its second half

7. Especially for the late tenth and early eleventh centuries, by comparison with Thietmar of Merseburg. Thietmar of Merseburg, *Ottonian Germany: The* Chronicon *of Thietmar of Merseburg*, trans. David A. Warner (Manchester: Manchester University Press, 2001).

are masterpieces of historical—and rhetorical—writing. The period beyond living memory, the age of tales, was a malleable one, and Cosmas availed himself of that flexibility to shape historical memory to the ends of his own narrative. Book 1 sets the tone for the *Chronicle of the Czechs* as a whole, establishing a style, key themes, and a clear narrative trajectory for all that follows.

Book 2 opens with a hero of almost mythic proportions, Duke Břetislav I. But its chief subject is conflict and cooperation: between the church and the ruler, and between brothers. The main events include Břetislav's successful invasion of southern Poland, the promulgation of laws promoting Christian mores, and the transfer of Saint Adalbert's relics from Gniezno to Prague; a dramatic fight with Emperor Henry III over the spoils from this raid; Břetislav's establishment of a rule of succession and the enthronement of his eldest son, Spitihněv, portrayed as a great patron of the see of Prague; the accession, after Spitihněv's early death, of his brother Vratislav and the life-long rivalry between him and his other brothers, Conrad, Otto, and Jaromír; Jaromír's appointment as bishop of Prague, Vratislav's establishment of a rival see at Olomouc, and the resulting conflict, pursued not only in Bohemia but also in Rome and the empire; the elevation of Duke Vratislav to the rank of king in 1086; and his subsequent struggles with his last living brother, Conrad, and his eldest son, Břetislav II. The dangers of divisiveness and the primacy of the see of Prague are the dominant themes of Book 2. Beginning with the accession of Duke Břetislav I in 1037 and ending with the death of the last of his sons in 1092, this period overlaps with the period of Cosmas's youth, his parents' and grandparents' generation. Near the end, he becomes a witness to and participant in the history he unfolds.

The last book treats events contemporary with Cosmas's mature adulthood in the first quarter of the twelfth century. It begins, like Book 2, with the uncontested succession to the throne in 1092 of an exemplary, idealized duke, Břetislav II, who rules a united Czech land and promotes Christianity. But Břetislav's assassination in 1100 ushers in twenty-five years of succession conflict, intrigue, and warfare among his younger brothers and cousins and their supporters among the Czech magnates. In a nutshell, although Bořivoj, the younger brother and designated heir of Břetislav II, initially succeeded him, he was soon challenged by his cousins, first Oldřich and then Svatopluk, who successfully deposed Bořivoj in 1107. Svatopluk was assassinated two years later, and while his younger brother Otto claimed the throne and Bořivoj attempted to return to power, Vladislav, another of the sons of Vratislav, bested them. Vladislav I reigned until 1125, while his brothers and cousins went in and out of favor, exile, and bids for the control of Moravia. Vladislav also briefly abdicated in Bořivoj's favor, in 1118, only to oust him yet again.[8] By virtue of the *Chronicle's* chronological structure, a variety of events intrude at random into this essentially political story: the deaths of bishops, the marriages of Přemyslid sons and daughters, border skirmishes, the arrival of crusaders in 1096, anti-Semitic violence and its aftermath, a miracle, a fire, the vagaries of the weather and harvests. All are events Cosmas experienced firsthand.

What holds together the wide range of material in all three books is a consistent style and tone, recurring motifs and language, and the author's own view of the events he reports. Cosmas is by no means a self-effacing writer; he often comments explicitly on the events at hand: "O exceedingly lucky *metropolis* Prague!" he rejoices, after Adalbert's relics have been installed there.[9] In addition, from the outset to the end, the speeches of the men and women who come to life on the chronicle's pages bear the strong imprint of the author's own judgments and opinions. "You will find no reason, my lord king, for war in these parts," Cosmas has Wirpirk, the wife of Conrad of Brno, say to her brother-in-law, King Vratislav. "You bring back no victory from this battle. You commit a war worse than civil. If you see us and our goods as booty for your warriors, you turn your spears against yourself since you despoil with bloody rapine your own brother, to whom you ought to be a

---

8. See my *Hastening Toward Prague* for an in-depth analysis of these political machinations (186–210).

9. 2.4.

guardian. He who attacks his own people goes against God."[10] This echoes a speech, earlier in Book 2, made to Emperor Henry III by Duke Břetislav I: "The wars you make, Caesar, will have no triumphs. Our land is your treasury; we are yours and wish to be yours. He who rages against his own subjects is known to be more cruel than a cruel enemy."[11] In both instances, Cosmas is obviously the ventriloquist.

The time of Cosmas's writing witnessed numerous political upheavals in the Czech Lands, most of them described grippingly in the chronicle that follows. But the *Chronica Boemorum* is much more than a narrative of these, and earlier, events. Scholars of medieval texts routinely class it within the subgenre of "national history."[12] Rightly so, because the opening stories about the origins of the Czechs and their rulers both assume and establish that a people is shaped by its shared past. The rhetoric of many pre-battle speeches, other appeals to unity, even the author's own acerbic asides about non-Czechs likewise betray—or, more likely, strive to construct— a sense of what we might call (only somewhat anachronistically) national consciousness. Whether Cosmas succeeded in inculcating this sensibility in others is debatable, but there is no question that he himself envisioned the nation as the object of the past he labored to discover and tell. In this he stood in a long line of medieval historians constructing the history of their people to meet contemporary political, ideological, and moral needs: from Jordanes and Bede before him to Saxo Grammaticus, Vincent Kadłubek, and many others after him. Scholars have long noted the intersection of history, community, identity, and politics in the context of Norman historiography before and during the twelfth century.[13] Unlike his

10. 2.45, including "war worse than civil" from Lucan. Lucan, *Pharsalia*, trans. Jane Wilson Joyce (Ithaca: Cornell University Press, 1993), 3.

11. 2.12, another quotation from Lucan *Pharsalia* 1.12.

12. For instance, Norbert Kersken, *Geschichtsschreibung im Europa der "Nationes" Nationalgeschichtliche Gesamtdarstellung im Mittelalter* (Cologne: Böhlau, 1995), 573–82; and Kersken, "High and Late Medieval National Historiography," in *Historiography in the Middle Ages*, ed. Deborah Mauskopf Deliyannis (Leiden: Brill, 2003), 181–215.

13. See R. H. C. Davis, *The Normans and Their Myth* (London: Thames & Hudson, 1976); Leah Shopkow, *History and Community: Norman Historians in the Eleventh and Twelfth*

near contemporary Orderic Vitalis, however, Cosmas could by no means draw upon a rich regional historiographical tradition; he was compelled to initiate one himself. The one historical work we know he possessed, the *Chronicon* by Regino of Prüm, is of an entirely different character: a universal history, situating the later Carolingians within a chronological framework stretching back to Augustus.[14] In writing his nation's first history, Cosmas worked independently—so far as we can tell—of models of national history per se.

As the quotations above attest, the *Chronica Boemorum* also has a strong political component. Its author shares this with many of his predecessors and contemporaries.[15] Whereas some historians worked to legitimate the political order through history, however, Cosmas seems neither to glorify the Přemyslids as a dynasty nor to sanction the rule of the reigning Duke Vladislav I. Instead, the opening chapters set a tone that is potentially critical of Přemyslid rulership, especially when exacerbated by dynastic strife.[16] Czech magnates and neighboring rulers, whose petty ambitions tended to worsen rather than improve such conflict, earn equal disapproval. Civil war appalled Cosmas, as it did one of his main literary influences, the Roman epic poet Lucan.[17] Yet Cosmas writes less in bit-

---

Centuries (Washington, D.C.: The Catholic University of America Press, 1997); Emily Albu, *The Normans in Their Histories: Propaganda, Myth and Subversion* (Woodbridge, UK: Boydell Press, 2001); and Nick Webber, *The Evolution of Norman Identity, 922–1154* (Woodbridge, UK: Boydell Press, 2005).

14. Regino of Prüm, *Reginonis abbatis Prumiensis Chronicon cum continuatione Treverensis,* ed. F. Kurze, *Monumenta Germaniae Historica, Scriptores Rerum Germanicarum* 50 (Hanover: Hahn, 1890). See also Dušan Třeštík, "Kosmas a Regino," *Československý časopis historický* 8 (1960): 564–87.

15. See Rosamond McKitterick, *History and Memory in the Carolingian World* (Cambridge: Cambridge University Press, 2004). See also, for a close study of a single late Carolingian author, Jason Glenn, *Politics and History in the Tenth Century: The Work and World of Richer of Reims* (Cambridge: Cambridge University Press, 2004).

16. My views on this disagree with current scholarship (cf. Třeštík, *Kosmova Kronika,* 181–82; also Kersken, *Geschichtsschreibung,* 581–82).

17. Although Cosmas may have known some ancient writers only from excerpts in grammar books and elsewhere, others he clearly had before him in their entirety: Virgil's *Aeneid,* Lucan's *Civil War* (a.k.a. the *Pharsalia*), Sedulius's *Paschale Carmen,* Boethius's *Consolation of Philosophy,* and Sallust's *War with Catiline.* See Antonín Kolář, "Kosmovy vztahy k antice," *Sborník Filosofické fakulty university komenského v Bratislavě* 3, no. 28 (1924): 21–99.

terness or despair than in real exasperation at such men and their deeds, and his political thinking goes well beyond mere partisanship for Bořivoj, Vladislav's rival. He was also personally committed to the parochial concerns of the church of Prague and its primacy over a single diocese comprising both Bohemia and Moravia; still, this by no means inspired him to compose an ecclesiastical history. Politics was what motivated Cosmas to write and politics was what he wrote chiefly about. The result is an account of the Czech past grounded in its present, set off from other peoples, meant as an exhortation to contemporaries to set a new political course for the future—if one he hardly expected to see.

Cosmas and His World

The *Chronica Boemorum* is the only source of information about Cosmas himself.[18] He was a high-ranking and probably influential figure in Czech ecclesiastical affairs. So far as we know, Cosmas spent nearly all his life and career at the cathedral in Prague. Born circa 1045, he was schooled there as a boy, and later recalled practicing his Psalms in the cathedral's crypt.[19] He must have been a child of notable intelligence and conspicuous promise. Though we do not know when, for how long, or under whose patronage, Cosmas pursued advanced studies in grammar at Liège, the preeminent center for learning in the eleventh-century German empire. He names his teacher as Franco, master of the Liège cathedral school from about 1058 to sometime in the 1080s, a man particularly renowned for his mathematical knowledge—though Cosmas himself

18. As a consequence, there is very little scholarly disagreement about the details of his life, with the exception of the uncertainties related to his time in Liège. A concise summary with an extensive bibliography is provided in Kersken, *Geschichtsschreibung*, 573–76. See also, in English, the recent article by Marie Bláhová, "The Function of the Saints in Early Bohemian Historical Writing," in *The Making of Christian Myths in the Periphery of Latin Christendom (c. 1000–1300)*, ed. Lars Boje Mortensen (Copenhagen: Museum Tusculanum Press, 2006), 83–119.

19. The commonly accepted estimated birth year is 1045, calculating back from his declaration in 3.59, a passage surely written soon before his death in 1125, that he was an "octogenarian." For the miracle of his boyhood, see 2.34.

seems to have been devoted especially to classical Latin literature, especially poetry.[20] In 1086, at a synod at Mainz, he witnessed an important imperial charter for the see of Prague, whether because he was already in Germany or as part of a legation sent from Bohemia.[21] This is the first time he figures as a witness to the events his chronicle reports.

Cosmas appears periodically throughout Book 3, usually involved in cathedral affairs, whether traveling in the company of an episcopal entourage or, once, in defense of the properties of the canons.[22] By his own report, he was ordained to the priesthood in 1099, together with Hermann, bishop-elect of Prague.[23] Cosmas was also married, to Božetěcha, and the father of a son, Henry—a situation not out of the ordinary for a cleric in Czech Lands, or in many other parts of Europe at this time, when the reform imposing universal clerical celibacy was just getting seriously under way.[24] The legal case he pursued on behalf of the canons, concerning a contested estate in Moravia, was resolved in 1110. Perhaps by then he had already become dean, a position second only to the bishop, responsible for overseeing the cathedral's liturgy and often also the management of the chapter's property and incomes. When Cosmas first began to write the *Chronica Boemorum* is uncertain, but Book 1 was finished circa 1120, and he was still adding chapters to the end when he died, as a self-proclaimed "octogenarian," on 12 October 1125.[25]

20. John Van Engen, *Rupert of Deutz* (Berkeley and Los Angeles: University of California Press, 1983), 44.

21. Below, 2.37.

22. The property dispute appears in 3.33, the traveling in 3.3. Consult the index for other self-referential instances.

23. Below, 3.9.

24. Božetěcha died in 1117, as noted in 3.43. In 3.51 Cosmas records the death of one Bertold and describes him as "a follower of my son, Henry." The word "follower" (*cliens*) suggests that Bertold was a warrior in Henry's retinue, which in turn suggests that Henry did not pursue the clerical career of his father. Beyond this remark no record of him survives.

25. In the Preface addressed to Gervasius at the beginning of Book 1, Cosmas declares himself to be writing during the reigns of four rulers, whose dates overlap

Writing as an old man, one who had witnessed a great deal, traveled in the Czech Lands and beyond, and shouldered significant responsibility, Cosmas surveyed the events of his lifetime from the very center—the summit, he might say—of his land. Prague was the undisputed political, ecclesiastical, economic, and intellectual capital of the Czech Lands.[26] There were other important commercial and administrative centers (Litoměřice and Žatec stand out) but none possessed the constellation of ecclesiastical institutions found at Prague. Probably none was wealthier than Prague and nearby Vyšehrad. Above all, Prague Castle was at the heart of the Czechs' political life: the site of the royal palace as well as of the bishop's cathedral church; the place to gather on the feast day of their heavenly patron, Saint Václav; and the location of an immovable stone throne, where dukes were made. Cosmas's own rootedness in Prague gave him a proximity to power that surely affects his chronicle. It also, significantly, left him blind to life in the regions beyond it. On the larger European scene, Cosmas was a provincial; at home, in the Czech Lands, he was a man of the capital.

Frustration with the political disruptions of the first decades of the twelfth century, and with his contemporaries, seems to have moved the elderly Cosmas to take up his pen. An equally compelling reason, clearly, was his desire finally to exercise as an author the love for Latin he felt as a reader. He has a gift as a storyteller, one he must have learned to exercise in other venues, though we cannot know them.[27] The prefatory letters attached to the *Chron-*

---

only in the years 1119–22; this is probably the time when Book 1 was *completed* and circulated. Books 2 and 3 must have been composed between that time and the death of Duke Vladislav in March 1125. At the end of 3.58 Cosmas declares: "Let this be the book's end, where our duke's end is." He nevertheless kept writing, adding four more chapters before his death in October that same year.

26. On Prague and other aspects of the social order, political life, and ecclesiastical affairs described below, see Wolverton, *Hastening Toward Prague*.

27. In this, Cosmas shares much with other historians of the period 950–1150, especially Liutprand of Cremona, Widukind of Corvey, and Richer—whom Beryl Smalley characterizes as "classicists, entertainers, and partisans." Smalley, *Historians in the Middle Ages* (London: Thames and Hudson, 1974), 79ff.

icle's three books as they circulated show that Cosmas addressed the work chiefly to his colleagues, prominent Bohemian clergymen whose erudition he respected (and whom he flatters, following the norm for such prologues). Taken together with his chronicle's sophisticated Latinity, this testifies to high standards of education prevailing in the Czech Lands, even if only within a narrow cadre of clergy. Cosmas must have been relatively close to court, given his rank and the proximity of the cathedral to the palace—and he may realistically have expected his words to reach the duke's ears, albeit through interpreters. While this sometimes makes him careful, he is never fawning.

What was his world like? What did he experience in his days? Like most historians, Cosmas mostly describes dramatic deeds and turning points. The steady progress of dukes and bishops, their accession and death, provides the framework for his view of past and present, as well as the chronology for his history. Military expeditions, offensive and defensive, provide the drama. Central Europe in these centuries was a world dominated by warriors. Czech magnates and commoners expected to be at war routinely: in their own defense, to seize spoils from others, to assist sworn allies, or, in their own land, to participate in succession contests, even open rebellion. As a cleric, Cosmas hardly participated in these military endeavors, but they were a staple of life in the eleventh and twelfth centuries, as were other incidental acts of violence. More routine for him was the liturgical year, the regular celebration of Christian feasts—Christmas, Easter, St. Václav's Day (29 September)—that brought clergy and laity together. Like the seasons and the cycle of agricultural work, these shaped the course of life year in, year out.

Looking back over his eighty years and the generations that preceded them, Cosmas could perhaps discern larger developments. The progress of converting a previously pagan people to Christianity stood out, and here Cosmas marks clear transitional points in his chronicle, key moments when Christian truth earned a victory over older beliefs. In Cosmas's understanding, the see of Prague (founded circa 973) played a crucial leading role in this process, as did certain Přemyslid dukes. Equally important were the early saints whose relics were preserved at Prague. Václav, himself a Přemyslid duke of Bohemia, was murdered and so martyred by his own brother in 929, to become the first and most important native saint. The second bishop of Prague, Adalbert, who fled his stubborn, barely Christian flock for Rome and was later, in 997, martyred as a missionary to the Prussians, also had a significant cult in the Czech Lands, at least after the translation of his relics to Prague in 1039. For Cosmas, however, most of Bohemia's pre-Christian tradition lies in the past, or in the remote countryside. By the time of his writing, after more than two hundred years of exposure to and progressive adoption of Christian mores and teachings, the Czech Lands seem to have been as fully Christian as many other parts of western Europe.

Decisively oriented toward Rome religiously, the Czechs had also long since achieved a rapprochement with neighboring powers, the Germans to the east, above all, but also the Hungarians to the southwest. The Poles to the north were another matter; Cosmas's generation, like the ones before it, would witness much conflict over territory among Czechs, Poles, and Germans, each capitalizing whenever possible on the other's internal instability. The Bohemians' involvement with their powerful neighbors to the west originated under Charlemagne (768–814). They could never be conquered outright, given Bohemia's mountainous geography, but they could be made to pay tribute and would serve alternately as allies and as duplicitous enemies of the eastern Franks over the subsequent two centuries. Cosmas declines to report these developments; he simply takes for granted the long-standing tributary overlordship of the German kings. Later events in Germany, most notably the civil wars of the 1070s, drew the Czechs actively into the internal affairs of the empire. Other circumstances, religious, economic, and intellectual, led them increasingly to travel: to the empire, to Rome, to Jerusalem. They would also bring, slowly at first, a variety of travelers and immigrants, including crusaders, to the Czech Lands. Population growth and a flourishing economy, hard to trace in our sources, must have accompanied all this.

The dukes of Bohemia oversaw this thriving society, dominating it in nearly every way. They had far-reaching rights over the land, its people, and its resources. The personal characteristics, abilities, and inclinations of individual dukes thus had a profound effect on Czech society—as did their quarrels, death and succession, or assassination. While one dynasty, the Přemyslids, dominated the ducal throne in this period (indeed until 1306), they did not, and could not, rule single-handedly. For this they relied on a broad range of freemen, from magnates of the highest rank by virtue of property or lineage, to younger, newer, lesser men. They manned the castles, filled the armies, guarded the borders, and gathered to advise the duke on regular and special occasions. Such men had a great deal vested in their lord, as well as a host of customary expectations of him; as a consequence, they were actively involved in determining succession to the throne in Prague or in deposing an unsatisfactory ruler. The *ducatus*, the duchy over which they fought, was understood to mean the office of the duke as well as the territory under his control. That territory, called here "the Czech Lands" for convenience, actually consisted of two separate parts, Bohemia and Moravia. Moravia was geographically distinct, separated from Bohemia by mountains and forests, and also oriented on a different river system, running southeast toward the Danube rather than northwest into the Elbe. However, from the mid-eleventh century it was controlled by the dukes in Prague, usually by grant to lesser members of the Přemyslid dynasty. The Czech Lands were not a feudal society per se, characterized by fief-holding or a titled nobility. Very little is known about land tenure or social relations among the peasantry, so we must be careful about what we assume by comparison with other regions.[28] Still, there is no question the Czechs shared much culturally with their German, Slavic, and Magyar neighbors, even as they lived according to their own

28. Once again, for a comprehensive analysis of these issues, see my *Hastening Toward Prague.*

native laws, customs, and social norms. *The Chronicle of the Czechs* is our chief window onto this society.

The Translation

All medieval texts, because copied by individual scribes by hand, show variations. No autograph, an original copy in Cosmas's own hand, survives for the *Chronica Boemorum*, allowing us to trace the nature of his revisions as he wrote or dictated.[29] Nor are there significantly different versions of his text.[30] The various additions and continuations that appear in certain manuscripts were clearly made by subsequent copyists, a process that seems to have begun immediately after Cosmas's death in 1125.[31] The earliest manuscripts date roughly to the late twelfth century, thus about fifty years after Cosmas's death. Not only was the *Chronicle* immediately circulated within Bohemia, it was moderately popular elsewhere in central Europe. More than a dozen manuscripts originating from the twelfth to the fifteenth century survive today in modern libraries. This is not always the case for medieval historical writings; some

29. As is the case for Richer (see Glenn, *Politics and History in the Tenth Century*). Jeff Rider has also studied the process of historical composition, though in the absence of an autograph, in *God's Scribe: The Historiographical Art of Galbert of Bruges* (Washington, D.C.: The Catholic University of America Press, 2001).

30. As, for instance, Ademar of Chabannes. Richard Landes, *Relics, Apocalypse, and the Deceits of History: Ademar of Chabannes, 989–1049* (Cambridge, Mass.: Harvard University Press, 1995).

31. Occasional scribes made additions to the text, in the margins or the body, to include information about people and places—usually their own—that they felt were unfortunately excluded from Cosmas's history. Two such writers, an anonymous canon at the collegiate church of Vyšehrad and an anonymous Benedictine monk (or monks) at Sázava, went further, writing historical accounts of the years after Cosmas's death. Since all these represent interpolations to Cosmas's original text, they are not included here in either the text or the notes. Together with other variants, the insertions are reproduced in the Bretholz edition (see the following note). However, the continuations by the anonymous Canon of Vyšehrad and Monk of Sázava are available in *Fontes rerum bohemicarum*, ed. Josef Emler (Prague: Nakladatelství Musea Království českého, 1874), 2:203–37 and 238–69, respectively.

of the most important to us now were virtually unknown in their own times. The more manuscripts, the more variants, the more the need for a critical edition of the original Latin text as near as can be reconstructed. For Cosmas's chronicle, we are very well served by the critical Latin edition published by Bertold Bretholz in 1923, the basis for the translation here.[32]

The Bretholz edition has helpfully traced Cosmas's copious citations from biblical, classical, and other late antique and medieval authorities. I have relied on these identifications and have consulted them systematically in preparing this translation.[33] Copious annotations from classical sources and the Bible are the result. Translators sometimes choose to bypass the potentially distracting apparatus necessary to convey the nature of these citations.[34] I include it here because I believe that as a writer, Cosmas was keenly attuned to the details of language, and the particular words and phrasings he found in his favorite religious and literary works influenced him deeply. They were as much the building blocks of his

32. Cosmas of Prague, *Cosmae pragensis chronica boemorum*, ed. Bertold Bretholz, Monumenta Germaniae Historica, Scriptores rerum Germanicarum, new series, vol. 2 (Berlin: Weidmann, 1923).

33. My renderings of the quotations from the Bible are based on the Douay-Rheims translation of the Latin Vulgate. However, since its language is somewhat stilted and old-fashioned, and thus reads awkwardly in context, I have rarely inserted language directly from the Douay-Rheims verbatim. Using the Douay-Rheims as a guide, as well as the more colloquial Oxford Revised Standard Version, the translations are essentially my own and aim to preserve the flow of Cosmas's own prose. I have treated the classical citations similarly, referring to an English translation for guidance without necessarily citing it exactly. I have normally preferred editions with facing pages showing Latin and English (usually the Loeb edition). In some instances—for Horace and Lucan, in particular—other, independent English translations were more suitable. Since Cosmas chiefly cites poets, and English translations of Latin poetry vary widely, it was sometimes necessary to consult more than one translation. Where English translations were unavailable or wholly unsatisfying, the reference here is to the Latin edition and the translations are my own.

34. They do not appear at all in the Czech translation, and only very rarely in the Polish translation: Karel Hrdina, trans., *Kosmova kronika česká* (Prague: Melantrich, 1950); Maria Wojciechowska, trans., *Kosmasa kronika czechów* (Warsaw: Państwowe Wydawnictwo Naukowe, 1968).

chronicle as the texts he consulted for historical facts. Moreover, in many cases, Cosmas clearly intended the words he borrowed from ancient authorities to resonate with his readers *as* citations, to trigger associations from their original contexts that would reinforce or ironically inflect their meaning in his own work. When Cosmas reaches for a more elevated register, he expects his audience to appreciate and understand it in manifold ways. For educated Christian clerics routinely reciting the Bible as part of the liturgy, even two words might suggest a meaningful comparison to the language and context of scripture. The same holds, though somewhat differently, for those ancient writers who formed the "core curriculum" to train future clerics across Catholic Europe to read and write in Latin. While it is customary to identify biblical references within the main text in parenthesis, I have placed them in the notes; Cosmas so frequently interweaves classical and biblical citations that it would give the reader an artificial impression to present them differently. Likewise, there is much cross-referencing in the notes, as Cosmas recycles handy phrases, repeated to provide continuity across the whole *Chronicle* but modified to endow each sentence with originality.

Cosmas's rhymed prose and occasional forays into verse are rendered as straight prose here. The usual reasons for this apply: in the hands of anyone other than a poet, translation in verse results in terrible English. Another reason is Cosmas's habit of inserting one or two lines of verse into the middle of a sentence, or interrupting several lines of verse with half a line of prose. Many of these verses are quotations or composites from classical poetry. Though clearly a fan of both epic and Christian poetry, Cosmas was less a poet himself (as he admits) than a dramatist or a storyteller. In a few instances, signaled in the notes, I judge Cosmas to have employed verse rather than prose self-consciously, to convey particular meaning.

I have provided a range of explanatory notes for undergraduates, for those unfamiliar with central Europe in the Middle Ages, and for scholars new to Cosmas. These identify people, explain technical terms, and indicate Cosmas's reliance upon older written texts. Their aim is to explain, just that, rather than to offer a kind of alternative or corrective narrative to Cosmas's. Though Cosmas is often factually mistaken, especially in Book 1, I have not made emendations to the body of the text. In those instances where Cosmas's confusion complicates the identification of specific individuals, I have explained the situation as succinctly as possible in the notes. The one consistent alteration to the original medieval text is the adoption of modern methods of dating; occasionally I have left in place Cosmas's astrological terminology, but otherwise all references to ides and *kalends* have been effaced in favor of the equivalents provided in the Bretholz edition. Overall, the annotations are designed to provide minimal guidance without offering interpretation. They do not engage in debates with, or heavily cite, the specialized literature. The bibliography, likewise, is not meant to be comprehensive of the matters treated in the chronicle; it is merely a list of works cited in the notes.

Significantly, the majority of the individuals mentioned here, including the addressees of Cosmas's prefaces, are unknown outside the *Chronicle.* Annotations have been provided only when other sources offer independent information about a person—a circumstance that chiefly applies to popes, saints, and non-Czech kings, bishops, and noblemen. Přemyslid rulers of Bohemia and Moravia are listed as part of this work's preliminary material and in the genealogical chart. A list of bishops of Prague and Olomouc is also provided. All these are key players in the story as it unfolds; as such they do not come in for annotations. Readers should consult the charts, use the index, and follow the cross-referencing should confusion arise. Likewise, most of the important place names mentioned can be found on the maps provided; others have been explained, where necessary and possible, in the notes. The maps were created specifically for this translation: they reflect Cosmas's worldview.[35]

35. I have relied particularly on the excellent map that accompanies Wojciechowska's Polish translation (see previous note).

Cosmas's choice of language opens a window onto medieval Czech social history. Translators are necessarily careful not to import anachronisms in the process of rendering Latin terms, themselves imperfectly equivalent to the vernacular words in everyday use. Thus it is expedient to clarify the translation of certain words that appear throughout the chronicle. For instance, *regnum* may be translated either "kingdom" or "realm," dependent as it is on the Latin verb for ruling, *regere*, which also gives rise to *rex*, king. Since Bohemia was not a kingdom but a duchy, it is rendered here as "realm." Cosmas also sometimes uses the familiar Roman phrase *res publica*, literally meaning "public affairs," as a singular noun to stand for the Czech polity. This is the phrase from which the English "republic" derives, but such a word obviously suggests a variety of inappropriate connotations. I have therefore retained the Latin in all instances.

Following other translators of earlier medieval texts, I have consistently rendered *urbs* and *civitas* as "burg."[36] I have generally translated *oppidum* as "fortress" and *castellum* or *castrum* (where it refers to a castle and not a military camp) as "castle." Since *oppidum* generally refers to a larger fortified settlement, a "fortress" is little different from a "burg." And while *castrum* sometimes refers to an isolated fortification, other times, again, the implication is the same as "burg." All these words indicate populated settlements surrounded by walls, but it is difficult to know whether they are military forts with garrisons, fortresses serving as administrative centers, castles that have acquired settlers within or immediately outside the walls, or larger urban and protourban economic centers. Above all, Cos-

---

36. David Warner puts it well in his Introduction to Thietmar's *Chronicon*: "As with other early medieval authors, Thietmar faced the challenge of trying to describe the institutions and practices of his own day with a language (Latin) developed in the far different circumstances of classical and late Antiquity. At times, this language was clearly inadequate. So, for example, Thietmar uses the terms *urbs* and *civitas* to describe everything from a bustling commercial or ecclesiastical centre to a fortress occupied by nothing more than a temporary garrison. Except where a locale can clearly be identified as an urban settlement (e.g., Madgeburg), I have employed the relatively neutral term 'burg'" (64).

mas does not deploy these terms systematically or consistently: he may refer to the same place as *civitas* or *urbs*, *urbs* or *oppidum*, in the course of a few chapters. Moreover, although sometimes a comment about a particular *civitas* seems to refer to the town and its population, more often the context suggests that the administrative authority over a town, conferred upon a magnate or lesser Přemyslid, is at issue—power that was probably wielded from, and physically symbolized by, the town's fortification.[37]

With regard to Prague, Cosmas's descriptions are often sufficiently specific to distinguish Prague Castle, located on a promontory on the left bank of the Vltava, from the urban settlement below it and across the river. Anyone familiar with the geography of today's Prague can immediately picture the castle's relationship to the town, albeit on a reduced, twelfth-century scale. Then as now Prague Castle housed both the ruler's palace and the cathedral church; it was also the site for a duke's enthronement and the home of the women's monastery dedicated to St. George. In many instances it is clear from the context that *urbs* means the castle proper: for instance, in reference to a siege or an event at the cathedral. In translation, I have nonetheless retained the usual "burg of Prague"; readers should themselves be able to infer when the castle is meant, with help from the annotations.

Metropolis is the only word Cosmas applies to towns very deliberately. It specifically signals a burg of particular preeminence, whether ecclesiastical or political. He applies it often to Prague, chiefly on what might be called state occasions—for instance, the enthronement of a duke or the return of a newly consecrated bishop. In these instances, *metropolis* again signifies Prague *Castle*, the location of both the ducal throne and the cathedral church. In medieval Latin, *metropolis* also regularly connotes an archepiscopal see (a metropolitan church), and Cosmas employs it in that sense as well, especially of Mainz, also of Gniezno. Since Cosmas uses the word *metropolis* in nothing like the modern sense, with connota-

---

37. See Wolverton, *Hastening Toward Prague*, 31–37. For this reason I have been more conservative in this translation even than Warner (cited in the previous note).

tions of territorial expanse and population size, I have generally left the Latin word in italics.

The ubiquitous term *miles* I have consistently rendered "warrior." I chose "warrior" over "knight," or even just "soldier," as the term that carries the least inappropriate baggage. The word "knight" might easily be misunderstood in light of feudal or chivalric ideals, anachronistic even for Germany in this period, rather than in the rudimentary sense of a mounted professional soldier.[38] Yet "soldier" perhaps fails to register the often elite nature of military service, conjuring instead any man with a ready weapon. "Warrior" seemed a safe middle ground, a word open to interpretation. Readers should remain aware, above all, that Cosmas's chronicle is our only source for what *miles* meant in a specifically Bohemian or Moravian context before 1125—whether in terms of military equipment and activity or social rank, lineage, and shared ideals—and that, as noted above, social conditions in the Czech Lands were not quite the same as those prevailing elsewhere.[39]

Nobilis translates as "noble," but it is hardly the primary designation for the social elite. Far more common are words like *proceres,* which I have generally rendered "leaders" or "leading men," and *seniores* or *maiores natu,* which literally means elders but substantially connotes the same as *proceres. Comes,* which in other regions might normally be translated "count," is always left untranslated, as the term does not carry the same hierarchical or vassalic connotations in the Czech Lands that it does elsewhere in Europe. Sometimes *comites* in the plural seems akin to *proceres,* but it is also used as an individual title for men of prominence.[40] Cosmas also routinely uses the word "satraps," which he takes from the Old Testament, to mean the same thing as *comites* or *proceres.* While "satraps" is unique to Cosmas, his use of *comes* accords with other mid- and late twelfth-century Czech sources.

38. Warner voices similar reservations in his Introduction to Thietmar's *Chronicon* (64).

39. Again, see my *Hastening Toward Prague,* esp. 37–41.

40. This usage persisted in the Czech Lands well beyond Cosmas's time and appears even in late twelfth-century charters (ibid., 45).

In most instances I have translated proper names according to ethnicity and relied on the standard modern usage within the specialized historiography (though no uniform standard exists per se). For Czech personal names I have taken Karel Hrdina's Czech translation as authoritative.[41] It is common practice to use English equivalents, such as Henry or Judith, where such exist, and that has been my habit here. In the specific case of *Odalricus*, an originally German name that was in common enough use in the Czech Lands to have shifted phonetically in accordance with Czech pronunciation, I have used different translations for German and Czech individuals: the holy bishop of Augsburg is called Ulrich, while the Přemyslid duke bearing his name is called Oldřich. This also has the advantage of avoiding confusion. The reader should likewise be able easily to distinguish the Czechs named Boleslav and Vladislav from Polish dukes named Bolesław and Władysław (though of course these names are the same and these men are often relatives named for one another). Place names are given according to modern usage unless otherwise appropriate or common English equivalents exist, such as for Prague (Praha in Czech).

Cosmas has frequent occasion to refer to German rulers, the Czech dukes' neighbors to the west, acknowledged by them as overlords. For those unfamiliar with medieval German history, it might be useful to explain that such men as Otto II or Henry III were both kings of the Germans *and* emperors of the Romans. They did not become emperors automatically upon their coronation as kings, however; a separate coronation was required, performed exclusively by the pope and in Rome. As a consequence, there was often a time lag before a king could assume the title of emperor. At the very least, an arduous journey across the Alps had to be arranged, leaving German territories to fend for themselves; uncooperative popes could create further difficulties. Nonetheless, all but one—Henry I (919–36)—of the medieval German kings was also crowned emperor. Cosmas is not particularly fastidious about

41. Hrdina, *Kosmova kronika česká*.

the titles he gives these rulers, calling some emperors or caesars before their formal assumption of the title, or kings as it suits him. However, mindful of the fact that Henry I was king but not emperor, Cosmas *numbers* the three eleventh-century emperors named Henry differently than is customary in modern scholarship (i.e., his Henry II is our Henry III). I have retained Cosmas's original number but also, to prevent confusion, provided the modern equivalent in brackets.

As a rule, throughout this translation square brackets in the text indicate my own insertions: for cross-referencing, as a quick clarification, or to emphasize the original Latin or relevant Czech word. Ordinary parentheses bracket Cosmas's own parenthetical statements.

One final word: I have made a conscious decision to translate this work's title, *Chronica Boemorum* as "The Chronicle of the Czechs," rather than as "The Bohemian Chronicle," or "A Chronicle of Bohemia" or "of the Bohemians." The Latin *Boemia*, for the crater-shaped region comprising the watershed of the Elbe River, originates with the ancient Romans and derives from the name of the Celtic inhabitants, the Boii, documented there as early as the second century BC. Although successive waves of migration displaced the Celts, medieval Latin authors retained the older name for the region, and both the English Bohemia and the German *Böhmen* are based on this usage of *Boemia*. The Slavic inhabitants of the place, however, call it *Čechy*. Whereas Latinate outsiders used *Boemii* or *Boemani* (with a number of spelling variations), the inhabitants call themselves *Češi*, with *Čech* the masculine singular form (hence English "Czech") and *Česka* the feminine. *Morava*, however, is territorially distinct from *Čechy*, though the inhabitants of Moravia are considered ethnically Czech. As a consequence, to translate *Boemii* as "Czechs" includes the residents of both Bohemia and Moravia, whereas rendering it "Bohemians" excludes the Moravians.[42] In the

42. Hence, in 1997, with the establishment of Slovakia as an independent state, the "Czecho-" parts of the former Czechoslovakia were officially designated the "Czech Republic."

chronicle, *Boemii* sometimes distinguishes Bohemians from Moravians, but usually it means Czechs. While Cosmas gives short shrift to internal Moravian developments, to be sure, he clearly understands both its inhabitants and their land as part of his story. This is the history of *both* a place *and* a people—as we will soon see—yet Cosmas's own title emphasizes the people: *Chronica Boemorum*, rendered here as *The Chronicle of the Czechs*.

THE CHRONICLE
OF THE CZECHS

✠ BOOK ONE

Prologue Addressed to Provost Severus[1]

To Lord Severus, provost of the church of Mělník,[2] endowed with both literary knowledge and spiritual understanding, from Cosmas, dean in name only of the church of Prague,[3] who after the contest of this life will have his reward in the celestial kingdom. I submit myself to your paternity with so much love and devotion of my mind that—I call God as my witness—I cannot speak, just as human reason cannot comprehend a love so great. True love can in no respect be kept one's own, private or hidden; it should be expressed to the one whom it loves with sincere affection. If true love had not been present, I would by no means have presumed to offer these, my senile delusions, to a man of such authority. Seeking something to offer you, I truly sought something pleasant or idle, but I find nothing as laughable as this little work of mine. If we laugh gently when we see someone dash his foot against a

1. Of the two prefatory letters here at the chronicle's beginning, this one was probably intended as a prologue to the whole text and was added at a point when Cosmas had all three books nearly complete. Notice that it stresses the author's old age.

2. The provost was the head of a collegiate chapter, rather like the abbot of a monastery, except that the members of the chapter were secular canons charged with ministering to the laity. The chapter at Mělník, an older castle situated at the confluence of the Elbe and the Vltava, was established sometime before the middle of the eleventh century. Typical of such early foundations, no early documentation exists. See Wolverton, *Hastening Toward Prague*, 115.

3. On Cosmas's rank as dean, see the Introduction. The remark here that he is dean "in name only" may suggest that, by the time this was written, he had effectively retired from his duties as dean, though he retained the formal rank and title.

stone,[4] you will see so many of my stumblings in this work and so many errors of the grammatical art that if you wished to laugh at every one, you would be able to do so beyond what is fitting to a human being. Farewell. Whether these senile trifles please or displease you alone, I ask that no third eye see them.[5]

Preface to the Work that Follows, Addressed to Master Gervasius[6]

To Archdeacon Gervasius,[7] fully imbued with the pursuits of the liberal arts and anointed with the wisdom of every kind of knowledge, from Cosmas, a servant of the servants of God and Saint Václav[8] (though he is hardly worthy to be so called): a gift

4. Mt 4:6 and Lk 4:11.

5. Here and elsewhere in his prefatory letters, Cosmas adopts a false humility that is entirely typical of medieval authors. This "humility trope," involving protestations of intellectual inadequacy, pleas for correction, and groveling flattery of the addressee, was a kind of literary etiquette, sincere in its insincerity. It was usually expressed in difficult, arcane Latin which belied the author's contradictory claims of inability to achieve a proper, erudite style. Readers should, therefore, not take too seriously Cosmas's request that Severus not share his laughable, error-riddled trifles with others, or similar statements in the prefaces that follow.

6. This prefatory letter was probably written when Cosmas circulated the first book (of the three he planned) among friends. The reign dates at the end point to its composition between 1119 and 1122. Most scholars consider this date when the letter was attached to a finished or nearly finished Book 1, rather than the point at which it was begun or substantially written.

7. A clerical office subordinate to the bishop with administrative authority within the diocese, whether over a particular subregion or the whole. The specific functions of an archdeacon in early twelfth-century Bohemia are unknown. The implication here is that Gervasius, like Cosmas, was a member of the cathedral chapter, though he may have had duties that kept him away from Prague regularly, hence the need for such a formal letter. As with the other men named in Cosmas's prefaces, we know nothing of Gervasius beyond what is written here.

8. Another way of indicating the cathedral church in Prague, which was originally dedicated to St. Vitus but was often known as well by the other martyrs buried there, Sts. Václav and Adalbert, both of them native Czechs. Wolverton, *Hastening Toward Prague*, 158.

of owed prayer and a pledge of mutual love. When you receive this little sheet, know that I have sent you a chronicle of the Czechs. I resolved to send it, although polished by no charm of grammatical art but arranged simply and scarcely in a Latin manner, to be examined by your singular prudence so that by your wise judgment it might either be rejected altogether, so that no one reads it, or if it is judged worthy of reading, it might be smoothed to perfection[9] by the file of your examination. What I especially ask is that, through you, it might be explained afresh in better Latin. For the only value I calculate in my work is that either you, on whom God conferred wisdom, or others who are more knowledgeable, might make use of my work as the material for demonstrating their own knowledge to posterity, thus making a great monument to their own names forever[10] (just as Virgil used the fall of Troy and Statius the Aeacidae).[11]

Therefore I have taken the origin of the narrative from the first inhabitants of the land of the Czechs. The few things that I learned from the fabulous stories of old men, I set out for the love of all good men, so far as I know and am able, not from the ambition of human pride but lest the tales fall altogether into oblivion.

I always burn to please the good and the skilled, and I am not afraid to displease the ignorant and the unschooled. I know several

9. Horace *Ars poetica* 294. Although Cosmas cites only two words, *ad unguem*, they indeed appear among Horace's comments on the virtues of revision—honing, sharpening, paring down the text. Horace, *The Art of Poetry*, trans. Burton Raffel, with James Hind and David Armstrong (Albany: State University of New York Press, 1974), 55.

10. Cf. Jdt 9:15, Ex 3:15, and Gn 12:2 (components of all three verses are here combined).

11. The Aeacidae are the lineage of warriors that included Achilles, the subject of Statius's unfinished epic poem *Achilleid*. At first glance Gervasius is here simply enjoined to use Cosmas's stories as the building blocks for his own literary works, as Virgil did with the tales of Troy and Statius for Achilles. Yet, since both those poets were working from one of antiquity's most revered and authoritative texts, Homer's *Iliad*, Cosmas may also be making bold claims for his own achievement under the guise of humility. See Gian Biagio Conte, *Latin Literature: A History*, trans. Joseph B. Solodow, rev. Don Fowler and Glenn W. Most (Baltimore: Johns Hopkins University Press, 1994), 487.

rivals exist and that they will die of laughter and scorn[12] when they have seen the form of this work. Such men are only taught to disparage others and know nothing good per se to bequeath themselves. Concerning such people, the prophet sings: "They are wise in doing evil, but do not know how to do good."[13] They only look at things with the eyes of Lynceus[14] and fix in their hearts by memory, as if in stone, which phrases were improper or where my drowsy mind faltered. What's to wonder at, when even good Homer nods?[15] I am neither frightened of their envious disparaging nor am I flattered by ironic fawning. Let those who want to, read it, and those who don't, cast it aside. But you, dearest brother, if you love me as your friend, if you are touched by my prayers, gird the loins[16] of your mind and take into your hand a scraper, an ink bottle, and a pen, so that you can scratch off what is superfluous and insert over it whatever is missing. By changing improper phrases to their proper ones, your skill should mitigate my stupidity. I am not embarrassed to be corrected by a friend, and so I beg to be improved by my friends with great affection.

This first book contains the deeds of the Czechs, so far as it was permitted me to know them, set in order until the time of

---

12. Cf. Ez 23:32 and Ps 43:14 in combination with Terence *Eunuch* 3.434, in *Terence*, ed. and trans. John Barsby (Cambridge, Mass.: Harvard University Press, 2001). Cosmas's Latin *emori risu subsannationis* draws on the biblical phrase *subsannationem et derisum* (i.e., scorn and derision) as well as on Terence's *risu emoriri* (died of laughter).

13. Jer 4:22.

14. One of the mythic Argonauts, known for his keen eyesight. The phrase is used by Horace, Boethius, and probably others.

15. Horace *Ars poetica* 359. Even as he confesses irritation at Homer's occasional failing, Horace's point is that even a poet as good as Homer did falter and that his doing so was understandable given the length of his poem. In Raffels's loose translation of Horace: "I scowl too, when even Homer nods, though [sleep] can't really be kept away from a really long poem" (25; cf. 58 for a literal rendering). In effect, Cosmas is claiming an indulgence for himself similar to the one for Homer, and chiding his detractors with Horace's exemplary attitude. Two sentences later he switches authorities and invokes verbatim Jerome's call to either read his text willingly or toss it aside (Jerome, *Praefatio Hieronymi in Ezram*, PL 28:1474).

16. 2 Mc 10:25 and often elsewhere.

Břetislav I, the son of Duke Oldřich. Because I was unable to uncover a chronicle, and thus to know when or in whose times the deeds took place that I will now relate, but I did not wish to invent the dates at the beginning of this book, I began to order the years of the Lord's incarnation only from the time of Bořivoj, the first Catholic duke.[17] Farewell. By your command I will either gird myself to disclose the rest, or I will halt my step[18] on the spot and put an end to my silly undertakings. Live, be well, and may you not reject my wishes, but fulfill them.

This chronicle was composed when Henry IV [V] reigned as emperor of the Romans and Pope Calixtus governed the holy church of God, in the time of Vladislav, duke of the Czechs, and also of Hermann, bishop of the church of Prague.[19] So too, it is given in what follows to all those wishing to know, in which years of Christ or indictions[20] the events occurred.

Here Begins the First Little Book of the Chronicle of the Czechs, Which Cosmas, Dean of the Church of Prague, Composed

1.1. After the effusion of the Flood, after the confusion of evil-minded men building a Tower, in divine revenge for such illicit and audacious deeds, the human species, which then consisted in about seventy-two men,[21] was divided into as many diverse kinds of languages as there were heads of men—as we learned from the

---

17. The first date provided by Cosmas is 894; see 2.14.

18. Virgil *Aeneid* 6.465, in *Virgil*, trans. H. Rushton Fairclough, rev. G. P. Goold, (Cambridge, Mass.: Harvard University Press, 1999).

19. Henry V (1106–25), Pope Calixtus II (1119–24), Duke Vladislav I (1109–17, 1120–25), and Bishop Hermann (1099–22). The overlap between these reigns is either 1119–22 or 1120–22, depending upon how seriously Cosmas interprets Vladislav's temporary abdication of the throne from 1117 to 1120.

20. A fifteen-year dating cycle originating in the late Roman Empire and used in the Middle Ages, especially to date various documents. Cosmas will never use it, though it appears in the imperial privilege of 1086 (2.37).

21. Cf. Gn 10, where Noah's sons' descendants, born after the flood, are listed.

historical account. Each and every man a fugitive and a wanderer,[22] they roamed throughout various regions of the earth, dispersed far and wide.[23] And even while weakening in body from day to day,[24] they multiplied, in generations and generations. Whence the human species, with God arranging everything according to his will, was so dispersed throughout the sphere of the earth that after many ages it came even into these regions of Germania. For this whole region, located under the north pole, extending from the Thanay [River Don] and into the west, is called by the general term "Germania" (although each of the places in it has its own name).[25] We mention these things so that we might better be able to accomplish what we declared as our intention. In the meantime, before we come to the beginning of the narrative, we will try to explain briefly the location of this Czech land and whence it was assigned its name.

1.2. In the division of the globe according to geometricians Asia comprises half of the world and Europe and Africa half.[26] In Europe is situated Germania, in whose regions, across the northern plain, is a place spread very wide, girded everywhere by mountains in a circle. They are stretched in a marvelous way around the whole land, so that to the eye, it is as if one continuous mountain circles and protects all that land.

At that time great solitudes of forest prevailed on the surface of the land, without human inhabitants,[27] but very loud with swarms of bees and the singing of birds. Flocks of animals wandered through

22. Gn 4:12, in reference to Cain.
23. Cf. Gn 11:8–9, in reference to the Tower of Babel.
24. Cf. 2 Kgs 3:1.
25. This sentence is lifted from Regino of Prüm, *Chronicon* (132), who is himself citing Paul the Deacon, *The History of the Lombards*, trans. William Dudley Foulke (Philadelphia: University of Pennsylvania Press, 1907), 1.
26. Cf. Sallust *War with Jugurtha* 17.3, in *Sallust*, ed. and trans. J. C. Rolfe (Cambridge, Mass.: Harvard University Press, 1931). Cf. also Isidore *Etymologies* 14.2.3, in Isidore of Seville, *Etimologías*, ed. and trans. José Oroz Reta and Manuel-A. Marcos Casquero (Madrid: Editorial Católica, 1982).
27. Cf. Jer 33:10, where the land is without animals as well.

the lonely places of the land, terrified by no one. Almost as in-numerable as the sands of the sea[28] or the forests, as many as there were stars in the sky, the earth hardly sufficed for them. Beasts of burden could hardly be compared to the number of locusts[29] jumping through the fields in summer. The waters there were very clear and safe for human purposes; likewise, the fish were sweet and healthy to eat. It was a wonderful thing, and you might well consider how high this region sits: such that no outside waters flow into here while so many streams, small ones and large, origi-nate from different mountains and are received by the larger river called the Elbe, to flow north to the sea.[30] And since at that time this region lay untested by the plow, and the man who would try had not yet entered it, it seems better to keep silent concerning its fertility or sterility than to speak in ignorance.

Seeking places suitable for human habitation, whoever the man was (it is uncertain with how many souls) who later entered these solitudes, he surveyed with keen sight the mountains, valleys, and wastes and, so I think, located their first settlement around Mt. Říp between two rivers, namely, the Ohře and the Vltava. He established their first dwellings and rejoiced in the guardian deities[31] that he had carried with him on his shoulders, now erected on the ground. Then the elder, whom the others accompanied as if he was their lord, spoke thus to his followers (among other things): "O com-rades,[32] you who have endured with me heavy burdens through lonely forests, halt your step. Offer a thankful libation to your gods,

---

28. 2 Kgs 17:11; 3 Kgs 4:20; also cf. Ps 77:27.

29. Cf. Jgs 6:5.

30. The whole Bohemian basin comprises the watershed of the Elbe, whose many tributaries originate in the encircling mountains just described, eventually flowing into the Elbe and thence north-northwest.

31. Cf. Virgil *Aeneid* 4.598 and 1.68.

32. While only the phrase "O comrades" is taken verbatim from Virgil (*Aeneid* 1.198), it may nevertheless be intended to remind readers of the Trojans' laborious search for a new home in Latium. Note also the repetition of the Virgilian "halt your step" (see above, n. 18) and the number of other phrases from the *Aeneid* in this chapter.

through whose wondrous work you have come to your fatherland, as once foreordained for you by destiny. This is it. This is that land which you often reminded me I promised you, a land subject to no one, filled with wild animals and fowl, wet with nectar, honey, and milk,[33] and, as you yourselves see, air delightful for living. The waters are abundant on every side and full of fish beyond measure. Here nothing will be lacking to you, because no one will hinder you. But since a region such as this, both beautiful and great, lies in your hands, think what name might be fitting for the land." Immediately they said, as if moved by a divine oracle: "Since you, O father, are called 'Bohemus,' where might we find a better or more fitting name than for the land to be called 'Bohemia'?"[34] Then the elder, moved by the divination of his comrades, began to kiss the ground for joy and, rejoicing, named it from his own name. Rising and stretching both hands palms upward to the stars,[35] he thus rose to say: "Greetings, fated land,[36] sought by our thousand prayers, once widowed of man in the time of the Flood. Now, as a kind of monument to men, keep us safe and our offspring plentiful from generation to generation."[37]

33. Cf. Dt 6:3, concerning the "land flowing with milk and honey." The addition of nectar comes from Ovid *Metamorphoses* 1.111: "Streams of milk and streams of sweet nectar flowed, and yellow honey..." Ovid, *Metamorphoses*, trans. Frank Justus Miller (Cambridge, Mass.: Harvard University Press, 1977), 1:11.

34. It is usually assumed that, rendered in Cosmas's native Czech, this elder's name was "Čech," since the Czech word for Bohemia is "Čechy." See, for instance, the Czech translation of this passage by Karel Hrdina, *Kosmova kronika česká*, 17. Cosmas, however, uses the Latin terminology to tell this story: thus "Boemus" and "Boemia." Medieval Latin writers adopted "Bohemia" and "Boemii" (or "Bohemani") from Roman geographers' descriptions of this region's earlier Celtic inhabitants, the Boii. Note that there are ample Virgilian parallels for naming places after people, not least the naming of Rome after Romulus (*Aeneid* 1.276).

35. Virgil *Aeneid* 1.93; see also David West's prose translation of the *Aeneid* (Harmondsworth: Penguin, 1990), 6.

36. Cf. Virgil *Aeneid* 7.120. Again, although only the "Greetings!" (Salve!) is verbatim, it is drawn from the passage in which Aeneas—with obvious parallels to the story here—cries: "Hail [Salve], land destined as my due! and hail to you, faithful gods of Troy! Here is our home, here our country!"

37. Lk 1:50.

1.3. The men of that time were so honorable in their mores, so simple and righteous, so loyal and merciful to one another, so moderate, sober, and continent, that if anyone tried to describe them to present-day men, who thoroughly represent the opposite qualities, he would be met with considerable irritation. Therefore, we omit these things and desire to say a few true things about the quality of that first age. How happy was that age,[38] content with moderate expense and not puffed up with swollen pride. They hardly knew the rewards of Ceres and Bacchus,[39] which were not available. They made their evening meal with acorns and wild game. Uncorrupted springs provided healthy drinks. Like the brightness of the sun and the moisture of the water, so the fields and the forests, even their very marriages, were held in common. For in the manner of cattle, they tried new lovers on various nights and, with dawn rising, broke the tie of the Three Graces[40] and the iron shackles of love. Wherever and with whomever they had spent the night, there they caught sweet sleep,[41] spread out on the grass[42] under the shade of a leafy tree. The use of wool or linen, even of clothing, was unknown to them; in winter they used the skins of wild animals or sheep for clothing.[43] Nor did anyone know to say

38. This first phrase matches the first line of meter 5 in the *Consolation of Philosophy*, book 2. The sentences that follow continue to cite and allude to Boethius's poem, which captures precisely the spirit Cosmas himself is striving for in this description: a nostalgic view of simpler times before greed led people to quarrel. Boethius, *The Consolation of Philosophy*, trans. S. J. Tester (Cambridge, Mass.: Harvard University Press, 1973), 206–9.

39. Meaning food and drink, with connotations of abundance and festivity. Ceres was the ancient Roman goddess of growth, harvest, abundance, etc., while Bacchus among the Romans was the god of fertility and wine. Given that the next sentence describes the people living off the more primitive fruits of hunting and gathering, this may be a reference to specific products of agriculture, thus bread and wine.

40. In myth, the Three Graces personify charm, grace, and beauty. Though something more specific seems to be implied here, I am not certain of its source.

41. Virgil *Aeneid* 4.555.

42. Ibid., 1.214.

43. Cosmas has lifted this description from a description of the Scythians found in Regino of Prüm's entry for 889 (*Chronicon*, 132). Regino is himself quoting verbatim from an account of the Scythians by a historian of the second or third century

"mine" but, in the likeness of monastic life, whatever they had the word "our" resounded in their mouth, heart, and deed.[44] There were no bars on their stables, nor did they close their gate to the poor, because there was no theft or robbery or poverty. There was no crime among them more serious than theft[45] or robbery. They saw the weapons of no people and themselves had only arrows, which they carried for killing wild animals. What more can be said?

Oh, alas! Prosperity gave way to the contrary, and communal goods to private ones. They avoided and fled secure poverty, once beloved, as if it were a muddy wheel, because in all of them lust for gain burned fiercer now than Etna's fires.[46] With these and similar evils emerging, they patiently endured from day to day worse and worse injury, which no one had ever incurred before, inflicted by one man upon another. And they had no judge or prince[47] to whom they could appeal their grievance. Later, they turned to someone in their tribe or generation, someone considered better in character and more distinguished by virtue of wealth. Without a tax collector, without a seal, of their own free will they came to him and, with their freedom whole, debated uncertain cases and injuries incurred.

One particular man had arisen among them, called Krok, after whom a castle is known to have been named, located in the forest adjacent to Ztibečná and now overrun by trees. He was a man

---

CE named Justin. *Epitoma historiarum philippicarum Pompei Trogi*, ed. Otto Seel (Stuttgart: Teubner, 1972), 2.103.

44. This echoes a famous passage on the ownership of property in Augustine's commentaries on John, specifically Jn 1:32–33: Augustine, *In Johannem Evangelium tractatus CXXIV*, ed. Radbodus Willems, Corpus Christianorum 36 (Turnhout: Brepols, 1954), 66–67.

45. Again, from Regino (*Chronicon*, 131) on the Scythians, again citing Justin, a little above the previous quotation (n. 43).

46. Having strayed, some sentences back, from a close paraphrase of Boethius, Cosmas returns now to cite the *Consolation of Philosophy*, book 2, meter 5, verbatim. Etna refers to the active volcano on the island of Sicily, the highest in Europe.

47. Cf. Acts 7:27.

absolutely perfect in his generations,[48] exceptional for his wealth in secular things, discreet in considering lawsuits. Like bees to their hive, so everyone, both from his own tribe and from the common folk of the whole province, flocked to him to sort out their lawsuits. Such a great man lacked manly offspring. Nevertheless, he fathered three daughters, to whom nature gave riches of wisdom no fewer than she was accustomed to give men.

1.4. The eldest of them was named Kazi, who surpassed Medea of Colchis[49] in herbs and song and the Paeonian master[50] in medicinal art, because she often made the Fates[51] themselves cease their unending work and oracles follow the commands of her song. Hence the inhabitants of this land, when they lose something and despair of its recovery, say the following proverb about her: "Even Kazi herself cannot get it back." Like the place where the daughter of Ceres was abducted by a tyrant,[52] her burial mound can still be seen today, heaped up very high by the inhabitants of the land in memory of their mistress, on the bank of the River Mže near the road which leads to the province of Bechyně, over the mountain called Osek.

Worthy of praise though second by birth, Tetka was a woman of keen discernment[53] lacking a husband. She built a castle on the River Mže, named Tetín after herself, well fortified by the nature of the place, with rocks reaching steeply to the summit. She taught the stupid and senseless people to adore and worship Oreads, Dry-

---

48. Gn 6:9, of Noah.

49. A mythic figure, sometimes a goddess, especially famed for her knowledge of potions; see nn. 65 and 69.

50. Paeonia is a region in Macedonia, but the word chiefly refers to Aesculapius, the healing hero, or his father, Apollo. Both Ovid (*Metamorphoses* 15.535) and Virgil (*Aeneid* 7.769) use the term in relation to healing with herbs.

51. A set of three goddesses that controlled every individual's destiny, down to the moment of death.

52. A reference to the mythical abduction of Proserpina, the daughter of Ceres, by Pluto, god of the underworld, which took place near Henna. Cf. Ovid *Metamorphoses* 5.391, though no burial mound is mentioned.

53. "Emuncte naris" from Horace *Satires* 1.4.8, in Horace, *Satires and Epistles,* trans. Smith Palmer Bovie (Chicago: University of Chicago Press, 1959), 52.

ads, and Hamadryads,[54] and established every superstitious sect
and sacrilegious rite. Like many villagers up until now, just like pagans, this one worships waters or fires, that one adores groves and
trees and stones, another sacrifices to mountains or hills, and still
another beseeches and prays to the deaf and dumb idols he has
made himself, so that they rule both his home and his own self.[55]

Younger by birth but older in wisdom, the third was called
Libuše. She built a castle, the most powerful then, next to the forest
which reaches to the area of Ztibečná, and called it Libušín after
her own name. She was truly a woman among women: cautious in
counsel, quick to speak, chaste in body, upright in character, second to no one in resolving the lawsuits of the people. Affable, even
lovable, in all things, she adorned and glorified the feminine sex
while handling masculine affairs with foresight. But because no one
is altogether blessed,[56] this woman of such quality and of so great
praise—alas the terrible human condition!—was a prophetess [phi-
tonissa].[57] Since she predicted many proven futures for people, that
whole people took common counsel and set her up as judge over
them after the death of her father.

At that time not a small litigation arose concerning the boundaries of a contiguous field between two citizens,[58] both among the
more eminent in wealth and birth, men who considered themselves
leaders of the people. They erupted to such a degree into mutual conflict that one flew at the thick beard of the other with
his fingernails. Exposing the sounds of their confrontation and

54. Mountains nymphs (oreads) and wood nymphs (dryads and hamadryads),
inhabiting trees and forests.

55. This sentence is modeled, with but a few verbatim borrowings, on Sedulius
Paschale Carmen 1.259, in Sedulius, *Opera Omnia,* ed. Johannes Huemer, Corpus Scriptorum Ecclesiasticorum Latinorum, vol. 10 (Vienna: Gerold, 1885).

56. Horace *Odes* 2.16.27, in *Odes and Epodes,* trans. C. E. Bennett (Cambridge, Mass.:
Harvard University Press, 1914).

57. For an extended discussion of the varied and complicated biblical and classical
usages of the word "phitonissa," see Geary, *Women at the Beginning,* 37–39; also n. 125,
below.

58. Cosmas's use of *cives,* here and elsewhere, derives from classical Roman authorities. It is meant as a general term, with no specific legal connotations of citizenship.

confounding each other disgracefully with a finger under the nose, they entered the court raving. Not without a great din, they approached the lady and asked humbly that Libuše resolve the undecided case between them by reason of justice. She, meanwhile—as is the wanton softness of women when they do not have a man whom they fear—reclined very softly deep in a painted coverlet, propped on an elbow, as if she had just given birth to a child. Walking on the path of justice,[59] not respecting men's persons, she brought the cause of the whole controversy that had arisen between them to a state of rectitude.

Yet he whose cause did not win the palm [of victory] in the judgment, more indignant than was fitting, shook his head three or four times,[60] foolishly hit the ground thrice with his staff, and with a full mouth, saliva sprinkling his beard, cried out: "O the injuries hardly to be tolerated by men! A woman full of cracks treats manly judgments with a deceitful mind. We know indeed that a woman standing or sitting on a throne knows little; how much less must she know when she is reclining on a coverlet? Truthfully, this posture is more suitable to the approach of a husband than to prescribing laws to warriors. They all have long hair, to be sure, but women are short on sense. A man should rather die[61] than suffer such things. A disgrace among nations and peoples, nature has forsaken us alone, who lack a ruler and manly severity, and whom feminine laws rule." At this the lady smiled, dissembling the insult made to her and concealing her heart's pain in feminine modesty. "It is," she said, "as you say: I am a woman, I live as a woman, and for that reason I seem to you to know too little. Because I do not judge you with a rod of iron[62] and since you live without fear, you rightly look down on me. For where fear is, there is honor.[63] Now, it is very necessary that you have a ruler fiercer than a woman. Just as the doves once spurned a white bird for a kite whom they had chosen as their king, so you spurn me. They appointed as

59. Cf. Prv 2:20.
60. Ovid *Metamorphoses* 2.49 and 1.179.
61. Terence *Eunuch* 7.773.
62. Ps 2:9.
63. Cf. Mal 1:6 and Rom 13:7.

their duke a much fiercer hawk, who, inventing crimes, began to kill both the innocent and the wicked.[64] From then until now, the hawk eats the dove. Go home now. I will accept as my husband whomever you should choose tomorrow as your lord."

Meanwhile, she summoned the aforesaid sisters, who stirred up matching rages. With their magical skill and her own, she made a fool of the people through everything. Libuše herself was, as we said above, a prophetess like Sibyl of Cumae, the other sister a sorceress of potions like Medea of Colchis, and the third an enchanter like Aeaean Circe.[65] What kind of counsel those three Eumenides[66] obtained that night and what kind of secret they carried out was then unknown. Nevertheless it was made manifest—clearer than light—to everyone in the morning, when their sister Libuše revealed both the place where the future duke was hidden and who he was by name. Who would believe that they would request their first duke from the plow? And who would know where plows the man who would become ruler of the people? What does prophetic rage not know? And what is there that magical skill cannot make happen? Sibyl was able to predict to the Roman people the course of their destinies almost to the day. She even—if we can believe it[67]—foretold of Christ. (A certain teacher inserted verses

64. Cosmas here alludes to a fable by Phaedrus, in which a kite (a kind of hawk) who is not swift enough to catch a flock of doves he desires instead persuades them to appoint him their king. He then devours all but one, who voices the moral of the story: "Deservedly does the doom of death await us, for letting this brigand be lord of our lives." Phaedrus, *The Fables*, trans. P. F. Widdows (Austin: University of Texas Press, 1992), 31. For a further warning of this sort, illustrated by another fable by Phaedrus with a similar theme, see 1.5 and n. 75.

65. The phrase "Aeaean Circe" is from Ovid *Metamorphoses* 4.205. The Sibyl of Cumae features in Virgil *Aeneid* 3.441 and 5.735. See also below, nn. 68–71.

66. The Eumenides are the Furies (also Erinyes) by another name, one sometimes taken as a euphemism, since it means "kind ones," to indicate the Furies in a more beneficent mode. Always female, though varying in number, the Eumenides were avengers of wrongdoing, especially of crimes beyond the reach of human justice. As personifications of vengeance, retribution, and blood curses, they were fearsome. However, they also stood for order, balance, and right.

67. This phrase, *si fas est credere*, appears in both Statius and Prudentius. In Prudentius it seems to signal something indeed incredible, whereas in Statius the tone is

about the coming of the Lord, composed by Virgil for the persona of Sibyl, in the words of his preaching.)⁶⁸ Medea was often able to lead Hyperion and Berecynthia back from heaven through her herbs and song; she was able to call forth rainstorms, lightning, and thunder from the clouds; she was able to make the Aegean king a youth from an old man.⁶⁹ By the song of Circe, the friends of Ulysses were transformed⁷⁰ into various forms of wild animals, and King Picus into the flying creature which is now called a *picus* [woodpecker].⁷¹ What wonder? How much did magi in Egypt do through their arts, they who performed almost every kind of wonder with their songs, as many wonders as Moses, God's servant, was said to have produced from God's power?⁷² Enough of that.⁷³

1.5. The next day, as was ordered, they convened an assembly without delay and gathered the people; at once, everyone came together into one. Sitting on the highest throne, the woman addressed the boorish men: "O most pitiable common folk, who do not know that you live free and that no good man gives up [freedom] except with his life.⁷⁴ You flee that freedom not unwillingly

---

more skeptical; the latter, "if we can believe it," has been adopted here. Prudentius *Contra Symmachum* 1.351, in *Prudentius*, ed. and trans. H. J. Thomson, 2 vols. (Cambridge, Mass.: Harvard University Press, 1949); and Statius *Thebaid* 2.595, in *Statius*, ed. and trans. D. R. Shackleton Bailey, 3 vols. (Cambridge, Mass.: Harvard University Press, 2003).

68. This must be based upon Augustine of Hippo's *Unfinished Commentary on the Epistle to the Romans* 3; the Virgilian line discussed there is *Eclogues* 4.4. *Augustine on Romans*, ed. and trans. Paula Fredriksen Landes (Chico, Calif.: Scholars Press, 1982), 55.

69. Hyperion, sometimes taken as equivalent to his son Helios, and Berecynthia, if equivalent to Cynthia (a byname of Artemis), probably represent the sun and the moon; this reading seems to fit the context here. The Aegean king made young again was Aeson, father of Jason. The story is recounted in Ovid's *Metamorphoses* (7.162–293), where it involves the moon, sun, and control of nature suggested by Cosmas.

70. Virgil *Eclogues* 8.70. The story of Ulysses' encounter with Circe appears in Ovid *Metamorphoses* 14.247–307.

71. The story of Picus and his companions, turned into various animals by Circe when Picus rejected her advances, appears in Ovid *Metamorphoses* 14.312–96.

72. Ex 4–11.

73. Horace *Satires* 1.4.63.

74. Sallust *War with Catiline* 33.4.

and submit your necks voluntarily to unaccustomed servitude. Alas, later you will regret it in vain, as the frogs regretted it when the serpent, whom they had made their king, began to kill them.[75] If you do not know what the rights of a duke might be, I will try to tell you in a few words. First, it is easy to appoint a duke, but difficult to depose one appointed. For he who is now under your power, whether you established him duke or not, when later he is established, you and everything yours will be in his power. In his presence your knees will tremble and your mute tongue stick to the roof of your dry mouth.[76] Because of great fright you will hardly respond to his voice, 'yes, lord, yes, lord,' when by his command alone and without your forejudgment he will damn this one and slaughter that one, order these sent to prison and those hung from the gallows. He will make you yourselves and from your midst, as he pleases, some slaves, some peasants, some taxpayers, some tax collectors, some executioners, some heralds, some cooks or bakers or millers. He will establish for himself tribunes, centurions, bailiffs, cultivators of vineyards and fields, reapers of grain, makers of arms,[77] sewers of various hides and skins. He will force your sons and daughters into obedience to him. From even your oxen and horses and mares and cattle he will take, at his pleasure, whichever are best. Everything yours, what is better in villages and in plains, in fields and meadows and vineyards, he will take away and reduce to his own use. Why do I delay with words? Toward what end do I

75. Phaedrus *Fables* 1.2, an Aesopian fable on the themes of liberty, tyranny, and making do with the status quo. In the fable, a group of frogs, frolicking in freedom, ask Jupiter for a king "who would curb their excesses by force." When he tosses them an inert log, they sport with it and then ask for a king less useless. The god next sends a snake, which immediately begins to eat the frogs. Though at first "their power of speech failed them," they later begged Jupiter for mercy. His answer was: "You were grudging and ungrateful when I gave you the good: so put up with the present, bad as it may be."

76. Ez 3:26.

77. From "tribunes" to "makers of arms": 1 Kgs 8:12. This scene in Cosmas is clearly modeled on the whole of 1 Kgs 8, where Samuel attempts to dissuade the Israelites from appointing a king.

speak, as if to frighten you? If you persist in what you have begun and do not swear your oath falsely, I will now announce to you both the duke's name and the place where he is."

At this, the base commoners[78] jumped up with a disordered shout; with one voice everyone demanded a duke be given to them. Libuše said to them: "Behold! Beyond those mountains"—and she pointed to the mountains with her finger—"is a river not yet large, named Bílina, on whose banks a village is to be found, Stadice by name. In its territory lies one newly cleared field, twelve paces in length and in width, which—wonder of wonders—while positioned in the midst of so many [arable] fields, yet pertains to no field. There your duke plows with two parti-colored oxen: one ox is girded with white and has a white head, the other is white from forehead to rear and has white rear feet. Now, if you please, take my ankle-length robe and mantle, and capes fitting for a duke, and go. Report my and the people's commands to that man, and bring back your duke and my husband. The name of the man, who will think up [excogitabit] many laws upon [super] your necks and heads, is Přemysl (for this name means, in Latin, 'thinking upon' [super-excogitans] or 'thinking beforehand' [premeditans]). His subsequent progeny will rule all this land forever and ever."[79]

1.6. Meanwhile, messengers were chosen, who would bring the lady's and the common folk's orders to the man. When Libuše saw them delaying, as if they did not know the way, she said: "What delays you? Go confidently: follow my horse. He will lead you on the right road and bring you back, because that road has been trod by him more than once." Empty rumor and false conjecture both fly[80] that, always at night, Libuše, on an imaginary ride, was accustomed to go there in the evening and return before daybreak. (Let Apella the Jew believe it!)[81] What then? Wise, though unedu-

---

78. Virgil *Aeneid* 1.149.

79. Ex 15:18 (though of the Lord).

80. "Rumor flies": Virgil *Aeneid* 3.121, and elsewhere.

81. Horace *Satires* 1.5.100. In context, this means something like "go tell that to someone more credulous."

cated, well aware of their ignorance,[82] the messengers proceeded, following the horse's footsteps. Soon they crossed mountains and eventually approached the village to which they went. One boy ran to meet them; they said to him, inquiring: "Hark, excellent boy! Is not that village named Stadice? If it is, is a man named Přemysl in it?" The boy said: "It is the village you seek. And behold, the man Přemysl goads his oxen in the field nearby so that he might finish more quickly the work he is doing." Approaching him, the messengers said, "Happy man! Duke produced by the gods for us!" As is the custom for peasants, it was not sufficient to have said it once, so with puffed out cheeks, they repeated: "Hail, duke! Hail, most worthy of great praise! Release the oxen, change your clothes, and mount this horse!" And they showed him the clothes and the neighing horse. "Our lady Libuše and all the common folk demand that you come quickly and take up the realm fated for you and your descendants. Everything ours and we ourselves are in your hand.[83] We elect you duke, you judge, you ruler, you protector, you our only lord."

At this speech, the foreseeing man, as if unaware of future things, halted and fixed in the earth the prod he carried in his hand. Releasing the oxen, he said, "Let us go to the place you came from." Immediately, quicker than can be said, the oxen vanished from his sight[84] and were never seen again. The hazel-wood prod which he had fixed in the ground produced three branches[85] and—what is more miraculous—leaves and nuts. Seeing such things happen thus, the messengers stood astonished. In turn thanking the visitors, Přemysl invited them to a meal, shook moldy bread and part of a cheese out of his cork-woven bag, put the bag on the ground for a table, and placed other things on the rough cloth. Then, while they were eating the meal and drinking water from

82. Gregory I *Dialogues* 2, prologue, in Gregory the Great, *Dialogues*, trans. Odo John Zimmerman (New York: Fathers of the Church, 1959).
83. Gn 47:(23–)25, concerning Joseph and the Jews' obligations to Pharaoh.
84. Jgs 6:21 and Lk 24:31.
85. Gn 40:10.

a jug, two of the branches (or two of the bushes) withered and died, but the third grew much higher and wider. Whence greater astonishment, mingled with fear, grew in the visitors. Přemysl said: "What are you astonished at? You should know that from our progeny many lords will be born, but one will always dominate. If your lady does not immediately hurry in this matter, but awaits the galloping fates awhile and does not quickly send for me, as many master's sons as nature produces, your land will have that many lords."

1.7. Afterward, dressed in a princely garment and shod with regal shoes, the plowman mounted his spirited horse. Still, not forgetful of his lot, he took with him his boots, stitched in every part from cork, and ordered them preserved for posterity. They are indeed preserved now and forever in the duke's treasury at Vyšehrad.

It so happened that, while they took a short cut, until now the messengers had not yet dared to speak more familiarly to their new lord. Just like doves when some falcon approaches them, they first tremble at it but soon become accustomed to its flight, make it their own, and love it.[86] Thus, while the riders chatted, shortened the trip with conversation, and lightened their labor by joking and with jesting words, one of them, who was more audacious and quicker to speak, said, "O Lord, tell us: why did you make us save those woven cork shoes, fit for nothing except to be thrown away? We cannot wonder at this enough." Přemysl said to them: "I had them saved and will have them preserved forever for this reason: so that our descendants will know whence they sprang, and so that they will always live trembling and distrustful, and will not unjustly, out of arrogance, oppress the men committed to them by God, because we are all made equals by nature. Now allow me to inquire in turn of you, whether it is more praiseworthy to be raised from poverty to honor or to be reduced from honor into poverty? Of course, you will tell me that it is better to be raised to glory than to

---

86. Alluding to the fable from Phaedrus already mentioned; see 1.4 and n. 64, above.

be reduced to indigence. Yet some people, born of noble parentage, are later reduced to base indigence and made wretched. When they proclaim their parents to have been glorious and to have had power over others, they are hardly unaware that they confound and debase themselves more when they lose through their own laziness what their parents had possessed through industry. Fortune always plays this game of chance with her wheel: now she raises these men to the pinnacle, and now she plunges those into the depths.[87] Whence it might happen that earthly honor, which brought glory for a time, is lost to disgrace. Truly, poverty conquered through virtue does not hide itself under a wolf's pelt but lifts up to the stars as a victor him whom it had once dragged to the depths."

1.8. After they had traversed the road and eventually arrived near the burg, the lady rushed to meet them, surrounded by her followers. With their right hands entwined, Libuše and Přemysl went indoors with great rejoicing, reclined on couches, refreshed their bodies with Ceres and Bacchus,[88] and gave themselves up to Venus and Hymen[89] for the rest of the night. This man—who is deservedly to be called a man [vir] from his force [virtus][90]—restrained this savage people with laws, tamed the untamed populace by his command, and subjected them to the servitude by which they are now oppressed. All the laws which this land possesses and by which it is ruled, he alone with only Libuše decreed.

1.9. One day, at the beginning of the new reign of laws, the

87. The *locus classicus* for Fortune's wheel is the first several chapters of Boethius's *Consolation of Philosophy*, book 2.

88. See above, n. 39.

89. Venus, the goddess particularly associated with sexuality and procreation; Hymen, the god of marriage. This is therefore a kind of euphemism: Libuše and Přemysl spent the night having sex to consummate their marriage.

90. Isidore *Etymologies* 11.2.17, with a more explicitly gendered emphasis: "Man [vir] is so called because in him there is more strength [vis] than in women; whence the word 'force' [virtus] also derives; or perhaps because of what a man does to a woman by force [vi]." The next line defines "woman" in terms of softness, which resonates with the charges against Libuše in 1.4: "Woman [mulier] is so called from softness [mollitia, also mollier]; if you remove a letter and change another in 'mollier,' that makes 'mulier.'"

aforesaid Libuše, excited by prophecy, with her husband Přemysl present and other elders of the people standing nearby, foretold thus: "I see a burg,[91] whose fame touches the stars,[92] situated in a forest, thirty stades[93] distant from the village where the Vltava ends in streams. From the north the stream Brusnice in a deep valley strongly fortifies the burg; from the south a broad, very rocky [*petrosus*] mountain, called Petřín from *petrae* [rocks], dominates the place. The mountain in that spot is curved like a dolphin, a sea pig, stretching to the aforesaid stream. When you come to that place, you will find a man putting up the doorway of a house in the middle of the forest. From that event—and since even a great lord must duck under a humble threshold—the burg you will build, you will call 'Prague' [Praha, from *prah*, threshold]. In this burg, one day in the future, two golden olive trees[94] will grow up; they will reach the seventh heaven with their tops and glitter throughout the whole world with signs and miracles. All the tribes of the land[95] of Bohemia, and other nations too, will worship and adore them, against their enemies and with gifts. One of these will be called 'Greater Glory,' the other, 'Consolation of the Army.'"[96]

91. Throughout this chapter Cosmas refers to Prague as *urbs* in Latin, which I have translated as English "burg," meaning a fortified place, whether a town or a stronghold. *Urbs* carries the connotation of a town, often a walled town, and Libuše does indeed seem to prophesy Prague's greatness as a city. However, the specific site described here accords precisely with the location of Prague *Castle*. The point of the story is to attribute prophetic origins to Prague Castle in particular, as the seat of ducal power and the location of Prague cathedral, where the relics of Sts. Václav and Adalbert were housed. By using "burg," I am trying to suggest both the castle specifically and the town that grew up around it. Already in Cosmas's day the town of Prague included what are today Malá Strana (Lesser Town), below the castle, as well as parts of Staré Město (Old Town) across the river.

92. Phrases akin to this are quite common, and can be found in Virgil, Ovid, Horace, and Sedulius. See Book 3, n. 180.

93. A stade is an ancient measurement of distance, approximately equivalent to five hundred feet.

94. Rv 11:4 and Zec 4:3.

95. Ps 71:17.

96. These are oblique references to Sts. Václav and Adalbert, based on the meanings of their Slavic names. "Consolation of the Army" (*voje útěcha*) is Vojtěch, Adal-

More was to be said, if the pestilential and prophetic spirit had not fled from the image of God. Immediately passing into the primeval forest[97] and having found the given sign, in the aforesaid place they built the burg of Prague, mistress of all Bohemia.[98]

At that time the maidens of that land, growing up without a yoke, pursuing military arms like Amazons[99] and making leaders for themselves, fought together like young soldiers and trod manfully through the forests on hunts. Men did not take them, but they took men for themselves, whichever ones they wanted and whenever they wanted. Just like the Scythian people, the *Plauci* or

---

bert's original given name (see 1.26). This same interpretation of "Vojtěch" appears in Bruno of Querfurt's *Life of Saint Adalbert* (*S. Adalberti pragensis episcopi et martyris, vita altera*, ed. Jadwiga Karwasińska, *Monumenta Poloniae Historica*, new series, vol. 4, fasc. 2. [Warsaw: Państwowe Wydawnictwo Naukowe, 1969], 3). Václav is a contraction of the longer Vaceslav (Latin Wenceslaus), i.e., "Greater Glory" (*více slávy*). Although Cosmas does so only rarely, Thietmar frequently offers similar explanations of contemporary Slavic personal names (e.g., *Chronicon*, 245); such interpretations must have been common and laid the basis for this prophetic riddle.

97. Virgil *Aeneid* 6.179.

98. Incidentally, the *Life and Passion of Saint Václav and His Grandmother Ludmila*, by Kristián (Christian), also presents the stories of Libuše and Přemysl, and of the foundation of Prague, although in much shorter form than Cosmas's version: "But the Slavs of Bohemia, who settled under Arcturus and venerated idols, lived like horses unrestrained by a bridle, without law, without a prince or ruler, and without a city. Roaming about sporadically like reckless animals, they inhabited only the open country. Finally, after being overtaken by a disastrous plague, they, as the story goes, turned to a prophetess [*phitonissa*] to request good advice and a prophetic pronouncement. And having received it, they founded a city and named it Prague. Afterward, they found a very discerning and prudent man named Přemysl, who merely spent his time plowing, and in keeping with the pronouncement of the prophetess, they appointed him prince or ruler, giving him the above-mentioned prophetess for a wife." Marvin Kantor, *The Origins of Christianity in Bohemia* (Evanston: Northwestern University Press, 1990), 168–69; cf. *Kristiánova legenda*, ed. Jaroslav Ludvíkovský (Prague: Vyšehrad, 1978), 16–18. Because the dating of Kristián's text remains controversial, it is unclear whether he was Cosmas's source or vice versa.

99. The famous women warriors of ancient Greek myth. In epic poetry, it is worth noting, "Amazons exist in order to be fought, and ultimately defeated, by men"—precisely what is about to happen here. *The Oxford Classical Dictionary*, 3d ed., ed. Simon Hornblower and Antony Spawforth (Oxford: Oxford University Press, 1996), 69.

the Pechenegs, man and woman also had no distinction in their dress.[100] Whence their feminine audacity grew so great that on a certain cliff not far from the aforementioned burg [Prague], they built themselves a fortress fortified by the nature of its location. It was given the name Děvín, from a maidenly word [i.e., *děva*, girl]. Seeing this, young men, many of them coming together at once, angry with the women and very jealous, built a burg among the bushes on another cliff, no farther than a trumpet call [from Děvín]. Present-day men call it Vyšehrad, but at that time it took the name Chrasten from the bushes [*chrasti*].

Because the maidens were often more clever at duping the young men, and because the young men were often stronger than the maidens, there was sometimes war between them and sometimes peace. At a time when they possessed peace between them, it pleased both parties to come together with food and drink as a token [of that peace]. For three days they engaged in festive sport—without arms—in an agreed-upon place. What more? In no other way could the young men have fun with the girls. And so, like rapacious wolves seeking food, they entered the sheepfold. They spent the first day merry, with sumptuous food and too much drink. While they wanted to quench their thirst, another thirst sprang up,[101] and the young men could hardly defer their happiness to the hour of night. It was night and the moon was shining in a cloudless sky.[102] Then, blowing a horn, one of the men gave the signal to the others, saying: "You have played enough, you have eaten and drunk enough. Arise! Golden Venus calls you with the hoarse rattle."[103] Immediately, each of the men carried off a girl.[104] Come morning and having entered into an agreement of peace,

---

100. On the Scythians Cosmas is here following Regino (*Chronicon*, 132), in turn citing Justin *Epitoma historiarum* 2.1. The reference to Amazons appears in Justin's original; the Petchenegs come from Regino. It is unclear who Cosmas means by the *Plauci*.

101. Ovid *Metamorphoses* 3:415.

102. Horace *Epodes* 15.1.

103. Adapted from Virgil (*Aeneid* 8:696); the previous sentence is verbatim from Horace (*Epistles* 2.2.214, loose translation).

104. Cf. Jgs 21:21.

supported by Ceres and Bacchus, the girls yielded the empty walls of their fortress to Vulcan of Lemnos.[105] Since that time, after the death of Prince[106] Libuše, the women of our people are under the power of men.

But since all men have a journey to make, where Numa and Ancus have gone before,[107] so Přemysl, now full of days,[108] who was worshipped like a god while living, was carried off to the son-in-law of Ceres[109] after he established the rule of laws. Nezamysl succeeded him in rule. When death took him, Mnata secured the princely rods. With him departing this life, Vojen took up the helm. After his fate, Vnislav ruled the duchy. When the Fates cut off his life, Křesomysl was placed on the summit of the throne. With him removed from our midst, Neklan obtained the throne of the duchy. When life left him, Hostivít succeeded to the throne. Silence reigns concerning both the life and the death of these princes. In part because they were like cattle, devoted to their stomachs and to indolence, uninstructed and unimproved. Contrary to nature's intent, the body was a source of pleasure to them and the mind a burden.[110] In part, too, because no one at that time commended their deeds to memory with a pen. But let us be silent about the

105. Lemnos is a volcanic island of the North Aegean, associated with the Greek god of fire, whose Roman equivalent is Vulcan; Vulcan, however, is particularly linked with destructive fire. In other words, this is an erudite way of saying that the castle of Děvín was burned down.

106. The word here is *princeps*, which seems to know no specifically feminine form at this time. Whether Cosmas assumes it will be read as akin to our "princess" or whether he is deliberately suggesting Libuše's virility as "prince" is an open question.

107. Horace *Epistles* 1.6.27. Pompilius Numa and Marcius Ancus were the legendary second and fourth kings of Rome.

108. Gn 25:8.

109. The son-in-law of Ceres refers to Pluto, king of the underworld. The phrase is taken from Juvenal *Satires* 10.112, in *Juvenal and Persius*, ed. and trans. Susan Morton Braund (Cambridge, Mass.: Harvard University Press, 2004). For some reason, Cosmas declines to name Pluto anywhere in his chronicle; instead, here and elsewhere, he employs this euphemism.

110. Sallust *War with Catiline* 2.8, verbatim from "devoted" to "burden," except for the addition of "they were like cattle." Cosmas deploys this phrase in much the same context Sallust does, thus loosely paraphrasing and adapting his source.

things that remain silent, and let us return whence we have deviated a little.

1.10. Hostivít begat Bořivoj, who was the first duke baptized by the venerable Methodius, bishop in Moravia at the time of Emperor Arnulf and of Svatopluk, king of that same Moravia.[111]

We judge it not superfluous to put in writing briefly in this little work of ours, in its place, what we heard from rumor's telling. Once long ago, at the time of Duke Neklan in olden days, a battle was fought in a field called Tursko between the Czechs and the Lučané (who are now, by present-day men, called the Žatčané, after the burg of Žatec). We do not want to pass over in silence why this nation was called the Lučané in ancient times. That province is divided into five regions. The first is situated around a stream called Hutná. The second is on both sides of the River Uzká. The third is stretched along the course of the stream Březnice. The fourth, which is also called Silvana ["forested"], is situated beyond the ends of the River Mže. The fifth, which is in the middle, is called Louka [*Luca*]. It is most beautiful in appearance, the most beneficial in its uses and very fertile, and also overabundant in meadowland—whence this region derives its name, because *louka* [*luca*] means "meadow." Since this region was first inhabited by men long before the burg of Žatec was founded, its inhabitants are correctly called "Lučané" after the region.

A duke named Vlastislav was in command of them. He was a warlike man, courageous in the weapons of war and crafty beyond measure in counsel. He could have been called quite lucky in battle if highest fate had not enclosed him within unlucky con-

---

111. Svatopluk, king of the Moravians (870–94). Arnulf, king of the eastern Franks (887–99). St. Methodius (d. 885), brother of Constantine (later called St. Cyril). Natives of Thessalonica, Constantine and Methodius were sent from Constantinople as missionaries to the Moravians, preached to them in the Slavic vernacular, and then traveled to Rome. Under Roman (i.e., Catholic rather than Orthodox) observance, Methodius was subsequently appointed archbishop of Sirmium in Pannonia, essentially Svatopluk's realm. Notice, however, that Methodius was already dead when Arnulf became king and that he could not have baptized Bořivoj in the year Cosmas gives below (1.14), 894.

fines. He frequently undertook war against the Czechs and, with Mars[112] favorable and with divine auspices, he always prevailed. Entering often, he cruelly laid waste to their land with killing, fire, and rapine.[113] He wore down the leaders of the people in their fortifications so much that, enclosed in a small fortress called Levý Hradec, they feared their enemies' attack on that fortress as well.

Vlastislav founded a burg, which he called by his own name, between two mountains, Medvěz and Připek, that is, on the border of two provinces, Bílina and Litoměřice. He garrisoned it with evil men in order to lay traps for the peoples of both provinces, because they had helped the Czechs' regions. Just as, in every vicissitude of affairs, prosperity lifts up a man's heart and adversity humbles it, so too, from the great prosperity that he always obtained in battle, the duke's heart was exalted and lifted up[114] so that he burned with an insolent mind to obtain all of Bohemia. Ah! The mind of man, ignorant of future things, is often deceived by its own augury[115] and often makes it so that the heart is lifted before a fall,[116] just as it is often humbled before rejoicing. Soon, puffed up with the swollen pride of arrogance,[117] wanting to know how great the strength of his military force, he sent a sword throughout the whole province with this princely decree: any man with a bodily stature surpassing the length of the sword who came out to the fight sluggishly on his command would be punished without a doubt by that very sword.[118] Quicker than it could be said, Vlastislav saw them assembled in the place agreed upon.

Standing in the middle of the rampart surrounded by a crown of people, leaning on a shield and brandishing a sword in his hand,

112. The Roman god of war and warriors.
113. Regino, on Magyar raids in 901 (*Chronicon*, 148).
114. 1 Mc 1:4.
115. Cf. 2.10, of Emperor Henry III.
116. Cf. Prv 16:18.
117. Regino (*Chronicon*, 134), where the phrase describes Svatopluk in 890 (see nn. 156 and 158).
118. Cf. the comparable threat made in 1 Kgs 11:7, whence Cosmas takes the phrase "whoever comes out." See also a similar threat made by Duke Břetislav I in 2.2.

he began thus: "O warriors, in whose hands is the final victory, in the past more than once you have conquered, and now you should finish the deed. What need is there for arms? You should pretend to carry arms to give the appearance of an army. But why not take falcons, hawks, owls, and every kind of flying creature with you instead, since that is more suited to fun and games. You will give them the flesh of your enemies to feed on, if it happens to be enough. With the god Mars and my lady Bellona,[119] who makes all good things for me, as witnesses, I swear on the hilt of my sword, which I hold in my hand, that I will put the pups of dogs at mothers' breasts in place of their children. Raise the signals[120] and toss off restraints. Delay is the bane of preparedness.[121] Go quickly now and conquer happily." Their cries rose up to the heavens.[122] The useful and the useless, the strong and the worthless, the powerful and the impotent resounded: "To arms! To arms!" The mangy mare and the spirited horse alike leapt into battle.

1.11. Meanwhile, a certain woman, one from the number of Eumenides,[123] summoned her stepson, who was just about to go to battle. She said: "Although it is not natural for stepparents to favor their stepchildren, nevertheless, remembering my connection to your father, I will make you safe so that you will be able to survive if you wish. Know that the Czechs' witches and ghosts have prevailed over our Eumenides in their prayers, whence victory will be granted to the Czechs, our men having been killed down to the last one. Here is how you might succeed in avoiding this calamity: kill whoever is opposite you in the first encounter and, cutting off both his ears, throw them into your purse. Then, with your unsheathed sword, mark the earth in the shape of a cross between both feet of the horse. By doing this, you will loose the invisible

119. Bellona was a goddess of war, variously described as the wife, daughter, or (most often) sister of Mars.

120. Is 13:2.

121. Lucan *Pharsalia* 1.281, verbatim from "toss" to "preparedness."

122. A conflation of Virgil *Aeneid* 2.313 and 2.338.

123. See above, n. 66.

bonds which make your horses (bound as they are by the anger of
the gods) fail and fall, as if exhausted from a long journey. Immediately mounting the horse, flee. If a great fear rushes after you,
never look back but quicken your flight. Thus you alone will barely escape. The gods who accompany you into battle are turned to
aid your enemies. For those unable to resist the Czechs, for those
indeed completely vanquished by the enemy: the one salvation of
the defeated is to hope for no salvation."[124]

Just as faithless men are always more prone to evil wherever
good men and good arts are lacking, some regions are inclined to
worse depravity. It was scarcely otherwise with this people [i.e.,
the Czechs]: devoted to empty rites, trusting more to lies, despair-
ing now of their men and military arms, they approached a certain fortune-teller, consulted her, and insisted she proclaim what
act should be performed in such a crisis and what results a future
war would achieve. As she was full of divination,[125] she did not
keep them long with this obscure riddle of words: "If you want
to obtain the triumph of victory, it behooves you first to follow
the commands of the gods. Sacrifice an ass to your gods, so that
they might be your refuge. Jupiter, the greatest, Mars himself and
his sister Bellona, and even the son-in-law of Ceres[126] order this
prayer to be made." The pitiable donkey meanwhile was sought
out, killed, and, as ordered, cut a thousand times into a thousand
pieces. More quickly than could be said, it was consumed by the
entire army. Having been endowed with courage from the eating
of the ass—rather like an omen—you could perceive the divi-
sions were cheerful and the men as ready for death as forest swine.
Just as the sun is brighter and more pleasant to view after a rain
cloud,[127] so too the army was more eager for the fight and bolder
after so much inactivity.

124. Virgil Aeneid 2.354 (cf. also West's prose translation of the Aeneid, 40).
125. The phrase here is plena phitone, which resonates with 1 Kgs 28:7: mulier habens
pythonem, translated as "a woman that has a divining spirit," or, more loosely, "a woman
who is a medium." Cf. phitonissa and phitonicus, used of Libuše, above, 1.4, and below, 1.9.
126. See above, n. 39.
127. Cf. 3.17 and n. 84.

1.12. Meanwhile, their duke, Neklan, more timid than a hare and quicker to flee than a Parthian,[128] became afraid of the imminent battle and, feigning an illness, hid in the aforesaid Levý Hradec. What should limbs do without a head, or warriors in battle without a duke?[129] There was, at that time, a certain man distinguished by the beauty of his body. Though in age and name he was a *tiro* [a new recruit], he was second in command after the duke. Tiro was known to fear not at all meeting a thousand attackers in battle and to yield to no one. Secretly the duke called this man to him and ordered him to put on his [Neklan's] armor. With only a few followers knowing it, he ordered Tiro to get on his master's horse and to lead the warriors into battle in his place.

Tiro came to the field agreed upon by both armies, which was not far from the burg, about two stades[130] distant. The Czechs were first to occupy the prominent hill in the middle of the field, from which they could see the advancing enemy. He who was taken for the duke, standing in a more prominent place, addressed the warriors. "If it were right for a duke to add strength to his warriors with words,"[131] Tiro said, "I would support you with many circumlocutions of speech. But because the enemy stands within sight and there is only a short time for exhortation, it is right for me to fire you up with but a few words. In war, the devotion to fighting is equal in all men, but the conditions for conquering are not equal. They fight for the glory of the few, but we fight for the fatherland and the people, for our liberty[132] and our final salvation. They fight to carry off another's goods, we to defend our

128. Horace *Odes* 2.13.17; also Virgil *Georgics* 3.31.

129. Cf. below, 2.48.

130. See above, n. 93.

131. Cf. Sallust *War with Catiline* 58.1, where Catiline declares that "words do not supply valour" and gives a long speech anyway.

132. Ibid., 58:11, slightly modified. Whereas in Sallust the exhortation is to fight "for country, for freedom, for life," Cosmas has swapped out "life" and inserted both the "people" and "final salvation" (with its clear Christian overtones, even though the story is set in pagan times). Cosmas also describes the enemy as fighting "for glory" rather than Sallust's "to uphold the power of a few men."

own sweet belongings and our dear wives. Take courage and show yourselves men,[133] for you have appeased your gods, whom you had offended until now, with the offerings with which they wish to be appeased. Be not afraid of their fear,[134] therefore, because in battle fear is detrimental to the spirit and is the greatest danger. Boldness is a bulwark,[135] and the gods themselves will aid the bold. Believe me, beyond that camp lies your salvation and glory. But if you turn your backs to the enemy, you will not escape death. Either death or what is truly worse than death will happen: they will violate your wives in your sight, by the sword they will slaughter your infants in their laps,[136] and they will give them puppies to nurse. There is only one power left to the vanquished: to deny the conquerors nothing."[137]

Meanwhile, approaching from the opposite direction, the duke of the Lučané, Vlastislav, a man most insolent in mind and with a most arrogant people (among whom, even today, to take pride in wickedness is inborn), when he saw that the enemy did not cede the field, ordered his own men to halt there for a moment. As if sympathizing with the fate of the enemy, he spurred their spirits with these words: "O the wretched gods of fearful men! They have occupied the hill in vain, they who lack strength and military skill. Nor will the hill help them if their courage is weak. Notice that they do not dare to meet you on a level field. Indeed, if I am not mistaken, they are now ready to flee. But before they flee, rush over them in a sudden attack, and do it in the usual way so that you trample them under your feet like paltry blades of grass. Take care lest you pollute brave spears with the blood of the cowardly. Instead send up the birds you carry in order to terrify the army like

133. 3 Kgs 2:2.

134. 1 Pt 3:14.

135. Cf. Sallust *War with Catiline* 58.2, with some rearrangement of key words: "in battle . . . spirit"; and 58.17, verbatim: "in battle the greatest danger" and "boldness is a bulwark."

136. Cf. Is 13:16.

137. Notice the parallel here with the last line of the speech given by the Lučan woman to her stepson in 1.11.

doves trembling before falcons." When this was done, there was such a density of various birds that the sky was darkened under their feathers as if under a rain cloud or during a dark storm.

Seeing this, the intrepid Tiro, interrupting the speech he'd begun, said to his men: "If by chance it happens that I die in battle, bury me on this small hill and build a mausoleum named after me forever." (Whence even today it is named: the tomb of Tiro, the fiercest soldier.) Immediately throwing himself, like a huge mass of rock which, broken off by lightning, rushes down from the summit of a high mountain through precipitous places, flattening all obstacles, in nearly the same way the strongest hero Tiro fell upon the closely pressed formations of the enemy.[138] And just like someone cutting tender poppies in a garden with iron, so he cut off the heads[139] of the opposing enemy with his sword until, covered in spears like a hedgehog, he fell in the midst of the carnage upon a great pile of the slain.

It is uncertain who was killed by whom or from what kind of wound, except we know this one thing for certain: that the Czechs achieved a triumph, having killed all the Lučané down to the last one, except the one whose stepmother once forewarned him going into battle. He, when he carried out his stepmother's commands, slipped away in nimble flight and was then provoked to return home. Behold! His wife had struck her breast in lamentation to the point of death. When, in order to see her, her husband laid bare her face—or something made in its likeness—her corpse was seen to have a wound in her feminine breast and shorn off ears. Recollecting what he had done in the battle, the man brought out of his purse ears with blood-soaked earrings and recognized her to be in the likeness of the man he had killed as an adversary in war.

1.13. Afterward, entering that land and laying waste to it without

138. Sallust *War with Catiline* 60.7, perhaps via Regino (*Chronicon*, 107).

139. Cf. Livy, *Ab urbe condita* 1.54.6, where King Tarquinius, walking in his garden, lops the heads off poppies with a stick. *Livy*, trans. B. O. Foster, vol. 1 (London: Heinemann/New York: Putnam, 1919), 189.

any resistance,[140] the Czechs destroyed burgs, burned villages, and seized many spoils. In the course of all this, they discovered Duke Vlastislav's son hiding at the house of a certain little old woman. When the Czech duke saw him, moved by compassion for him,[141] he had mercy on his young age and small size (although he was a pagan, he was like a good Catholic). Building a new burg named Drahuš in a flat place along the banks of the Ohře (next to the region of Postoloprty, where the monastery of St. Mary can be found today), he surrendered it and the boy to a guardian, named During, to whom his father had earlier entrusted him. During was from a people in Sorbia,[142] exceeding other men in wickedness, a man worse than the worst man and crueler than any beast. All this was done on the advice of the *comites* so that the scattered people would not fly to the master's son—indeed their prince—like bees flock to their little queen. Moreover, the native common folk might not so quickly conspire with a foreigner. And if they should ever desire to rebel, they could easily be captured in that flat place. With these things having been arranged thus, the Czechs returned to their own land with great happiness and brought the victorious eagles[143] back to their own stations.

Meanwhile that wicked Sorbian, worse than an unbeliever,[144] cruelly perpetrated a cruel crime. One day fishermen announced that there was a large school of fish in the calm water under the new ice. Indeed, it was clear ice which the wind had not yet spoiled nor dust sullied. That second Judas, During, supposed that this was a fitting time to carry out the evil deed against the life of his lord, which he had conceived a short time earlier with a wicked mind and a wicked spirit. To the boy whom he planned to murder with deceit, he said: "Let's go fishing." When they arrived, he said to him: "O my little lord, look at the fish swimming under the

140. Jgs 18:7 and 2 Par 28:20.
141. Lk 7:13.
142. Cosmas consistently uses the term "Sorbia" to designate the Mark of Meissen.
143. Lucan *Pharsalia* 1.339.
144. 1 Tm 5:8.

ice, more than one thousand of them!" When, just like the boy
he was, he childishly bent his knees to look at the fish under the
ice, untroubled, During took an axe to his tender neck.[145] Whom
his enemy had spared, his own guardian murdered. Everyone fled
from such a sight. Worse than a parricide, what he was not able to
complete with one blow of the axe, he did with a small knife, cutting off the head of his little lord as if he were a piglet.[146] Hiding
it under a cloak, he—unlucky in his crime—wrapped it in a clean
linen cloth[147] as if in honor of his lord, in order to bring it to the
duke who had entrusted the boy to him.

Hoping that immense rewards would follow such a deed, During brought the grisly gift[148] without delay. He found the duke
in his palace at Prague, sitting in council with all of his *comites*.
Thinking it best to report his wicked deed in the midst of everyone, he entered and greeted the duke. Standing, he waited to be
greeted in return and, when he was given the freedom to speak,[149]
he said: "Behold what I and I alone have done with my axe, so that
you might all sleep untroubled on either ear.[150] Often a single tiny
spark, which the caretaker of a house incautiously leaves under a
weak ember, ignites a great fire[151] and it envelops and burns not
just the house but also the very lords of the house. Taking care

145. This passage repeatedly plays on the words *securus* (safe, carefree, untroubled)
and *securis* (an axe, especially an executioner's axe).

146. Compare this description with the execution of Mutina's small sons, in 3.24.

147. Mt 27:59.

148. This, *funesta dona*, is from Lucan, from the same line cited below (n. 152).
More important, this whole section is closely modeled on a very similar incident in
book 9 of the *Pharsalia* (which opens with reference to a *dira dona*, a gruesome gift) in
which Caesar is brought the head of his son-in-law Pompey, wrapped in linen, with
assurances that the murder was committed for his own security and with requests
for remuneration. See Lucan, *De bello civili*, ed. D. R. Shackleton Bailey (Stuttgart:
Teubner, 1988), 262–65.

149. Virgil *Aeneid* 1.520.

150. Terence *Self-Tormenter* 341, though Cosmas has swapped *otiose* (soundly, at ease,
without fear) for *securi* to keep up his wordplay (see n. 145 above). Barsby indicates
that this is a proverbial expression (*Terence*, 1:214–15).

151. Sir 11:34.

and looking to the future, I have extinguished the spark that would harm you and have protected you and your descendants from the disaster to come, as if forewarned by a divine oracle. You, who are the heads of the land, find a name for this deed. If it was worthy, make it so that everyone knows how much I have merited. And if you say it was a crime, you should give me more because you yourself did not commit the crime.[152] Should you have spared the infant when his father wanted to kill your infants and put puppies to suck from your wives? Surely, ravening wolves [deserve] neither sweet meats nor a sweet law. Behold the avenger of his father's blood,[153] who would have harmed you someday, lies vanquished without your blood. Go and take his realm in leisure instead, so that you might possess it more happily, without anxiety, forever."

Immediately he produced on a dish the delicate head, from which nothing of a living man had yet been extinguished except only this: that he was deprived of his voice. The duke became greatly frightened, the hearts of the *comites* trembled, and a confused murmur quivered in the air. Then the duke turned his head from the horrific gift and opened his mouth to say these words: "Take your gift out of our sight, criminal.[154] Your crimes are beyond measure and will neither find favor nor be found worthy of defense. Neither a fitting sentence nor a comparable punishment for this disgraceful act can be thought up. Do you think that I could not[155] have done what you did, if I had wanted to? It was licit for me to kill my enemy, but not for you to kill your lord. The sin you committed is greater than can even be called a sin. Certainly, whoever kills you or condemns you to be killed, incurs not a single sin but a double sin because it is both a sin for you to be killed and a sin that you killed your lord; and for both sins, he will carry a triple sin. Truly, if you hoped for some payment from us for this crime so immense, know that this is given to you

152. Cf. Lucan *Pharsalia* 9.1031–32.
153. Juvenal *Satires* 10.165 (*sanguinis ultor*).
154. Lucan *Pharsalia* 9.1063, though Cosmas has swapped "minion" for "criminal."
155. Mt 26:53.

as your great reward: you may choose the death you prefer from among three. Either throw yourself from a high rock, hang yourself by your own hands in some tree, or end your wicked life by your own sword." To this the man said, sighing: "Alas, can a man be considered worse off than when he finds himself beyond hope?" Leaving immediately, he hanged himself by a noose in a tall alder tree; whence that alder, for so long not chopped down (since it was next to the road), is called "During's alder."

Since these things are said to have occurred in ancient times, we leave it to the reader to judge whether they are fact or fiction. Now let our pen—though blunt, nevertheless devoted—sharpen itself for setting down those things worthy of memory which the true report of the faithful recommends.

1.14. 894.[156] Bořivoj was baptized the first Catholic duke of the holy faith. In the same year, Svatopluk, the king of Moravia—as it is commonly said—fled in the midst of his army and was never seen again. But the truth of the matter is that he came to himself[157] when he recognized that he had unjustly taken up arms against his lord emperor and fellow-father[158] Arnulf, as if forgetting his benefice. For Svatopluk had subjugated not only Bohemia but other regions as well, from there all the way to the River Oder and toward Hungary to the River Gron. Having repented,[159] with no one knowing of it in the darkness, he got on his horse in the middle of the night and, passing through his camp, fled to a place on the side

156. This chapter shows Cosmas reworking Regino of Prüm's description of relations between Svatopluk and Arnulf. The date, 894, and the last two sentences of this chapter come from Regino's account of Svatopluk's death in that year (Regino, *Chronicon*, 143). The comment that Svatopluk had rebelled against Arnulf after gaining control of Bohemia is derived from Regino's entry for the year 890, though Cosmas has modified Regino's version of events (134).

157. Lk 15:17.

158. The Latin is *compater*, which Cosmas uses (also in 3.22 and 27) to indicate that two men are linked by one's status as godfather to the other's child. Here it further testifies to Cosmas's familiarity with Regino's entry for 890, which describes how Svatopluk became godfather to Arnulf's illegitimate son and gave him his own name—usually rendered in the Germanic spelling, Zwentibold (Regino, *Chronicon*, 134).

159. Mt 27:3, in reference to Judas's repenting his betrayal of Jesus.

of Mt. Zobor, where three hermits had once built a church with his money and assistance in a great forest inaccessible to men.[160] When he arrived there, he killed the horse in a secret place in the forest, buried his sword in the ground, and, with the light of day dawning, approached the hermits. Without their knowing who he was, Svatopluk was tonsured and dressed in hermit's garb. As long as he lived, he remained unknown to everyone. He told the monks with him who he was only when he realized death was at hand—and died immediately thereafter. His realm was held by his sons for a short, but less happy, time. With the Hungarians plundering part of it, the eastern Germans another part, and the Poles another part, it was subsequently laid waste by enemies.

1.15. Bořivoj begat two sons, Spitihněv and Vratislav, by a woman named Ludmila,[161] the daughter of Slavibor, castellan of Pšov. When Bořivoj went happily the way of all flesh,[162] Spitihněv succeeded to his father's principate. After his death, Vratislav obtained the duchy. He took a wife named Drahomiř from that hardest of people, the Liutizi, and she herself was harder than stone[163] toward believing; she was from the province called Stodor.[164] She bore two sons, Václav, pleasing to God and men, and Boleslav, accursed by fratricide.

But how Duke Bořivoj, with the grace of God preceding and following him everywhere, came to the sacrament of baptism, and how the holy religion of the Catholic faith grew from day to

160. Mt. Zobor outside Nitra, where by Cosmas's time there was indeed a Benedictine monastery for men. Pál Engel, *The Realm of St. Stephen: A History of Medieval Hungary, 895–1526*, trans. Tamás Pálosfalvi, ed. Andrew Ayton (London: Tauris, 2001), 43.

161. Ludmila is today revered as a saint, though there is some question of when in the Middle Ages her cult began. Notice that Cosmas makes no suggestion of sanctity here, although later (3.11) he describes a relic of hers at St. George's monastery.

162. Cf. Gn 6:12 and 3 Kgs 2:2.

163. Dt 32:13.

164. Thietmar of Merseburg equates "Stoderania" with "the land of the Hevelli," a west Slavic people living along the Havel River, north of Sorbia and south of the Liutizi, a Slavic confederation in the region between the Elbe and the Oder. Thietmar, *Chronicon*, 172.

day[165] in these parts through his successors, and which duke as a
believer first built which or how many churches in praise of God, I
have chosen to omit rather than to inflict disgust upon my readers,
because I have already read it in the writings of others: some in the
privilege of the Moravian church, some in the "epilogue" of that
land and of Bohemia, some in the life or passion of our most holy
patron and martyr Václav.[166] For foods that are eaten more often
are detestable. The deeds we considered above were done between
those years which we have noted below [in the next chapter, i.e.,
between 895 and 928]; I was not able to determine in which [spe-
cific] years or times these deeds might have been done.

1.16. 895. 928.

1.17. 929. On 28 September, Saint Václav, duke of the Czechs,
martyred by fraternal deceit in the burg of [Stará] Boleslav, happily entered the eternal chamber of heaven. Boleslav was hardly
worthy to be called the brother of that holy man. How he deceit-
fully invited his brother to a feast where he schemed instead to kill
him in order to seize control of the realm, or how he disguised
his fratricidal guilt before men if not before God, I consider sufficiently set out in the celebration of the passion of that same holy
man. After the short span of his life, Boleslav, another Cain, alas
obtained the duchy so wickedly taken up.

A distinguished child of Duke Boleslav was born of an excellent wife at this feast, the one at which the execrable fratricide oc-

165. Pss 60:9 and 95:2.
166. This Václav (also known as Wenceslas) is the same man mentioned above
as the son of Vratislav and Drahomiř. He was murdered, as Cosmas will note in
a moment, by his brother Boleslav on 28 September 929 and, so far as we can tell,
was almost immediately venerated as a martyr by Bohemia's nascent Christian community. By Cosmas's time, several accounts of Václav's life and passion (i.e., his martyrdom) had been written, both in Latin and in Old Church Slavonic. For a concise
description of the Václav legends, see Gábor Klaniczay, *Holy Rulers and Blessed Princesses:
Dynastic Cults in Medieval Central Europe*, trans. Éva Pálmai (Cambridge: Cambridge University Press, 2000), 100–108; also Wolverton, *Hastening Toward Prague*, 149–56. English
translations of the *vitae* of Czech provenance are available in Kantor, *Origins of Christianity*.

curred (as we said above); from this event, he was endowed with the name Strachkvas, which means "terrifying feast."[167] For what more terrifying feast could there be than one where fratricide was perpetrated? Therefore Duke Boleslav, conscious of the evil committed, fearing the punishments of Tartarus,[168] and always thinking with a shrewd mind how God might be able to be placated for this crime, made a vow to the Lord, saying: "If[169] this son of mine should survive, I promise him to God with all my heart. Let him be a cleric and serve Christ all the days of his life, for my sin and for the people of this land."

1.18. Afterward, remembering his vow, his father sent him to Regensburg, placing him under the monastic wings of the abbot of St. Emmeram the martyr[170]—since he was already a docile boy, much loved by his parents, and his father could not bear for him to study before his eyes. There he was trained in ecclesiastical and monastic decrees, there dressed in a monk's habit, and there nourished until he reached a man's strength. The course of the rest of his life will be sufficiently elaborated in what follows.

Concerning the deeds of Duke Boleslav I was able to find nothing worthy of report except one thing that I decided to lay out before you as worthwhile. Prevented by death, Václav, the servant of God, left a church in the *metropolis* of Prague,[171] constructed in honor of the holy martyr Vitus but not, however, consecrated. Since he deemed it worthy of consecration, Duke Boleslav humbly sent messengers with great rewards and greater promises and

167. No son of Boleslav I named Strachkvas, born on the day of Václav's martyrdom and designated for the church, is known from other sources. Bruno of Querfurt, however, mentions a brother of Boleslav II named "Christian" who was a monk (*Vita Adalberti* 15).

168. The lowest region of the underworld, a mythical place of severe punishment.

169. Jgs 11:30: "He made a vow to the Lord, saying: If . . ."

170. The venerable Benedictine monastery in Regensburg, established ca. 739.

171. Here and at the end of this chapter, Cosmas describes Prague as a "metropolis," which connotes grandeur as well as ecclesiastical primacy. However, the physical location of this event is Prague Castle. The remains of this large rotunda church associated with St. Václav lie underneath the present cathedral.

inducements to a bishop named Michael, who was then ruling the church of Regensburg and who fulfilled his request but barely carried it out.[172] The bishop would scarcely have agreed to it, except he determined it to be in memory of the soul and for the salvation of his friend Václav, now slain. For the man of God, Václav, while he lived in the flesh, had cherished him with great affection as if he was a spiritual father as well as a most beneficent bishop. Bishop Michael had likewise adopted him as his most beloved son,[173] often instructing him in the fear and love of God, and as often sending him gifts, which the new church of Christ especially needed at that time. As soon as the duke had achieved his wish, all the devoted common folk and magnates and clergy rushed to meet the arriving bishop and received him with great honor and rejoicing in the buildings of the *metropolis* of Prague. What more? Having dedicated the church of St. Vitus the martyr on 22 September, the bishop happily returned home.

1.19. 930. Otto, son of Emperor Henry, married Edith, daughter of the king of the English.

931. Emperor Henry made the king of the Abotrites and the king of the Danes Christians.[174]

932. On 4 March, the body of St. Václav the martyr was transferred from the fortress of [Stará] Boleslav to the burg of Prague

172. Michael was bishop of Regensburg from 942 to 972. *Handbuch der bayerischen Kirchengeschichte*, vol. 1, ed. Walter Brandmüller (St. Ottilien: EOS Verlag, 1998), 1213. Since Michael was not bishop of Regensburg in 929, Cosmas may simply have mistaken the name of the bishop who consecrated the Church of St. Vitus. More likely, some tradition Cosmas "was able to find" preserved Michael's name, as well as the date 22 September, but not the year. Typically for Cosmas when he is uncertain of a date, he simply inserts the event at the outset of Boleslav I's reign. Since Václav was killed on 29 September and the church was consecrated on 22 September, Cosmas probably does not mean to suggest that the latter took place in 929. He may, however, want the reader to infer that it took place before 932, the date he gives for the removal of Václav's remains from Stará Boleslav to Prague, since it would have been inappropriate to move such precious relics to an unconsecrated church.

173. Est 2:15 (cf. also Est 2:7).

174. These entries for 930 and 931 are lifted verbatim from the anonymous continuation of Regino of Prüm's *Chronicon* (158).

owing to the hatred of his envious brother. Indeed, his brother
Boleslav, becoming worse and worse from day to day, pricked by
no sort of penance for his crime, with a haughty mind, did not accept that God manifested innumerable miracles through the merits
of his martyr Václav at his tomb. Boleslav secretly ordered faithful
followers of his to transfer Václav's body to Prague by night and
bury it in the ground of the church of St. Vitus so that, if God
should manifest any wonder to the glory of his saints, it would be
ascribed not to his brother's merits but to St. Vitus's.

The rest of his evil deeds I either found unworthy of report
or I was unable to discover them for certain. One of his crimes,
which he committed back in the days of his youth, was nevertheless sufficiently bold and memorable that I wanted to report it to
your charity. This Duke Boleslav—if someone who was an impious tyrant, more cruel than Herod, more savage than Nero, excelling Decius in the enormity of his crimes and Diocletian in his
barbarity[175] (whence, it is said, he earned for himself the nickname
"the Cruel") could even be called a duke—was so severe that he
ruled nothing with counsel, nothing with reason, but did everything for his own will and on impulse. Whence it happened that
he conceived in his mind that he might build a burg for himself in
the Roman manner. Boleslav immediately called the leaders of the
people into one and to a man. Leading them into a wood on the
River Elbe and specifying the place, he opened up to them the secret of his heart: "Here," he said, "I desire and command that you
build for me the walls of a burg in the Roman manner very high
and in a circle." To this they said: "We, who are the mouth of the
people and hold the rods of dignities, we refuse you, because we
neither know nor desire to carry out what you order. Our fathers
did no such thing before. Behold, we stand in your presence and we
submit our necks to your sword rather than to such unbearable servitude. Do what you wish, but we will not obey your commands."

175. According to Christian tradition, Herod "the Great" (40–4 BCE), the Jewish king of Palestine under the Romans, ordered the massacre of the innocents after
Jesus' birth (see Mt 2:16–17). Nero (37–68 CE), Decius (249–51), and Diocletian
(284–305) were all Roman emperors notorious for their persecution of Christians.

Then the duke broke out in awful anger and, springing up, stood on a decayed tree trunk, which fortunately lay there in the woods, and with his sword unsheathed said: "O lazy sons of lazy fathers, if you were not half-men or more vile than the dregs,[176] you would confirm those words by deeds and test whether it is easier to submit your necks to the sword or to the bond of servitude." It was a thing worthy of a stage play and a bold duke's act of insolence to be marveled at. For if there were a thousand armed right hands on one body, such a crowd of men could not have trembled so much. When the duke saw that they were paler than boxwood[177] from fear, he seized one who was first among the elders. Taking him by the hairs of his head[178] and striking him as hard as he was able, he cut off his head as if it were a tender poppy.[179] Then he said, "I wish it and I will do it. Let my will be reason enough."[180] When the rest of them saw this, repenting[181] late, they fell at the duke's knees begging forgiveness with tears. "Now, lord," they said, "spare us, the guilty. We will now obey your commands in all things. We will now do whatever you want and more, lest you be more cruel to us." And immediately they built a burg at the duke's will with a thick high wall in the Roman style, just as is seen today. It is called Boleslav after its founder.[182]

1.20.[183] 933. The Hungarians returned, through Italy, laying waste to the eastern Franks and the Alemanni, as well as Gaul.

176. The word here is *peripsima,* meaning the filth that comes off when scouring something. 1 Cor 4:13.

177. Ovid *Metamorphoses* 11.417.   178. Ez 8:3.

179. See above, n. 139.

180. Almost verbatim from Juvenal *Satires* 6.223.

181. See above, n. 159.

182. Presumably Mladá (Young) Boleslav, since the burg of Stará (Old) Boleslav was already in existence at the time of Václav's martyrdom and this story seems to postdate that event, presuming Boleslav's rule as duke. However, Cosmas says specifically that this incident occurred in Boleslav's youth, so perhaps he does mean Stará Boleslav here.

183. The material in this chapter is again taken from the continuation of Regino's *Chronicon* (159–65). Although Cosmas decided to leave the years after 951 blank, the continuation describes events down to 967.

934. With considerable slaughter, King Henry overthrew the Hungarians and captured many of them.

935. King Henry was struck down with paralysis.

936. King Henry died. His son, Emperor Otto, succeeded him.

937. Arnulf, duke of the Bavarians, died.

938. The Hungarians were again laid waste by the Saxons with considerable slaughter. And the sons of Duke Arnulf rebelled against King Otto.

939. King Louis married Gerberga, the widow of Gisalbert.

940. The duchy of Lotharingia was entrusted to Henry, the king's brother, and, in that same year, he was expelled from there.

941. Henry, the king's brother, conspired with certain Saxons against the king, but he was unable to do any harm.

942. A star resembling a comet was seen for fourteen nights and an immeasurable mortality of cows followed.

943. Duke Otto died; Conrad, the son of Werner, succeeded as duke.

944. With considerable slaughter, the Hungarians were massacred by the Carinthians.

945. Bertold, duke of the Bavarians, died; Henry, the king's brother, succeeded him.

946. King Louis was expelled from his kingdom by his own men.

947. Lady Edith the queen died.

948. A synod was held in Ingelheim by thirty-four bishops.

949. A daughter, Mathilda, was born to Liudolf, the king's son.

950. Boleslav, duke of the Czechs, rebelled against the king. The king assailed him with a strong force and subjected everything to his authority.

951. King Otto went to Italy.

952. 966.

1.21. 967. On 15 July Duke Boleslav, whose nickname was "the Cruel," lost with his life the duchy that he had wickedly bought with his brother's blood. His son of the same name, but with good mores and a pious way of life altogether different from his father's, succeeded him as duke. O the miraculous mercy of God! O how incomprehensible are his judgments![184] Behold, just as grapes issue forth from a bramble bush, a rose from thorns, or a noble fig from thistles,[185] so a worshipper of Christ was born of a fratricide, a lamb from a wolf,[186] a gentle ruler from a tyrant, a pious second Boleslav—a duke second to no one in probity—from the impious Boleslav. Having the same name as an evil father did not contaminate him, in whom burned a true love and pure delight in Christ. Just as, by contrast, many people are allotted the names of saints but nonetheless do not achieve sanctity, because neither sanctity nor iniquity is found in a name but instead in the merit within a man.

1.22. That prince, Boleslav II, was a most Christian man, a Catholic in faith, a father to orphans, a protector of widows, a comforter to the grieving, a pious supporter of clergy and pilgrims, an exceptional builder of God's churches.[187] As we read in the privilege of the church of St. George,[188] that faithful man built twenty churches for the Christian religion and generously endowed them with all the necessities that pertained to ecclesiastical uses.

He had a sister named Mlada, a virgin devoted to God, learned in sacred letters, given over to the Christian religion, gifted with humility, charming to talk to, a generous patron of paupers and orphans, and adorned with every kind of integrity of character. When she went to Rome for the sake of prayer, she was received benevolently by the pope. Living there for some time, she was imbued fully with monastic discipline. Finally, the lord pope, upon the advice of his cardinals and indeed wanting to help the new church by his beneficent judgment, consecrated her as abbess, having changed her name to Mary, and gave her the rule of St. Benedict and the abbatial staff.

184. Rom 11:33.

185. Cf. Mt 7:16 and Lk 6:44 (although, when Jesus asks, "Are grapes gathered from thorns?" and so forth, he gives an answer contrary to Cosmas's point here, namely, that bad trees do *not* bear good fruit).

186. Cf. Lk 10:3: "I send you as lambs among wolves."

187. Cf. Regino's description of Louis on his death in 874 (*Chronicon*, 107).

188. A document since lost; no privileges pertaining to St. George's survive from Cosmas's time or earlier.

Afterward, having received permission and apostolic blessing to bring this new and holy monastic rule to Bohemia, the new abbess rode back to her sweet fatherland with her companions very delighted. She went to the royal burg of Prague[189] and Duke Boleslav honorably received his long-missed and most beloved sister. Holding hands, they passed under the royal roof,[190] where they rested for a time, enjoying each other's conversation. She reported to her brother the many things worthy of mention or wonder she saw and heard in Rome. Moreover, she presented him with letters addressed to him on behalf of the pope, whose formulation was like this:[191]

John, servant of the servants of God, to Boleslav, nourished in the Catholic faith, apostolic blessing. It is just for benevolent ears to accommodate just petitions, because God is justice and those who love him will be justified and for those who love God's justice all things work together for good.[192] Our daughter, your relative named Mlada (who is also Mary), among other petitions not to be refused, brought entreaties, sweet to our heart, on your behalf: that, with our approval, it might be permitted for there to be a bishopric in your principality to the praise and glory of the church of God. We received it gladly and gave thanks to God, who always enlarges his church everywhere and extols it in all countries. Whence, by apostolic authority and the power of St. Peter, prince of the

189. Key words from "giving her" to "Prague" have been lifted from chapter 8 of the *Vita Adalberti* by John Canaparius. Johannes Canaparius, *Vita antiquior (passio sancti Adalberti martiris Christi)*, ed. G. H. Pertz, Monumenta Germaniae Historica, Scriptores 4 (Hanover: Hahn, 1841), 584.

190. Virgil *Aeneid* 6.13.

191. This letter, which authorizes the establishment of an episcopal see at Prague, is considered a forgery, whether fabricated by Cosmas himself or found by him among the cathedral archives. The pope named here is John XIII (965–72), although scholarly consensus dates the see's foundation to circa 973. Cosmas's confusion may result from some tradition, perhaps this very forgery, ascribing its foundation to John XIII, whom Cosmas otherwise knew had died in 972. Note also that below (2.37) Cosmas describes a privilege issued by a Pope Benedict (VII, presumably) to St. Adalbert that also involves Otto I, which cannot be correct. See also 1.24, n. 199, concerning some difficulties with the dates for Thietmar, Prague's first bishop.

192. Rom 8:28.

apostles, whose vicar we are, although unworthy, we approve and highly praise, and indeed put in writing, that there be an episcopal see at the church of Sts. Vitus and Václav, martyrs, and also that a community of nuns be established at the church of St. George the martyr under the rule of St. Benedict and in obedience to our daughter, Abbess Mary. Not according to the rite or sect of the people of Bulgaria or Russia, nor in the Slavic language, but rather following apostolic laws and decrees, at the will of the whole church you should choose someone more preferable for this work, a cleric well educated in Latin letters.[193] He should be capable of cutting through the fallow land of the heart of the gentiles with the plowshare of the word, sowing the wheat of good work, and bringing back bundles of the fruit of your faith in Christ. Farewell.

Immediately, as was ordered, on the advice of the duke and abbess, the church of St. Vitus was decreed to have a future bishop. For the present, the church of St. George the martyr[194] was given to Abbess Mary, the duke's sister.

1.23. A certain man from Saxony of marvelous eloquence and knowledge of letters, by the name of Thietmar, a priest by promotion and a monk by profession, had come to Prague once in earlier days for the sake of prayer. When he came to the attention of Duke Boleslav II, within a short time he obtained his considerable favor and friendship. And since he knew the Slavic language perfectly, the duke summoned him through his messengers. Boleslav convened the clergy, leaders, and people of the land and, through his own entreaties and admonitions, he brought it about that everyone by common assent elected Thietmar as their bishop. On the next day, as pleased the duke, everyone chose Thietmar as bishop by favorable acclamation.

Then he was sent, on behalf of the duke and the entire clergy and people, to the most Christian Emperor Otto, son of Emperor

193. The implication here is to prohibit the liturgical use of the Slavic vernacular, originally pioneered by Sts. Constantine (Cyril) and Methodius with papal approval that was subsequently withdrawn.

194. This women's convent was thus the oldest monastic establishment in the Czech Lands. It is located within Prague Castle, immediately behind St. Vitus's cathedral.

Henry,[195] with these letters: "O most glorious emperor and special cultivator of the Christian religion: mercifully accept our prayers and those of the entire clergy and people and accept this man named Thietmar, approved by all, whom we chose as our pastor. We humbly entreat that he be ordained bishop by your most holy commendation and command." Then the emperor, as a lover of divine law, with the counsel of the dukes and princes but especially the bishops, and taking thought for the salvation and newness of these Christian people, ordered the archbishop of Mainz, who presided at court then,[196] to ordain him bishop.

Then the new bishop, garlanded with a mitre,[197] returned joyfully to his new diocese of all Bohemia. When he arrived at the *metropolis* of Prague, he was enthroned by everyone next to the altar of St. Vitus, with the clergy singing "Te Deum laudamus." The duke and the magnates resounded with "Christus keinado," etc., while the simpler and unlearned people cried "Krlessu" [*Kyrie eleison*].[198] Thus, according to their custom, they spent that entire day in good cheer.

968. *Comes* Vok died.

1.24. After this, Bishop Thietmar consecrated churches built by the faithful in many places to the praise of God and, baptizing a great number, made the gentile populace faithful to Christ. After not many days, namely, on 2 January 969, he was freed from the

195. Otto I, king of the Germans from 936 to his death in 973, emperor after 962.

196. In 967 the archbishop of Mainz was Wilhelm (954–68); his successors were Hatto II (968–70), Rupert (970–75), and Willigis (976–1011). The comment that the archbishop "presided at court then" is perhaps intended to explain why the new diocese of Prague was subordinated to the archdiocese of Mainz, with which it is not contiguous, rather than Salzburg or Magdeburg. No extant source addresses this issue. Nevertheless, the sees of Prague and, later, Olomouc were suffragan to Mainz until the establishment of an independent archbishopric at Prague in 1344.

197. A liturgical headdress, pointed, with two strips of cloth hanging down the back, normally reserved to bishops.

198. Thietmar of Merseburg describes the missionary bishop, Boso, teaching Slavic converts to sing *Kyrie eleison* (Greek for "Lord, have mercy"), as well as their mockery of it (*Chronicon*, 119). This might explain Cosmas's description, here and elsewhere (1.42, 2.4., 2.14, and 3.27), of the Czech people singing *Kyrie eleison* or crying out "Krleš" (which he glosses once as equivalent to *Kyrie eleison*) on public occasions.

bonds of flesh, paid his debt, and returned a hundredfold increase to Christ.[199]

1.25. Meanwhile, returning from the castles of philosophy where he had fought for more than ten years, and bringing with him no small quantity of books, a worthy hero appeared named Vojtěch, by rank still a subdeacon. Solicitous, like a tender lamb among sheep, he performed the funeral rites fitting for the death of their shepherd.[200] Continuing in prayers both day and night,[201] he commended the spirit of their common father to God with abundant alms and holy prayers. Duke Boleslav and his magnates, seeing him to be devoted to such good work and hoping that he would be more devoted in the future—and with the grace of the holy spirit inspiring them—grabbed the strongly resisting youth, brought him into their midst, and said: "Whether you like it or not, you will be our bishop. You will be called bishop of Prague however unwillingly. Your nobility, your character and deeds accord perfectly with the honor of the pontificate.[202] You are known to us from head to toe.[203] You know well how to show us the path which leads to the heavenly fatherland.[204] We must want to fulfill your commands so far as we are able. All the clergy proclaims you worthy and the entire populace proclaims you suitable to be bishop." This election took place not far from Prague, in the fortress of Levý Hradec, on 19 February in the same year in which Bishop Thietmar died.

1.26. At that time, returning from the Saracen war, the most excellent Otto II, a lover of peace and worshipper of justice, went to the burg of Verona.[205] More glorious than his most glorious father,

199. This date is probably incorrect, though it fits with the confused chronology associated with the founding of the bishopric of Prague; cf. 1.22, n. 191. Modern scholarly consensus holds that Thietmar was consecrated bishop (by Archbishop Willigis of Mainz) in 976 and died in 982.

200. Cf. Mt 9:36: "he had compassion for them . . . like sheep without a shepherd."

201. 1 Tm 5:5.

202. Canaparius *Vita Adalberti* 7.

203. Cf. Horace *Epistles* 2.2.4, where the adjective is "handsome."

204. Heb 11:16.

205. Otto II, king of the Germans and Roman emperor (961–83); he shared both titles with his father until 973.

Otto I, he was the most victorious victor in every battle. A Slavic retinue went to him with the elected bishop of Bohemia, bringing an embassy on behalf of the duke and a petition from the entire clergy and people, that by imperial command he might confirm their common election. Therefore, the most serene emperor, condescending to the worthiness of their petition, gave him the ring and pastoral staff on 3 June.[206] Archbishop Willigis of Mainz,[207] who by chance was there and whose suffragan[208] he was, consecrated him bishop by order of the emperor, with the name Adalbert. (Some time before, Archbishop Adalbert of Magdeburg,[209] confirming him with chrism, had called him by that name, his very own.)

Consecrated on 11 June, he rode into his sweet fatherland[210] with

206. Episcopal investiture was a procedure whereby a king conferred the insignia of episcopal office, the ring and staff (or crozier), upon a bishop-elect, often in exchange for oaths of fealty and in conjunction with the grant of land and temporal authority from the king. This secular ceremony invariably took place *before* the candidate was liturgically consecrated bishop by his ecclesiastical superior in a church. For a description of the process and its political significance in the empire, see I. S. Robinson, *Henry IV* (Cambridge: Cambridge University Press, 1999), 114–15. Although Cosmas would have it occur in 969, scholars date Adalbert's investiture in Verona to 983. See Karl Uhlirz, *Die Jahrbücher des Deutschen Reiches unter Otto II und Otto III*, vol. I, *Otto II: 973–83* (Leipzig: Königliche Akademie der Wissenschaften, 1902), 185. This would accord with Cosmas's remark (derived from Canaparius 8) that Otto was "returning from the Saracen war," which must refer to the important battle at Crotone in July 982. See Gerd Althoff, *Otto III*, trans. Phyllis G. Jestice (University Park: Pennsylvania State University Press, 2003), 29.

207. Archbishop Willigis of Mainz (975–1011).

208. In the hierarchy of the Catholic Church, the bishop oversees all ecclesiastical affairs, legal and theological, within his diocese (territories usually with well-defined, even long-standing boundaries). These bishops are *de iure* subordinate to a specific archbishop. Among other aspects of his oversight, the archbishop may summon his subordinate bishops to synod to give him advice, i.e., suffrage, hence the term for the bishops who answer to a particular archbishop: suffragan. As noted above (n. 193), bishops of Prague were suffragan to the archbishops of Mainz.

209. Archbishop of Magdeburg (968–81).

210. The words "sweet fatherland," as well as half the individual words from the start of this chapter to this point, are lifted from Canaparius and rearranged (*Vita Adalberti* 8). The parenthetical note about Adalbert's confirmation is half-quoted from earlier in the same vita (3).

his followers and, as he came to Prague with bare feet and a humble heart, he occupied the episcopal throne with the clergy and all the people singing for joy. With the advice of this noble shepherd Adalbert and by the intervention of the aforementioned Abbess Mary, his dear sister, Duke Boleslav granted to both in willing piety whatever the bishop of Prague possessed as his own up to that time or might obtain for his episcopate, as well as whatever the abbess chose to be given or made over for the benefit of her convent. And he confirmed it for both by the holy authority of the canons.

1.27. 970. 971. 972. Saint Ulrich left this world.[211]

977. Doubravka died. Since she was a very impudent woman, when she married the duke of Poland as a woman already advanced in age,[212] she removed the *peplum* from her head and put on a maiden's crown, which is the great insanity of woman.[213]

978. 979. 980. 981. Slavník, the father of Saint Adalbert, died. Concerning his habits and life, although many things shine forth as worthy of memory, we will nevertheless mention only a few of them, interrupting our undertaking. In his visage, he was a man most pleasant to everyone; in his mind, most serene in counsel; in his speech, most charming; in his riches, both worldly and spiritual, he was wealthy. In his house shone honor and genuine love, rectitude of judgment and a multitude of magnates. Among his works was knowledge of the law, refreshment of the poor, consolation for the grieving, refuge for pilgrims, and the defense of widows and orphans.

The distinguished *metropolis* of this duke was Libice,[214] located where the stream Cidlina loses its name as it enters the freer waters of the River Elbe. His principality had these boundaries: in the

211. Bishop of Augsburg (923–73).

212. Gn 18:11, in reference to Sarah.

213. The daughter of Duke Boleslav I of Bohemia and sister of Boleslav II; she married Duke Mieszko of Poland in 965. Thietmar of Merseburg credits her with converting her husband to Christianity (*Chronicon*, 191–92).

214. Cosmas's use of *metropolis* here suggests that Libice was, in effect, Slavník's capital, akin to the role Prague played for the Přemyslid dynastic rulers.

western region, facing Bohemia, the streamlet Surina and a castle situated on Mount Osek next to the River Mže; in the region to the south, facing the east Germans [Austrians], the boundary burgs Chýnov, Doudleby, and Netolice up to the middle of the forest; toward the rising of the sun, facing the realm of Moravia, the castle below the forest called Litomyšl up to the Svitava streamlet in the middle of the forest; likewise in the north, facing Poland, Kłodzko castle next to the River Nysa. Here Duke Slavník, as long as he lived, lived happily.

1.28. 982. 983. 984. Otto II, caesar of Rome, died. Bishop Adalbert of Prague truly was a familiar of this emperor, dear to him for his devotions—so much so that during the Easter feast, which the king celebrated in the palace of Aachen before all the bishops, he raised Adalbert to the highest dignity, namely, Adalbert placed the crown on the king and celebrated the major mass (which it was only permitted for an archbishop to do). After the feast, when he had already received permission from the caesar to return to his fatherland, the emperor called him aside in secret and, confessing his sins, he commended himself to his prayers in pious remembrance.[215] Moreover, Otto gave him the vestments in which he had celebrated Mass at Easter, namely, an alb, dalmatic, chasuble, cope, and towel;[216] these Adalbert kept in memory of him. They are

215. The only time Otto II celebrated Easter in Aachen was in 975 (Uhlirz, *Jahrbücher des Deutschen Reiches*, 1:61). He died in December 983. On the anniversary of his death in 984, his widow asked Adalbert for memorial prayers on Otto's behalf and gave the bishop generous gifts (Althoff, *Otto III*, 49; cf. Canaparius *Vita Adalberti* 586–87). This last occasion perhaps explains the origin of the vestments reverently preserved at Prague, with an alternative story about them developing later.

216. The alb was an ankle-length undergarment, white, belted at the waist, worn by all ranks of clergy. The dalmatic was worn over the alb, chiefly by bishops and deacons; it was somewhat shorter, with wider and shorter sleeves. Moreover, it was never worn in penitential seasons. The same holds for the chasuble, an overgarment worn by the celebrant of the Mass; this was a tent-like cloak, put on over the head and draped on the shoulders and arms. The cope was a semicircular cloak that fastened at the neck, often with a hood; it was first worn as an outer garment to protect against the inclement weather, then retained for warmth in cold churches, whence it eventually assumed a ceremonial function. Janet Mayo, *A History of Ecclesiastical Dress*

honorably preserved still today in the church of Prague and called "the vestments of Saint Adalbert."

985. 986. 987. Střezislava, the venerable mother of Saint Adalbert and a matron pleasing to God—so much so that she is said to have been worthy of a holy child—died.[217]

988. 989. 990. With the abbot unaware of who he was, Saint Adalbert was made a monk at St. Alexius in Rome.

991. 992. 993. 994.

1.29. I think that I should not pass over what I see others have omitted.[218] Seeing that the flock committed to him would always go off a precipice and that he could not steer it onto the correct path, and fearing that he might also perish with this dying people,[219] Bishop Adalbert did not dare remain with them any longer, nor could he further endure to offer his preaching in vain. When the time came that he wished to take a trip to Rome, fortune appeared by chance in the form of that same Strachkvas, whom we discussed above [1.17]. He came from Regensburg with the permission of his abbot to see his sweet fatherland, his relatives, and his brother, the duke of Bohemia. The man of God, Bishop Adalbert, sought him out in secret and had a conversation with him, complaining a great deal about the faithlessness and wickedness of the people, the incestuous bond and especially the illicit dissolution of impermanent marriages, the disobedience and negligence of the clergy, and the arrogant and intolerable power of the *comites*. He laid bare every intention of his heart[220] down to the last: that he wanted to go to Rome to consult the pope and never return to this rebellious people.[221]

(New York: Holmes and Meier, 1984.) The *faciterium* here is probably a sort of towel used in the liturgy, though the word could also denote a handkerchief or towel that was a symbol of investiture (equivalent to *facitergium*).

217. Some of the language here is borrowed from Regino's entry for 851 on the death of Irmengard (*Chronicon*, 75).

218. As Cosmas himself has signaled here, the story that follows is attested nowhere in the hagiographic or historical writings pertaining to Adalbert. This is true of all the references to Strachkvas in this section.

219. Cf. Gn 19:15, of Lot leaving Sodom.

220. Heb 4:12.   221. Ez 2:3.

Among other things, he added these words to those, "It is good that you know yourself to be the brother of the duke, and that you take your origin from the lords of this land. These common folk prefer that you rule and prefer to obey you more than me. With the advice and aid of your brother, you will be able to suppress the arrogant, censure the negligent, correct the disobedient, and thunder at the unfaithful. Your worthiness and knowledge, and the holiness of your way of life, very much agree with episcopal governance. That this might be I grant you, with God's will and my power. And I will intercede before the pope with all my prayers, so that it might be permitted for you to be bishop here, even with me still living." He put in Strachkvas's lap the bishop's staff, which by chance he was holding in his hand. But that man threw it to the ground as if in a rage and added these words more: "I do not want any distinction in the world, I flee from honors, and I despise worldly pomp. I judge myself unworthy of the episcopal summit, nor able to bear the great burden of pastoral care. I am a monk; I am dead; I cannot bury the dead."[222] To this the bishop responded: "Know, brother, know: what you do not do now to your good, you will do later to your very great evil." After this, as he proposed, the bishop traveled to Rome and abandoned his disobedient people to their own commands.

Because at that time Duke Boleslav was not in his own power but in that of the *comites*, the *comites*, turned to the hatred of God, the worse sons of evil fathers, perpetrated a very bad and evil crime. On a certain feast day, they secretly broke into the burg of Libice, where the brothers of Saint Adalbert and all the burg's warriors stood, like innocent sheep, celebrating the feast with the holy solemnities of the Mass. Like savage wolves, the *comites* broke through the walls of the burg, killing everyone to a man, male and female.[223] Having beheaded the four brothers of Saint Adalbert with all their children before the altar itself, they burned down the

---

222. Cf. Mt 8:22, where Jesus responds to a disciple who asked leave to bury his father before following him, "Follow me, and let the dead bury their dead."

223. Gn 1:27.

burg, bathed the streets in blood, and returned cheerful to their own homes loaded with bloody spoils and cruel plunder.[224] In the burg of Libice the five brothers of Saint Adalbert were killed in the year 995; their names are Soběbor, Spytimír, Dobroslav, Pořej, Čáslav.[225]

1.30. After these deeds were carried out, Duke Boleslav consulted with the clergy, then turned anxiously to the metropolitan [archbishop] of Mainz with these words: "You should either return our pastor Adalbert to us, which we prefer, or you should ordain someone else for us in his place, which we ask reluctantly. Given the novelty of the faith still among this people, if the watchful protection of a shepherd[226] is not present among them, this sheepfold of Christ will become sumptuous food fitting for a ferocious wolf." Then the archbishop of Mainz, worried that the people recently acquired by Christ would relapse into their old sacrilegious rites and perish, sent legates to the pope[227] and called upon him to either send back to the widowed church in Prague her husband[228] or permit someone else to be ordained in his place.

The servant of God, Adalbert, freed from the care of his flock by the lord pope's order, was living in the monastery of Saint Alexius in the company of the senators of heaven within the lovely

224. Loosely modeled on Regino (*Chronicon*, 151).

225. There is a clear discrepancy in these sentences between Cosmas's statement that Adalbert's *four* brothers were beheaded and his list of the *five* brothers killed. Noticing the difference, scribes occasionally corrected or elided the former number. Bruno of Querfurt describes this massacre, stating at the outset that Adalbert had five brothers, one of whom was away in the retinue of Bolesław Chrobry of Poland; he then explains clearly that four were killed by Duke Boleslav II's army, while the fifth brother was put to the sword subsequently (*Vita Adalberti* 21–22). Cosmas may have garbled the information in paraphrasing Bruno; or the error might have been introduced by an intermediary source (listing the brothers' names, for instance, which are not mentioned in either Bruno's vita or that of John Canaparius).

226. Cf. Lk 2:8 and Jn 10:11.

227. Pope John XV (985–96); the archbishop of Mainz is still Willigis (above, n. 196).

228. Cf. Canaparius *Vita Adalberti* 22: "Pragam suo pastore viduari." In fact, the first part of Cosmas's chapter 1.30 matches Canaparius 22 closely in content, although Cosmas has rewritten it thoroughly to accord with his own style.

court of the Elysian Fields.[229] The lord pope and his pious abbot
consoled this gloomy man with friendly words of this sort:[230] "O
sweetest son and most beloved brother, we entreat you for the love
of God and we implore you for the love of your neighbor that
you properly return to your diocese and diligently take back the
governance of your sheep. If they listen to you, thank God; if
they do not listen to you, flee those who flee you, lest you perish
with the dying,[231] and you will have license to preach to foreign
peoples." Very much cheered by the decision that a license to teach
foreign peoples was given to him, but still in considerable gloom,
the bishop left that sweet community of brothers.

With a bishop of the highest discretion, named Notharius,[232]
Adalbert approached the archbishop of Mainz in his palace and
asked whether he might learn, through messengers, if his flock
would accept him. What his flock responded when this was done,
for what reason they would not accept him, to which peoples he
went thence, in what frugal ways he spent all the days of his episcopate, and with how much probity of character he glittered, whoever reads his life or passion can know.[233]

It does not please me to say a second time what has already
been said. Strachkvas, the duke's brother, whom we mentioned
above [1.29], seeing the bishop repudiated by his own people, as if
this were by rule and law, was inflamed with swollen pride to gain
the bishopric. And since it is easy to compel a willing man, the
wicked people immediately raised that simpleton and sycophant

229. The ancient Greek and Roman paradise, where the good and distinguished
go after death.
230. Virgil *Aeneid* 5.770, together with Juvencus 2.321, in *Libri evangeliorum quattuor*,
ed. Karl Marold (Leipzig: Teubner, 1886), 39.
231. Again Gn 19:15; see above, n. 219.
232. This is usually interpreted to mean Bishop Notger of Liège (972–1008), but
the identification remains uncertain.
233. Two lives of St. Adalbert were composed ca. 1000: the first by John Canaparius at the monastery of St. Alexius in Rome; the second by Bruno of Querfurt,
based in Merseburg, who was familiar with the Canaparius version. As the notes
above indicate, Cosmas knew both, though he preferred Canaparius and drew on his
language at various points in his chronicle.

into the bishop's chair. For thus by his providence, thus God often allows the power of depraved men to take over. So, in this irregular election, the games of the son-in-law of Ceres prevailed. For this Strachkvas was well dressed in his clothes, puffed up in his mind, dissipated in his behavior, wandering in his eyes, empty in his words, a hypocrite[234] in his habits, chief of all error and leader of evil men in every bad deed.

It is a shame to relate much[235] about Strachkvas the pseudo-bishop; a few things will suffice for many. He came to the archbishop of the see of Mainz,[236] where everything that was to be done was carried out in the order that it was accustomed to occur. After the episcopal examination, with the chorus singing the litany, when the archbishop, adorned with the symbols of his office, was prostrate on the carpet before the altar and behind him Strachkvas, who was about to be ordained, was prostrated in the middle, in between two suffragans—alas, a fearful situation!—Strachkvas was seized by an evil demon. And what the servant of God once predicted to him in secret was laid bare before the clergy and all the people. Let it suffice to have inserted this much.

1.31. 996. Afterward, the remarkable standard-bearer of Christ, Bishop Adalbert, caught Hungary and likewise Poland in the nets of faith.[237] Finally, while he was sowing the word of God in Prussia, he happily ended this present life in martyrdom on Christ's behalf, on 23 April. (That year Easter was 25 April.)

997. The oft-mentioned Duke Boleslav, seeing that the Prague church was widowed of its shepherd, sent his legates to Emperor Otto III,[238] asking that he give the Bohemian church a bridegroom

---

234. Cf. Is 9:17 for *hypocrita*.

235. Sedulius *Paschale Carmen* 1.276.

236. Given the date, this implies Archbishop Willigis (above, n. 196).

237. Adalbert's connection with Hungary is noted by Bruno (*Vita Adalberti* 16); a later tradition has him St. Stephen's godfather (Engel, *Realm of St. Stephen*, 42). On his preaching in Poland on way to the Prussians, cf. Bruno *Vita Adalberti* 23. Bolesław Chrobry famously redeemed the martyr's body from the Prussians and buried it at Gniezno; cf. 2.4, below.

238. Otto III (983–1002), king of the Germans and Roman emperor.

worthy of its merit, so that the flock recently delivered to Christ would not return to the original rites of vanity and to iniquitous acts. Moreover, he asserted that no cleric worthy of episcopal office was to be had in all of Bohemia at that time. Soon the august Caesar Otto, who was most experienced in divine and human affairs, assenting to their petition, began to consider carefully which most capable man among his clerics he would send for work so arduous. By chance, present in the royal court was a chaplain, named Thieddag, upright in his deeds and honorable in his mores, especially learned in the liberal arts, of Saxon stock and perfectly instructed in the Slavic language. Because fate offered this man, every senator in the royal hall and the very happy emperor himself chose and commended him as bishop of the church of Prague. Sending him to the archbishop of Mainz, Otto ordered that he should be quickly consecrated bishop.

998. On 7 July Thieddag was consecrated. He was honorably received by the people and clergy of the church of Prague and enthroned with great rejoicing at the horn of the altar[239] of Saint Vitus. The duke rejoiced, because the good shepherd smiled upon his flock and the joyful flock played with their new shepherd.

1.32. That most excellent prince, Boleslav, ruled the duchy for thirty-two years after the death of his father. He was a most ardent executor in matters of justice, of the Catholic faith, and of the Christian religion, and in his presence no one gained ecclesiastical or worldly office by means of money. He was also, as the matter shows, a most victorious victor in battles, but a most merciful indulger of the vanquished and a particular lover of peace. The treasures most important to him were the instruments of war and the sweet pursuits of arms; for he loved the stiffness of iron more than the shimmer of gold. In his eyes, no one useful was displeasing and the useless never pleased. Boleslav was terrible to his enemies and mild to his own people.

This most glorious duke had joined himself in matrimony to Emma, who was more noble than others by birth, but also—what

239. Ex 29:12.

ought to be praised more—more distinguished than many in the nobility of her character. From her Boleslav received two sons of the finest talents, namely, Václav and Boleslav. Václav exchanged this fragile life for eternity at a young age. Boleslav, however, after the death of his father, assumed the governance of the princely seat, as will be set out in what follows.[240]

1.33. It happened that when the days of the aforementioned Duke Boleslav [II] drew near to an end—when he would exchange eternal life for death—he summoned his surviving son of the same name. With his wife Emma and a great crowd of magnates present, he addressed his sweet son, so far as he was able, with sobbing interrupting his words. "If it is right," he said, "for a mother to offer gifts of wisdom to the child of her womb, like breasts of milk, it is not by nature—for man was created to have dominion in creation.[241] Nevertheless, God granted some of his gifts to men like Noah, Isaac, Tobias, and Matthew. And at the very least God blessed those whom those men blessed. God also granted them, destined for a life[242] of good living, perseverance. And so it is also today, my son: if the mercy of the Holy Spirit is not present, the boasting of my words is of little use. 'I made you duke,' God says, 'Do not exalt yourself but be as one of them.'[243] In other words, if you feel yourself higher than others, nonetheless recognize yourself to be mortal. And look not to the glory of the office to which you have been raised in the world, but focus on the work that you will carry with you to the netherworld. Write God's precepts on your heart,[244] and do not disregard your father's commands.

"Frequently visit the thresholds of churches, worship God,[245] honor his priests. Be not wise in your own eyes[246] but consult

---

240. Most of this paragraph is lifted, with only small modifications, from Regino's entry for 876, describing the death of Louis the German, whose wife was also named Emma (*Chronicon*, 110–11).

241. Wis 9:2.

242. Cf. Acts 13:48.

243. Sir 32:1, where it reads "ruler" (*rector*) instead of "duke."

244. Prv 7:3.   245. Rv 22:9.

246. Prv 3:7.

many men if they are wise in the matter. [Cultivate] as many as you please but take pains about whom. Discuss everything with friends,[247] but first consider them. Judge justly,[248] but not without mercy. Do not look down upon widows or strangers[249] standing at your door. Love money but scarcely love its form.[250] The *res publica*, although it might be greatly augmented, will quickly diminish to nothing through the false form of coin. This is something, my son, that Charles understood, the wisest king and most powerful in his army (hardly to be compared to us very humble men).[251] When he arranged for his son, Pippin,[252] to be raised to the throne after him, he bound him for this reason with a frightful oath: that there should never be deceitful or crooked valuing of weights or money in his realm. Certainly no disaster, no pestilence, no death, nor even if enemies laid waste to the whole land with rapine and fire, nothing would harm the people of God more than frequent change and fraudulent worsening of the coinage. What plague or act of the infernal Furies[253] plunders, ruins, and weakens Christians more severely than the master's fraud in the coinage? Afterward, with justice growing weak and wickedness stronger, not dukes but robbers arise, not rulers of the people of God but vile tax collectors, the greediest men without mercy. Not fearing that God sees everything,[254] they will be in the devil's snare, changing

247. Cf. Prv 25:9.   248. Jer 11:20.
249. Ps 93:6.

250. This is verbatim from the popular collection of aphorisms, wrongly attributed in the Middle Ages to Cato. It is, however, but the first of two lines, which read: "Love money but scarcely love its form. No one holy or honorable strives to have it." *Disticha Catonis* 4.4, ed. Marcus Boas (Amsterdam: North-Holland, 1952), 197. The same line appears in Bruno's *Vita Adalberti* 11.

251. Charles "the Great," usually called Charlemagne, king of the Franks (768–814) and Roman emperor (after 800).

252. Pippin was king of Italy (781–810) under his father Charlemagne's aegis, at which time he issued a silver penny. Pierre Riché, *The Carolingians: A Family Who Forged Europe*, trans. Michael Idomir Allen (Philadelphia: University of Pennsylvania Press, 1993), 321. Cf. below, 2.8 and n. 72.

253. Also known as the Eumenides; cf. above, n. 66.

254. Est 16:4.

the money three or four times per year to the ruin of the people of God.[255] By means of such worthless skills and through arrogance toward the laws, they will constrict the boundaries of this realm and the resources of the people, which I expanded through God's grace[256] to the mountains beyond Cracow, named the Tatras. For the riches of the common folk are the praise and glory of a king; poverty brings harm not to the slave but to his lord."[257] He was going to say more, but the late hour limited the prince's speech. More quickly than it was said, he fell asleep in the Lord[258] and a great lamentation was made over him.[259] The day of his death was 7 February 999.

1.34. In that same year, Gaudentius (who is also called Radim), the brother of Saint Adalbert, was ordained bishop of the church of Gniezno.[260]

How much this most glorious duke, Boleslav II—whose memory is blessed[261] and truly can hardly be lamented enough today—expanded the boundaries of his duchy by his sword,[262] apostolic authority bears witness in the privilege of the bishopric of Prague.[263] After his death, his son, Boleslav III, succeeded as duke, as was related above; but he did not hold the acquired borders with the same good results nor with his father's auspices. For the Polish duke, Mieszko (no other man was more deceitful than him!), soon took the burg of Cracow by deceit and all the Czechs whom he found there were put to the sword.

Two brothers, the glory of their fecund mother, were born to

255. Cf. 1 Tm 6:9.
257. Lucan *Pharsalia* 3.152, verbatim.
259. Acts 8:2.

256. Cf. Dt 12:20.
258. Acts 7:59.

260. Archbishop of Gniezno (ca. 999–1006 or 1012 or 1022). Cosmas is here either glossing over, or perhaps ignorant of, what most historians take to be a significant moment in the reign of Otto III: his visit to the tomb of St. Adalbert in Gniezno in 1000, his reception there by the Polish duke, Bolesław Chrobry, and the creation of an *arch*bishopric at Gniezno. Althoff, *Otto III*, 90–107.

261. Sir 45:1.

262. Regino, concerning Karlomann on his death in 880 (*Chronicon*, 116).

263. Presumably the 1086 privilege; cf. 2.37.

Duke Boleslav by his noble wife: Oldřich and Jaromír.²⁶⁴ As a youth Jaromír was raised in his father's hall, but Oldřich was sent in his boyhood to the court of the Emperor Henry [II], where he learned their customs and cleverness, as well as the German language.

Not long after this, the aforesaid dukes Mieszko and Boleslav came together to parley in an agreed-upon place. With peace between them, faith having been given and strengthened by an oath, Duke Mieszko invited Boleslav to condescend to come to his feast. Since he was a dove-like man without bile,²⁶⁵ Boleslav said that he wanted to do everything with the advice of his familiars. But what plague is more harmful than familiar enemies?²⁶⁶ Because he was not able to go against their deceitful plans, which were already his fate—ah, the prophetic mind of the duke—he summoned the more noble men and those in the realm he was about to leave behind who seemed more faithful to him. Then he addressed them with these words: "If, by chance, something untoward should happen to me in Poland, beyond faith and hope, I commit this son of mine, Jaromír, to your faith and bequeath him to you as duke

264. Here begins a section where Cosmas is held to be almost completely wrong, chiefly by comparison with Thietmar of Merseburg, who was both contemporary with the events in question and personally familiar with all the protagonists; the scholarly consensus is universal in preferring Thietmar's facts over Cosmas's. The struggles for the Bohemian throne in this period were intimately tied to Polish-imperial relations, especially the aggrandizement of the Polish ruler Bolesław Chrobry, who briefly gained control of Prague. Since the political machinations lasted for more than a dozen years, they are too complicated to summarize here. Two basic points are relevant here: First, Thietmar reports that Oldřich and Jaromír were the *brothers* of Duke Boleslav III, not his sons (*Chronicon*, 221). Second, in all the chapters that follow Cosmas incorrectly attributes the deeds of Bolesław I Chrobry (992–1025), to his father, Duke Mieszko (950s?–992).

265. The absence of bile (*sine felle*) as a fundamental characteristic of doves is a commonplace in Christian literature; cf. Isidore *Etymologies* 12.7.61.

266. Cf. Boethius, *Consolation of Philosophy*, book 3, prose 5: "What plague is more able to hurt a man than an enemy who was once a familiar friend?" Since this is the last line of a chapter wholly devoted to critical questions on the power of kings and their opportunistic associates, Cosmas surely intends for this citation of the "punch line" to call to mind Boethius's larger moral.

in my place." With the affairs of the realm thus arranged, the man who was about to be deprived of his sight went under a sinister omen and entered the burg of Cracow to attend the feast of the perfidious Duke Mieszko. Soon, during the midday meal, peace, faith, and the law of hospitality were broken: Duke Boleslav was seized and deprived of his eyes, and all the rest of his men were either slaughtered, slain, or shoved in prison.

Meanwhile, the domestic and familiar enemies of Duke Boleslav, a hateful people and an evil generation,[267] the Vršovici, worked an abominable evil,[268] unheard of since back when the world began.[269] The first among them, or rather the head of all evil, was Kohan, a most criminal man and the worst of all bad men. He and his relatives, evil men, arrived with the duke's son, Jaromír, at a place for hunting called Veliz. Rumor now spread about the duke in Poland, and after they heard what had been done, they said, "Who is he [Jaromír], a little man worth less than seaweed,[270] who ought to be greater than us and called lord? Is not a better man to be found among us, who might be more worthy to rule?" Ah, wicked mind, wicked spirit! That which the sober mind ruminates over, the drunk does openly. As their iniquity kindled and took up the horn of wine, they seized their lord and savagely tied him up. They affixed him, nude and lying on his back, to the ground by his arms and feet with wooden nails and then leapt, playing at military leaps, leaping over his body on horses for some time.

One of Jaromír's servants, named Dovora, seeing this and quickly running to Prague, announced to the duke's friends what had been done. That same hour, without delay, he led them to the disgraceful triumph. When the evildoers[271] saw armed men rushing upon them unexpectedly, they fled like bats through the hidden recesses of the forests. The duke's friends found him half-dead,

267. Mt 12:39.
268. Prv 10:29.
269. Jn 9:32; also Regino (*Chronicon*, 131) on the Magyars.
270. Horace *Satires* 2.5.8, and Virgil *Eclogues* 7.42.
271. 1 Mc 3:6.

badly mutilated by flies (for a multitude of flies rose above the nude body, like a swarm of bees). Untying him and placing him on a cart, they bore him away to the burg of Vyšehrad. For his merit, such thanks was rendered to Dovora, the servant, a friend of the duke worthy of every praise: by the voice of the herald, it was proclaimed throughout markets everywhere that both Dovora himself and his future descendants would be among the freeborn and noble forever and ever. In addition, they gave to him the office of hunter, which pertains to the court of Ztibečná—and which, from that time until now, his descendants have possessed through the generations.

1.35. While these things were happening in Bohemia, Duke Mieszko, coming with a strong Polish force, invaded the burg of Prague and held it for the space of two years, namely, the years 1000 and 1001.[272] But the burg of Vyšehrad, faithful to its duke, remained undaunted and unconquerable.

During this time, the same Duke Mieszko sent messengers to the emperor, promising and giving him infinite amounts of money, so that he might send to prison in chains the son of Duke Boleslav, named Oldřich, then in the emperor's service. O invincible hunger for gold,[273] where is the most powerful law of the Roman Empire? Behold a possessor of gold, crushed by gold's weight: an emperor, corrupted by gold, obeys a duke's orders and so a deliverer of prisons becomes a torturer. It is no surprise that he obeyed the duke, since in our times, Vacek, born under a peasant millstone, dragged Henry III [IV], the most powerful king, into Bohemia with a golden chain, just like a dog.[274] O undignified crime! A lord of lords[275] obeys what a slave of slaves orders. The king thus sent

272. By comparison with Thietmar of Merseburg, these dates are incorrect. The standard chronology asserts that Bolesław Chrobry blinded Boleslav III in 1003 and was subsequently in control of Prague and Bohemia for about a year (*Chronicon*, 225 and 245–47).

273. Virgil *Aeneid* 3.57.

274. There is some wordplay here that does not come through in the English: between Latin *mola* (millstone), and *molossus* (Molossian hound).

275. Rv 17:14, though there obviously in reference to God as lord of lords.

Bořivoj, a duke strictly just,[276] a truthful man, to prison continuously chained at the knees as if he were an iniquitous and lying man. But this will be fully written out in pen in its place [3.32].[277]

1.36. In the year 1002, with Christ now looking down upon the Czechs and Saint Václav aiding his people, Duke Oldřich returned to his fatherland and entered a most fortified castle named Dřevíč. (It is unclear to us whether he escaped secretly by flight or was sent away by order of the emperor.) From there he sent a warrior faithful to him and suggested that, entering the burg of Prague at night, they might terrify the incautious enemy with a trumpet noise. His loyal follower soon carried out his orders: climbing at night to a higher point (called Žiži) in the middle of the burg, he blew a trumpet and repeated, shouting with a clear voice: "They are fleeing! The confused Poles are fleeing shamefully! Invade! Invade eagerly, armed Czechs!" At that voice, dread and trembling came upon them [the Poles][278] because of the wondrous permission of God and the intervention of Saint Václav. Everyone fled in different directions: one, forgetting himself and his weapons, jumped nude onto his nude horse and fled; another, just as he slept, hastened into flight without trousers. Fleeing, several men were thrown off the bridge because the bridge was broken up by enemies in ambushes. With others fleeing on the broken road which is commonly called "the tail of the burg," and with countless men having been overwhelmed in a confined back gate there on account of the narrowness of the exit, Duke Mieszko himself barely escaped with a few men. And thus it was as it usually is when men flee out of fear: they trembled even at the motion of the air[279] and that trembling increased the fear in them. So, with no one pursuing them,[280] it seemed to them that the stones and

276. 2 Mc 10:12; also Horace *Odes* 3.3.1.

277. Although this seems to refer to 3.32 below, where Cosmas describes Henry IV's role in the deposition of Duke Bořivoj in 1110, others are named (not Vacek) as the *comites* instrumental in bringing him to Bohemia.

278. Ex 15:16.   279. Cf. Virgil *Aeneid* 2.728.
280. Lv 26:17.

the walls were crying out[281] after them and pursuing those fleeing. After daybreak, Duke Oldřich entered the burg of Prague and, on the third day, with those same familiar enemies (about whom we spoke above [the Vršovici]) fraudulently suggesting it, he deprived his own brother Jaromír of sight.[282]

No offspring was born to him from his legitimate marriage on account of the infertility of his wife, but from a certain woman named Božena (who was also called Křesina) he begat a son of the most extraordinary beauty whom he caused to be called Břetislav.[283] One day when he returned from hunting through a peasant village, he saw the woman we mentioned washing clothes at the well. Looking at her from head to toe[284] inflamed him beyond measure with love.[285] Indeed, the appearance of her body was remarkable: brighter than snow, softer than a swan, more splendid than ancient ivory, more beautiful than a sapphire.[286] Sending for her immediately, he took her as his, although he did not dissolve his old marriage. At that time—and as was pleasing to him—it was permitted to have two or three wives. Nor was it a sin for a man to abduct the wife of another, or for a wife to marry another's husband. What is now considered modest was then a great dishonor, namely, if a husband lived content with one wife or a wife with one husband. For they lived like brutish animals having spouses in common.

1.37. In the same year, Emperor Otto III migrated from this world in order to live in heaven where every Christian lives. His son, Em-

281. Hb 2:11.

282. According to Thietmar, it was *Jaromír* who regained Prague from Bolesław Chrobry with the help of the German king, Henry II (*Chronicon*, 245–47). As duke of Bohemia, Jaromír was subsequently very active in frontier wars and politics as Henry's ally. Then, in *1012*, Oldřich ousted him from power virtually in Thietmar's presence (ibid., 285, 292).

283. Except for changing the names, Cosmas has taken this sentence verbatim, again, from Regino's entry for 880 on Karlomann (*Chronicon*, 107; see above, n. 262).

284. See above, n. 203.

285. Ovid *Metamorphoses* 10.253.

286. Song of Thr 4:7, although "softer than a swan" is an addition from Ovid *Metamorphoses* 13.796.

peror Henry [II], succeeded him.[287] Among the other great things that he did[288] in his life in the name of Christ, he built a castle on a certain mountain, purchased at no small price from the owner of the place, named Poppo, whence it took the name "Bamberg," which means "Poppo's mountain."[289] There he also established a bishopric which he endowed to such an extent with resources and pontifical honors that, in all of eastern Francia, it was considered not the last bishopric but second (after the first). He also built there a temple of astonishing magnitude in honor of the holy Virgin Mary and St. George, the martyr of Christ. He likewise augmented it with endowments for the church, ornaments of gold and silver, and other regal splendors, so much so that it seems to me better to remain silent about these things than to speak insufficiently, or more than is considered useful.

Nevertheless, I will report one beneficial deed among the many. Not far from the aforementioned burg, there was a certain anchorite, a monk of holy virtues. Often the emperor, pretending as if he wanted to go hunting, would create some pretext to go to him secretly, with a single follower, and commend himself to his prayers. When the emperor learned that the anchorite wanted to go to Jerusalem for the sake of prayer, he committed to him a golden chalice for the Lord's body and blood. Because of its great size, the chalice had two handles on each side (which we commonly call ears) so that it could more easily be lifted. The emperor com-

287. Otto III died young, unmarried, and without offspring. His successor, Henry II (1002–24), was his second cousin, as Otto's grandfather and Henry's grandfather were brothers. Karl J. Leyser, *Rule and Conflict in an Early Medieval Society* (Oxford: Blackwell, 1979), xii–xiii.

288. Cf. Dt 10:21 or Ps 70:19.

289. For the association of Bamberg, a contraction of Babenberg (as Cosmas spells it) with the Babenberger lineage, descendants of a ninth-century Poppo (or sometimes, as Cosmas has it, Pabo) and later dukes of Austria, see Karl Lechner, *Die Babenberger: Markgrafen und Herzöge von Österreich, 976–1246* (Vienna: Böhlau, 1976), 30. Cosmas is substantially correct in his etymology though certainly mistaken in assuming that Henry purchased the castle from Poppo; Bamberg had long since passed out of Babenberger hands.

manded and requested that he dip it with a threefold immersion in the River Jordan, where Christ was baptized by John,[290] and gave him as much money as he needed for the road. What more? The man of God went to Jerusalem and did as ordered, dipping the chalice three times in the waves of the Jordan.

Afterward, returning through Constantinople, he crossed through Bulgaria. There, a certain hermit was living a holy life. Coming to him, the Jerusalem farer humbly asked, after many pleasant and holy conversations, that he pray to God for the safety of Emperor Henry. The hermit said to him: "It is not necessary to pray for his safety because he has now been transferred from this vale of tears[291] to the rest of the blessed." The anchorite pressed and asked the hermit to tell him how he knew that. The hermit said: "Last night, while I was neither fully awake nor totally asleep, a lofty vision raised me to a large field, very broad and extremely wide, and pleasant. There I saw evil spirits[292] most terrifying, out of whose mouths and nostrils sulfurous flames discharged, and who dragged Emperor Henry unwillingly by his beard as if to trial. Others, poking his neck with iron forks, happily clamored: 'He is ours. He is ours.' Saint Mary and Saint George followed them from a distance, as if they were sad and as if they wanted to snatch him away and dispute with them, until a pair of scales, whose capacity was wider than two miles, was suspended in the middle of the field. On the left, the malicious party placed great, immense, innumerable weights, which were his evil works. But on the other side, I saw Saint George place a great monastery with its whole cloister; I saw golden crosses heavy with precious stones; I saw such an abundance of things filled with gems and gold; I saw golden candelabra and censers and countless *pallia*,[293] and whatever else good

290. Mk 1:9.   291. Ps 83:7.
292. Lk 8:2.

293. The *pallium* (pl. *pallia*) was a mark of rank and honor granted by the pope to metropolitan archbishops and occasionally other bishops. In shape, it was a circular band of white wool worn across the chest and shoulders, with two long strips that hung vertically down the front and back. Censers, also known as thuribles, were used to burn and waft incense during the liturgy.

the king had done in his life. But still the malicious party weighed more, and clamored: 'He is ours. He is ours.' Then Saint Mary took a great golden chalice from Saint George's hand, shook her head three times,[294] and said: 'Certainly he is not yours but ours.' Then with great indignation she threw the chalice against the wall of the church and one handle of the chalice was broken. At its ringing, the fiery army immediately vanished. Saint Mary took the emperor by the right hand and Saint George took him by the left and they led him, so I believe, into the celestial residence." The Jerusalem farer, brooding in his heart upon the things that were said, reached down into his pack and found the chalice's handle broken, just as the hermit had predicted. To this day, it is kept in the monastery of Saint George in Bamberg as evidence of this great miracle.[295]

1003. Here the Vršovici were killed.[296]

294. See above, n. 60.

295. By "monastery" Cosmas means the cathedral church, which is indeed dedicated to St. George, together with Sts. Laurence, Peter and Paul, Killian, and the Virgin Mary. The story of a battle for Henry's soul and a broken chalice preserved in the cathedral is similar in some elements to one reported by Leo Marsicanus, an eleventh-century chronicler at Montecassino. There Henry's soul is claimed by demons on his deathbed until his good and bad deeds are placed in a balance, including the Bamberg chalice, which tips the balance toward the good. The chalice subsequently falls out of the balance and is broken. Although Leo notes that the church in Bamberg is dedicated to St. George, it is St. Laurence who figures with the angels in the vision. Leo Marsicanus, *Chronica monasterii casinensis,* ed. W. Wattenbach, Monumenta Germaniae Historica, Scriptores 7 (Hanover: Hahn, 1846), 658–59. Still another, pared-down version appears in Henry's vita (*Die* Vita sancti Heinrici regis et confessoris *und ihre Bearbeitung durch den Bamberger Diakon Adelbert,* ed. Marcus Stumpf, Monumenta Germaniae Historica, Scriptores rerum Germanicarum in usum scholarum, vol. 69 [Hanover: Hahn, 1999], 304–7). Since there are no verbal borrowings, and only Cosmas's version includes the hermit, the trip to Jerusalem, the Virgin Mary, and St. George and their dialogue, it seems likely that these stories are all based on an oral kernel associated with the famous chalice; it is also possible that Cosmas knew the Montecassino text that seems to precede the others and yet chose to tell the story differently. On the political and religious significance of Henry's foundation of the see at Bamberg, and the large church where his tomb would lie, see Stefan Weinfurter, *Heinrich II (1002–1024): Herrscher am Ende der Zeiten* (Regensburg: Pustet, 1999), 250–68.

296. This entry has always puzzled scholars, because another massacre of Vršovici is described in great detail for the year 1108; cf. 3.23. Moreover, Cosmas uses vivid

1.38. 1004. Benedict was martyred with his companions.[297] In the times of Emperor Henry [II], who ruled the Roman Empire after Otto III, five monks and hermits—true Israelites[298]—lived in the regions of Poland: Benedict, Matthew, John, Isaac, Christian, and a sixth, Barnabas. No deceit was found in their mouths,[299] nor depraved work[300] in their hands. Concerning the life of these fathers, I prefer to write little rather than much, because it is always taken as more pleasant when food is offered more sparingly.

Their way of life was laudable, acceptable to God, admirable to men, imitable to those willing to follow it. Toward this end we admire the merits of the saints, so that we might render ourselves admirable by imitating them. Indeed, we can compare the five men not inappropriately either with the five porticos by the pool[301] or with the five wise virgins overflowing with the oil of mercy,[302] be-

---

language in reference to this clan at many points in his chronicle, making this spare note seem incongruous. Perhaps he found it in one of his sources, an annal or necrology, but did not know what to make of it.

297. These martyrs are certainly the same as those described by Bruno of Querfurt in his *Vita quinque fratrum eremitarum*, ed. Jadwiga Karwasińska, Monumenta Poloniae historica, new series, vol. 4, fasc. 3 (Warsaw: Państwowe Wydawnictwo Naukowe, 1973). Bruno's version, which is clearly connected to his Life of Adalbert, emphasizes the tradition of eremeticism associated with Romuald and others around Rome in the reign of Otto III, as well as the missionary impulse to evangelize the Slavs and other pagan peoples. Cosmas's account shows no obvious reliance on Bruno's text in the form of verbal borrowings. Moreover, by dramatically reducing the story to an account of the brothers' asceticism and their murder, he eliminates much of Bruno's narrative and nearly all of the main themes of his vita. Still, the core elements of the story here accord with Bruno's version: the brothers' names, the monetary gift, murder by thieves. Cosmas's inclusion of the martyrs here stems from the fact that their remains were transferred from Gniezno to Prague with the body of St. Adalbert in 1039 (below, 2.5). As elsewhere, he names Mieszko in place of Bolesław Chrobry.

298. Jn 1:47.   299. 1 Pt 2:22.
300. Jas 3:16.

301. Jn 5:2. Here and with reference to the next note, Cosmas is clearly comparing comparable sets of five. However, the verses of John he alludes to here (2–9) describe these porticos by the pool as housing a variety of invalids, one of whom, in need of help but not receiving it, was healed by Jesus.

302. Mt 25:2, though again Cosmas is referring more broadly to verses 1–13, which comprise part of Jesus' description of the kingdom of heaven, wherein the five vir-

cause, as paupers themselves, they paid the expenses of mercy for
Christ's paupers, whom they cared for in their lodgings as much
as they could. The power of abstinence was such in them that one
would eat food twice and another only once on the Sabbath, and
no one did so during the day. Moreover, food to them was veg-
etables produced by their own hands. They seldom had bread, and
never fish. It was not permitted for them to eat legumes or millet
except on Easter. They drank pure spring water, and that only in
measure. A meal of meat was abominable to them and the sight
of women detestable. Their clothes were rough and harsh, woven
from a horse's tail and mane. For the support of the head in bed
they used a rock, and for a couch a mat—and this was very old
and there was only one. Nor was there any rest; they stood for the
entire night, mourning both their own crimes and guilt and those
of the common folk. Sometimes their chests, black and blue with
frequent beating, resound; sometimes their weary bodies sweat with
uncountable genuflections; and sometimes, with hands spread and
eyes raised, each works at his prayers with strained breathing—in
order to live in heaven. They never spoke with one another except
to an arriving guest, and very little even to him. Truly they are doers of the law, not hearers.[303] Truly, crucifying themselves with the
world's vices and desires,[304] and bearing Christ's cross[305] in mind
and body, they offered a grateful sacrifice to God not of another's
cattle but of their own bodies, because every day they were flogged
in turn. It was their custom once each day, after prime,[306] to rend

gins wise enough to bring oil for their lamps were prepared to go to the wedding
banquet when their heavenly bridegroom arrived.

303. Cf. Rom 2:13: "For it is not the hearers of the law who are righteous in God's
sight, but the doers of the law who will be justified."

304. Gal 5:24.

305. Jn 19:17.

306. Clergy were expected to pray the divine office (or hours), a set round of
psalms and other prayers, over the course of the day at set times. These then became
a convenient way of marking the time of day, even outside a purely religious context.
Though there was some variation in different periods and regions, the hours and
their modern equivalents are roughly: matins (before dawn), lauds (dawn), prime

their backs all the way to the bottom.[307] Falling on his face,[308] brother said to brother, "If you spare me, you sin; when you touch me, spare me not." Standing with the flog, the other responded: "As you wish, let it be done!" He beseeches Christ and flogs his brother, saying, "By these deeds, let Holy Christ discharge your crimes." Then falling in turn, he offers his back in turn. While another scourges a brother, he sings not "That hurt, brother," but either "Miserere mei, Deus" or "Benedicite."[309] For what someone suffers willingly, he endures easily.

Gazing down from on high on their suffering, their innocence of life, and their persistence in faith and works, God wished to reward them now for their holy labors and, as it were, to guide them back to their rejoicing fatherland by a wondrous path.[310] Duke Mieszko, hearing of their good reputation and their holy way of life, went with a few followers to commend himself to these holy men. Since he recognized their need, he gave them a great abundance of money, namely, a purse full of one hundred marks. Receiving from them fraternity and community of prayers, he commended himself to them and very much asked that they perform memorials for him. Then he went off happy to his hall.

But because they had never had such a thing, the brothers did not know what they should do about the money. They stood dumbstruck (since already for half a year they had said nothing to each another). One of them opened his mouth and said: "The weight of silver and gold is the snare of death.[311] The lovely places of Elysia will not easily lie open to those for whom the stinking

---

(6:00 A.M.), terce (9:00 A.M.), sext (noon), nones (3:00 P.M.), vespers (sunset), and compline (bedtime).

307. Cf. Mt 27:51.

308. Gn 17:3.

309. "Miserere mei, Deus" (i.e., Have mercy on me, God) are the opening words of Psalm 50. "Benedicite" (Bless you [Lord]) is the first word of the canticle sung by the three boys in Nebuchadnezzar's furnace (Dn 3:26ff.); it was sung frequently as part of the medieval liturgy.

310. Cf. Wis 10:17.

311. Ps 17:6 and Prv 21:6.

moneybag overflows; infernal punishments replete with horror will instead crucify them in Etna.[312] Without a doubt this is a temptation of the enemy of humankind, in order to make us enemies to Christ. For whoever is a friend of the world becomes an enemy of God.[313] Indeed, those who do not keep his commandments speak against God.[314] God says: 'No one can serve two masters.' And, as if to explain, he added: 'You cannot serve God and Mammon.'[315] We, who until now were free in our poverty, will now be slaves to Mammon. Does the bearer of gold not tremble at the motion of gold? Will not the empty-handed traveler sing before the thief?[316] Won't thieves come often to us and kill us on account of it or, not finding it, go away, sometimes having beaten us,[317] sometimes having accepted our blessings? Surely the rumor now flies throughout the world that we love the world and things of the world.[318] Money itself, which is known never to be silent, clamors against us. And in time, a vile band of robbers will be at the gate, because what lords do many people know. Yea rather, this poultice of death, this nourishment of the wicked, this loss of the soul[319] should be quickly thrown away, and this silver returned to him whose it is."

So they sent one of the brothers, named Barnabas (who always handled external matters), to speak these words to the duke on their behalf: "Although we are sinners and unworthy, nevertheless we keep the memory of you continuously in our prayers. We never had money, nor do we want to have it. Our Lord, Jesus Christ, exacts from us not silver but double the sum of good works. If a monk has a penny, he is not worth a penny. Behold what is yours and take back the money. It is not permitted for us to possess forbidden things."

---

312. Elysia and Etna stand in for heaven and hell. For Elysia, see n. 229 above; for Etna, n. 46.

313. Jas 4:4.

314. Cf. Ex 16:28.

315. Mt 6:24.

316. Juvenal *Satires* 10.22, verbatim.

317. Cf. Lk 10:30.

318. 1 Jn 2:15.

319. Mk 8:36.

A hostile band appeared immediately after Barnabas departed for the duke's court (on the first vigil of the night) and, suddenly rushing in the doors of the house, found the five hermits singing and making melody to the Lord.[320] With swords thrust at the brothers' throats, they said: "If you want to live with good peace, give us now the silver you have and spare yourselves. For truly we know that you have the king's money." But the brothers swore to God as their witness, firmly denied it, and said: "The money you seek is now in the duke's treasury, because we did not need it. If you do not believe us, behold our house: search as much as you please, just do not do evil to us." Those men, harder than stones, said: "There is no need for words; either give us the duke's money or you will come under an awful sentence of death." At once, they bound them cruelly and inflicted diverse punishments upon them throughout the entire night, until finally they all fell at once by the edge of a sword.[321] Thus the wrath of the wicked[322] transported them to the kingdoms of heaven. These five brothers—Benedict, Matthew, Isaac, Christian, and John—suffered on 11 November 1003.

1.39. 1005. 1006. Snatched up by a fever, Princess Emma, gem of the female sex, was snatched away from the bonds of flesh. I either saw, or remember myself having seen, her epitaph, which proclaimed in these little verses: "Behold Emma, who was like a gem, lies as worthless ashes.[323] Say, I beg: 'Be patient[324] with her soul, Lord.'"

1007. 1017. On 11 June, Thieddag, the third bishop of the church of Prague, died. This Thieddag was a fitting successor of the holy Bishop Adalbert: virginal in his body, golden in his character, and shining in his deeds. Following the footsteps of his predecessor, he pursued the disgraceful deeds of the common folk entrusted to him. He bore martyrdom—if not in his body, nevertheless in his mind. Neither did he die in the fashion of men, but, having

---

320. Eph 5:19.
322. Cf. Prv 11:23.
324. Sir 3:15.

321. Sir 28:22.
323. Ovid *Metamorphoses* 7.521.

followed the lord, he both sleeps and rests in peace.[325] Ekkehard succeeded him as bishop in the year 1018.

1019. 1020.

1.40. Meanwhile the duke's son, Břetislav, crossing over from boyhood into youth, will go from virtue to virtue.[326] Prosperity of work, height of body, beauty of form, greatness of both physical strength and wisdom, fortitude in adverse times, and mildness in prosperous ones all belonged to him above others.

At the same time, in the German regions, there was a certain very powerful count, nicknamed "Otto the White," springing from royal blood through his paternal lineage.[327] A single daughter was born to him, named Judith, with beauty that surpassed all the girls under the sun.[328] Her good father and her better mother (from whom she learned the Psalter) gave her to a monastery which is called Sweinbrod, a place most fortified by its situation and its walls.[329]

But what towers, even the highest, or what extremely strong walls can withstand love and keep out a lover? Love conquers all; king and duke yield to love.[330] Therefore, Břetislav, the most handsome youth, the bravest hero, hearing from many people about the excessive beauty, probity of character, and generous parentage of the aforesaid girl, could not keep his spirit in bounds and began to think within himself[331] whether he should try to seize her by force

325. Ps 4:9.

326. Ps 83:8.

327. Otto "the White" is probably Otto of Schweinfurt (d. 1057), the son of Henry (d. 1017), count of Schweinfurt and margrave of the Bavarian Nordgau (north of Regensburg). Judith was not Otto's daughter, however, but his sister, the daughter of Henry. Otto did have a daughter Judith, but she lived until the early 1100s, whereas Břetislav's wife died in 1058 (below, 2.17). See Herwig Wolfram, *Konrad II, 990–1039: Kaiser dreier Reiche* (Munich: C. H. Beck, 2000), 243–44. No genealogical links between this family and the royal Ottonian line are known.

328. A conflation of Ovid *Metamorphoses* 1.338 *(sub Phoebo)* and 4.55 *(praelata puellis)*.

329. Sweinbrod is taken in the modern literature to be the monastery of Schweinfurt (in Franconia, between Bamberg and Würzburg).

330. Virgil *Eclogues* 10.69.

331. Dn 4:16.

or negotiate a marriage with gifts. But he preferred to act manfully than to submit his neck in supplication. Indeed he weighed carefully the arrogance innate to Germans and the fact that, puffed up with pride, they always regard the Slavs and their language as an object of contempt. Yet the more difficult the path to love, the more robust a fire the son of Venus produces in the lover. Set ablaze with the fire of Venus, the mind of the youth rages, just as Etna roils with fires. And he intoned this speech to himself: "I will either accomplish this excellent marriage or I will be sunk in perpetual mockery if it cannot be, if she should not be mine: Judith, product of a noble family, an admirable virgin, very lovable, brighter than the light of the sun, dearer to me than life.[332] Let never-ending praise be to God that she lives among us."

At once Břetislav ordered those among his followers whom he knew to be readier with their arms and more faithful to him, men proven and better able to bear the labor, to be fitted out with horses. He pretended he would go quickly to the emperor and to return more quickly. The men carried out their orders,[333] but they did not know what their lord was attempting. They marveled among themselves that they traveled so quickly. In about seven days, arriving like guests, they entered the atrium of the aforesaid convent. The duke's son had ordered all of his men not to make known to anyone who he was or where he came from, but to treat him as one of them. The Ithacan went to track down the son of Thetis by adroit cleverness, and the Trojan shepherd did not fail to carry off the daughter of Tyndareus from Amyclae.[334] But this youth Břetislav exceeded both of them in the impetuosity and the

332. Virgil *Aeneid* 5.725.
333. Ovid *Metamorphoses* 3.154.
334. Amyclae was part of the realm of Menelaus, obtained by marriage with Helen, the daughter of Tyndareus; Helen was later abducted by Paris, "the Trojan shepherd," instigating the Trojan War. The "Ithacan" here is Ulysses, sent in the midst of the war to fetch Achilles, the son of Thetis, who had withdrawn from the fight to mourn Patroclus. That these epic figures are named only indirectly may play on the fact that Břetislav is about to carry out an equally heroic abduction without anyone knowing his name.

immensity of his bold deed. After permission to spend the night there was granted to them, like a wolf when it walks around the sheepfold searching for the place where he might rush in to snatch the plump lamb, so the hero Břetislav, circling the monastery with his keen eyesight and his illustrious spirit, wanted to rush in with force but did not dare, because he did not have a sufficient number of warriors with him.

By fortunate chance a feast day arrived and behold, the virgin Judith, wished for by a thousand wishes, exited the monastery with the other girls her age, as tender girls are accustomed to strike the bells in the middle of the church at vespers. When the most daring abductor saw her, made unthinking before his joy, like a wolf who rushes from hiding and seizes a lamb and then, conscious of the deed, flees, tucking its tail and seeking a farther hiding place,[335] so Břetislav fled with the abducted virgin. When he came to the door, he found it bound with a chain thicker than a miller's rope and the way out blocked. With sharp sword drawn, he immediately cut it like a stem; a section of it can be seen to this day as evidence of his very strong blow. But with the rest of his companions knowing little of this and still remaining in their tents, they were seized by enemies rushing in; some had their eyes plucked out and their noses cut off, others their hands and feet mutilated. The duke, with a few of his men and his abducted virgin, barely escaped through the shadows of the night. The virgin Judith was carried off in the year 1021.

And lest the Germans be given a genuine opportunity for reproaching the Czechs, as for some injury done, the hero Břetislav immediately took the direct road to Moravia with his new bride, having paid his respects to his father, Duke Oldřich. Earlier his father had given all of that land into his power, all the Poles having fled from the burgs, among whom many—hundreds and hundreds—he had ordered captured and chained in a line, to be sold in Hungary and beyond. For the truth of the matter is that, just

---

335. Cf. Virgil *Aeneid* 11.820.

like the burg of Prague,[336] so too the Poles had taken all of Moravia by force after the death of Boleslav II.

1022. A persecution of Christians was carried out in Poland.

1023. On 8 August, Ekkehard, the fourth bishop of the church of Prague, crossed over from this light to reign in a life never ending. This bishop was resolute against the powerful, yet pious and mild toward the humble and gentle. He was a most eloquent preacher, a lavish giver of alms, a faithful dispenser of wheat by the measure to the Lord's household.[337] This bishop established that, as a tithe, each person—whether powerful, rich, or poor, whether he possessed arable land from his benefice or his allod—would pay the bishop two measures of five palms and two fingers, one of wheat and the other of oats. Previously, as had been established by the first bishop, Thietmar, they gave two stacks of the harvest as a tithe (a stack, we say, holds fifty handfuls).

After Ekkehard's death, Izzo obtained the bishopric; he was ordained on 29 December that same year by the Archbishop of Mainz.

1.41. 1024. King Henry died on 12 July.[338]

1025. King Bolesław died on 17 June.[339]

1026. . . .

1030. In this year Duke Břetislav overthrew the Hungarians with considerable slaughter and laid waste to their land all the way to the burg of Esztergom.[340]

In that same year, on 30 January, Izzo, the fifth bishop of the church of Prague, crossed over from this world and enjoys his pleasant reward. He was of noble birth, but was more noble in his work, one who did first what he taught should be done. For no one

336. Cf. 1.35.

337. Cf. Lk 12:42.

338. Henry II (1002–24), king of the Germans and Roman emperor.

339. This presumably refers to the Polish ruler, Bolesław I Chrobry, though Cosmas omits mentioning his assumption of the royal title in the year 1000 (see above, n. 260) and, throughout the chronicle, mistakenly attributes most of his deeds to his father Mieszko (above, n. 264).

340. Continuation of Regino (*Chronicon*, 159); cf. above, 1.20, concerning 934.

knew his own dwelling better than the prison and the hospice were known to him. Nor was it hidden from him how many heads of men were supplied life or how many souls death sent to dark shadows. Moreover, he was accustomed to feeding forty paupers daily; procuring food and drink in abundance, he blessed and cheerfully distributed it himself.[341] The beauty of his body was also remarkable and his head of hair was whiter than a swan—whence he got his nickname: he was called Bishop Izzo "the White and Charming."

Bishop Severus succeeded him, sixth in line. In the time of his youth, he shone with a marvelous elegance of agility. Surpassing everyone—however many were at the duke's court—in his obedience, he offered industrious service to his lord, especially pleasing because it was loyal. He was first in the duties of clerics but was no less devoted to the pursuits of laymen. This *comes* was always present at hunts, inseparable from the duke. Indeed he was present first at the killing of a wild sylvan boar; cutting off its tail, he cleaned and prepared it as he knew the duke wanted and then gave it to the arriving duke ready for eating. Whence Duke Oldřich is often said to have declared: "O Severus, I tell you truly: for such sweet food, you are worthy of a bishopric." And so, with endeavors of this sort, he had the duke's favor and pleased everyone.

1031. On the Feast of the Apostles, Saints Peter and Paul, Severus was ordained bishop by the archbishop of Mainz. In that same year, Spitihněv, the son of Duke Břetislav, was born.

1032....

1037. Duke Boleslav [III], whom Mieszko deprived of sight, died.[342]

1.42. In that same year, on 9 November, Duke Oldřich left earthly kingdoms and achieved heavenly ones. Then Jaromír, whom we mentioned above, bereft of light, whom Duke Oldřich had planned to carry in chains to Lyše, hearing that his brother had departed this world, rose early[343] and ordered himself brought to Prague in a

341. Cf. 1 Cor 13:3.   342. See above, 1.35.
343. Cf. Prv 11:27.

cart. When he arrived there, he found his brother already conveyed to the monastery of St. George. Standing next to the bier at his funeral, he moved and struck the heart of everyone standing around with a lament of this sort: "Woe is me! What will I say except, more often, 'woe is me'? Woe is my brother. Alas, the dreadful possibility of bitter death.[344] Behold, you lie dead, not I. And now you rejoice, having deserted this land's lofty throne.[345] Three days ago the third noble duke, today you are an immobile trunk, tomorrow you will be food for worms, and afterward fine dust and an empty tale.[346] Now, I know that you would want to return my eyes if you could, since your deeds, whether good or bad, now lie naked and open.[347] But, brother, I forgive you now with all my heart,[348] so that omnipotent God might spare you through his piety and your spirit might afterward rest in peace."

After the funeral rites were completed, [Jaromír] took his little brother Břetislav and led him to the princely seat.[349] Just as they always do in the election of a duke, they scattered ten thousand coins or more among the people in the chambers of the upper hall, so that they might not crush the duke on his throne but rather chase the strewn coins. Next, when the duke had been placed on the throne and all was silent, Jaromír took the right hand of his nephew and said to the people: "Behold your duke!" And they cried together three times: "Krlešu!" (that is, *Kyrie eleison*).[350]

344. Virgil *Aeneid* 2.274 *(hei mihi!)* and 12.879 *(conditio mortis)*.

345. Silius Italicus *Punica* 17.143, in Silius Italicus, *Punica*, trans. J. D. Duff (Cambridge, Mass.: Harvard University Press, 1934).

346. This represents a fusion of Is 5:24 ("will be like dust"), Jb 30:19 ("you have become like dust and ashes"), and Persius *Satires* 5.152 ("you will be ashes, a ghost, a tale").

347. Heb 4:13.

348. Cf. Mt 18:35. See also below, Book 2, n. 26.

349. Really his nephew. A comment like this is no mistake, since Cosmas himself states explicitly that Břetislav was Oldřich's son. "Brother" is often used, in this chronicle and other twelfth-century texts, to indicate members of the Přemyslid line with a claim to the ducal throne (cf. 3.5, n. 60). The diminutive here is both a reminder of Břetislav's relative youth and an endearment.

350. See above, n. 198.

And again Jaromír spoke to the people: "Approach from the Muncia clan! Approach from the Tepca clan!" and he called by name those who were more powerful in arms, better in faith, stronger in war, and more prominent in wealth. And sensing them to be present, he said: "Since my fates have not permitted me to be your duke, I designate this man as duke for you and praise him. You should obey him as befits a duke and show him the fidelity owed to your prince. I warn you, son, and again and again repeat the warning:[351] worship these men like fathers, love them like brothers, and keep their counsel in all your dealings. To them you commit burgs and the people to be ruled; through them the realm of Bohemia stands, has stood, and will stand forever.[352] And those who are the Vršovici, the worthless sons of evil fathers, the domestic foes of our lineage, familiar enemies, avoid and turn away from their company like a muddy wheel, because they were never faithful to us. Behold, they first bound and variously mocked me, their innocent prince, and afterward they arranged, by the lies and deceitful counsels[353] innate to them, that a brother deprive a brother—me—of these very eyes. Keep always in your memory, my son, the proclamations of Saint Adalbert—that, on account of their cruel deeds, they would bring ruin upon themselves three times—which he confirmed with his holy mouth and for which he excommunicated them in church. Those things which, by the will of God, have now been done twice, the fates are still anxious to have happen a third time."

Hearing this, the Vršovici were cut to the heart, [ground] their teeth against him, and growled like lions.[354] After not many days, Kohan, whom we mentioned above [1.34], sent his executioner: when the blind man went out to purge his belly in the night, he pierced him through with the sharpest dagger, from his posterior

---

351. Virgil *Aeneid* 3.436.   352. Dn 2:44.
353. Prv 12:5.

354. Cf. Acts 7:54 and, for the lion, Prv 19:12. I have modified Cosmas's Latin a bit, since it literally says "growled their teeth against him like lions," which reflects the conflation of these passages but makes no sense in English.

all the way to his inner stomach. And thus, like a martyr of God, the just man, Duke Jaromír died on 4 November 1038.

So far this first book has contained the deeds of antiquity. Because, as blessed Jerome says, things seen, heard, and fabricated are related differently, the things we know better, we also express better.[355] So now, with God and Saint Adalbert helping, the spirit is moved to tell[356] those things which we ourselves saw, or which we heard truthfully from those reporting what they saw.

Here ends Book 1 of the Chronicle of the Czechs.

355. Jerome *Against Rufinus* 2.25.61, in Jerome, *Apologie contre Rufin*, ed. and trans. Pierre Lardet (Paris: Cerf, 1983), 176. Cosmas has copied these lines from Regino's entry for the year 813, which includes the attribution to Jerome, and where he too declares himself to be turning to events of his own time (*Chronicon*, 73). The third category, of things "fabricated" (*ficta*), is Cosmas's own addition to this otherwise verbatim quotation from Regino quoting Jerome.

356. From the opening line of Ovid's *Metamorphoses.*

✠ BOOK TWO

Here begins the Proemium, Addressed to Clement, Abbot of the Church of Břevnov

To Clement, the spiritual father of the monastery of Břevnov,[1] thus possessing a name drawn from reality [i.e., clemency] while always engaging deeply in theory, from Cosmas, hardly worthy to be called dean, the partnership of the angelic senate. Turning things over in my mind, I resisted sending a thing so worthy of charity to a man of such holiness that indeed weights of gold and silver are of no account to him and only those things that are spiritual please him. Still I considered it best merely to follow your will. I understood through your cleric named Deocarus, who secretly made it known to me in private, that you willingly desired to see the scribbles I had once written for Gervasius. Invigorated by the opportunity, indeed compelled by the persuasion of a dear friend, I presume to lay out for your paternity not only what you desired but even a second little book—as I call it—of this same story. It is likewise a digest—from the time of Břetislav, the son of Duke Oldřich, up to his grandson of the same name, the son of King Vratislav—so far as I was permitted to know it.

Although, O venerable father, you should not cease to drink up the divine scriptures and you should always drain the deep

---

1. The oldest Benedictine monastery for men in Bohemia, located a short distance from Prague Castle. Its foundation is associated with St. Adalbert. See Wolverton, *Hastening Toward Prague*, 115, also the map on 117. As usual, we know nothing more of Clement than what is stated here.

springs of philosophy, nevertheless do not disdain to cleanse your holy lips[2] with this weak liquid. It often happens that after strong wines and soporific drinks, sometimes a natural thirst is incited in a man and a draught of clear liquid is more agreeable than sweet drinks. It also often happens that a warrior of Mars, who labors in arms, rejoices to join in maidenly dances or tries boyish games with a hoop.[3] So, O most holy father, forsake now lofty, syllogistic volumes and read through this little work of mine, childish in sensibility, rustic in style. There you will find several things worthy of scorn and derision,[4] things you should by all means commit to memory so that, with the wisdom God conferred on you, you might someday correct them to perfection.[5] Since in certain places you will find verses not quite metrical, you should know that when I made the verses, I was well aware of my ignorance.[6] Farewell.

2.1. And so Duke Břetislav, now vigorous in his father's seat, treads in the footsteps of his forefathers with deeds well pleasing to both men and God, and surpasses them in reaching the height of virtues. Just as the sun hides and weakens the light of the stars by its power and the moon by its excessive brightness, Břetislav—like a new Achilles, a new Diomedes[7]—diminishes and obscures the powerful actions and most victorious palms of his ancestors with new triumphs. For God conferred such grace upon Břetislav that all the unfailing virtues which he grants particularly to individual men, he lavished generally upon him. Indeed Břetislav received such an accumulation of virtues that he surpassed Gideon in his vigor in warfare, exceeded Samson in bodily strength, and went before Solomon in the special privilege of wisdom. Whence it happens that he was a victor in all his battles, like Joshua, and richer in gold

---

2. Cf. the opening line of the Prologue to Persius's *Satires* (Braund, *Juvenal and Persius*, 45).

3. Cf. Horace *Odes* 3.24.55.   4. See Book 1, n. 12.

5. See Book 1, n. 9.   6. See Book 1, n. 82.

7. Like Achilles, Diomedes is a Greek (Achaean) hero who plays a prominent role in the epics of the Trojan War.

and silver than the kings of Arabia.[8] With his inexhaustible riches flowing everywhere and since he never ceased to bestow rewards, Břetislav might be compared to the water which is never lacking in a river.

To him his wife Judith, most noble in lineage, most fertile bearer of offspring, bore five youths distinguished in body and preeminent, like the mountains of Emathia,[9] singular in wisdom, comparable to no one in honesty, and acceptable in character, easily pacified toward transgressors, praiseworthy for the collective honor of their virtues. The firstborn was Spitihněv, the second by birth, Vratislav, the third in line, Conrad, the fourth by birth, Jaromír, the fifth and last, Otto, the most comely. Their lives and glory will be described sufficiently in the appropriate places, as the abundance of words flows. While they were yet boys but excelling in manly endeavors, their father very much marveled, perceiving the brothers to be surpassing in excellence and equal in nobility.[10] Her joys tortured their mother[11] not at all, since Judith was glad about the great progress of her sons and their magnificently glorious estate.

2.2. At that time, with the most noble duke of Poland removed from this light and his sons Bolesław and Władysław still in infancy and taking milk at the breast, Kazimierz was the one hope of salvation for the Poles, all fleeing to different places in wretched flight.[12] Noticing this, Duke Břetislav—in the fourth year of

8. Cosmas here compares Břetislav to four heroes of the Old Testament (Gideon, Samson, Solomon, and Joshua), whose legendary qualities are duly noted. On the gold of Arabia, see Ps 71:15.

9. Emathia here refers not to the fields of Lucan's *Pharsalia* (1.1), but to mountains in Macedonia.

10. Horace *Satires* 2.3.243: *par nobile fratrum.* Usually translated "a noble pair of brothers," it refers here to five.

11. Statius *Achilleid* 1.183.

12. Cosmas is confused: the unnamed Polish duke who died was Mieszko II (1031–34); Kazimierz I "the Restorer" (1034–58) was his son and successor; and Bolesław and Władysław were the names of *Kazimierz's* own sons, though they were not born until 1041 and 1042, respectively. Moreover, Kazimierz was unable to assume power in 1034 after his father's death, being instead driven into exile. The resulting inter-

his reign as duke—thought it would be best for him not to miss an opportunity to damage his enemies, more precisely to revenge the injuries Duke Mieszko had once inflicted on the Czechs.[13] As quickly as he was able, having taken counsel with his men, Břetislav ordered them to invade [Poland]. Sending throughout the province of all of Bohemia a collar of twisted cork as a sign of his command, he immediately pronounced a terrible sentence: that, once the signal was given, whoever came out to camp sluggishly would know without a doubt that he would be hanged by such a collar in the gallows.[14] They gathered into one in an instant—in the twinkling of an eye[15] and to a man[16]—and Břetislav entered the land of Poland, widowed of its prince, and invaded it as an enemy.

Like a huge storm, he raged, raved, and leveled everything. Thus he devastated villages with murders, rapine, and fires, and broke into fortifications by force.[17] Entering from the summit, he overthrew their *metropolis*[18] at Cracow and seized its goods. He even uncovered in the treasury old treasures stolen from ancient dukes, namely, an infinite quantity gold and silver. He set fire to the rest of the burgs and destroyed them to the ground.

When they came to the castle of Giecz, the castellans, together with those villagers who had taken refuge there, unable to endure the duke's assault, came out to meet him. Bearing a golden rod,

---

regnum ended only in 1040, when Kazimierz was restored to the throne with German assistance. Aleksander Gieysztor, "Medieval Poland," in Aleksander Gieysztor et al., *History of Poland,* trans. K. Cekalska (Warsaw: Państwowe Wydawnictwo Naukowe, 1968), 65–66.

13. Cosmas is referring to events ca. 1000 (above, 1.34–35). There, as here, he confuses Duke Mieszko I with his son, Bolesław Chrobry, who, according to Thietmar, was responsible for the blinding of Boleslav III and the subsequent conquest of Bohemia.

14. Duke Vlastislav of the Lučané issues a similar summons in 1.10 (see n. 118). "Hanged on the gallows" is taken from Est 7:10.

15. 1 Cor 15:52.

16. Ps 13:1 and Rom 3:12.

17. These sentences combine borrowings from two separate passages in Regino (*Chronicon,* 41 and 148); the latter also appears in 1.10 (see n. 113).

18. *Metropolis,* which in Cosmas's usage implies either political or ecclesiastical pre-eminence, here suggests that Cracow was a kind of capital for the Poles.

which was the sign of surrender, they humbly asked that Břetislav transfer them peacefully to Bohemia with their cattle and the rest of their belongings. The duke, acquiescing to their requests, later led them into Bohemia and gave them not a small part of the forest called Černín.[19] He established one overseer and judge from among them and decreed that both they and their descendants should live forever under the law which they had had in Poland. They are called "Hedčané" to this day, the name derived from the burg.[20]

2.3. Not far from the aforesaid burg [Giecz], they came to the *metropolis* of Gniezno,[21] strong by virtue of its location and the defenses in front of the walls but easily captured by enemies because few citizens were inhabiting it. At that time, a most precious treasure lay there, in the basilica of the holy Mary, ever-virgin Mother of God,[22] namely, the body of the most blessed martyr, Adalbert. The Czechs soon took control of the burg without Mars [i.e., without a fight], and with great joy went in the entrance of the sacred church. All other booty neglected, they demanded that only the precious mass of the holy body, which suffered on Christ's behalf, be given to them.

Their bishop, Severus, observing their boldness, sensing their will to be primed for anything, right or wrong,[23] tried to recall them from illicit deeds with words such as this: "My brothers and sons of the church of God, it is not as easy as you think for any mortal to presume brazenly to touch the holy earth of a body filled with God's virtues. For I am very afraid that we might be smitten either by insanity, blindness,[24] or some debility of limbs, if we presume brazenly to do it. Therefore, first fast for three days,

19. Southwest of Tetín perhaps.

20. Modern Polish and Czech pronunciation obscures Cosmas's etymological point, which is clearer in the Latin original, where Giecz is spelled "Gdec," and Hedčané "Gedcane."

21. Gniezno is probably called a *metropolis* here on account of its religious significance and its status as an archepiscopal see.

22. The cathedral church in Gniezno, dedicated to St. Mary and St. Vitus.

23. A combination of Lucan *Pharsalia* 5.313 and 6.147.

24. Cf. Dt 28:28.

do penance for your sins,[25] renounce all the abominations which God abhors in you, and promise with all your heart[26] that you will not commit them any more. I hope in the mercy of God[27] and our patron, Saint Adalbert, that we will not be deprived of the hope of our petition if we persist in the assiduous saying of prayers[28] and in the devotion of faith." But the words of the bishop seemed to them an idle tale.[29]

They covered their ears and rushed[30] immediately to take the holy body. Because it was kept behind the altar next to the wall, it could not be pulled out without the altar's being destroyed; these profanities were carried out with an unrighteous hand and a bestial mind. Yet divine vengeance did not delay. For in the very act of their brazenness, they stood there with senses stupefied, having neither voice nor sense nor sight for a space of almost three hours, until they again regained their original faculties by God's grace. Although repenting late,[31] they soon fulfilled the bishop's commands and the more manifestly they were chastised by divine will, the more devotedly they persisted, untiring in prayers, fasting for three days, and asking forgiveness.

2.4. On the third night, the holy Bishop Adalbert appeared in a vision to Bishop Severus (who was resting after gathering for matins)[32] and said: "Say this to the duke and his *comites:* 'Your Father in heaven will grant what you ask,[33] if you do not repeat the evil deeds which you renounced at the baptismal font.'" In the morning, when the bishop made this known to the duke and his *comites,* they were immediately gladdened. Entering the Church of St. Mary, they lay prostrate on the ground before the tomb of Saint Adalbert, pouring out a single prayer together for a long time. Then the duke rose and, standing in the pulpit, broke the silence with his voice:[34] "Do

25. Jer 8:6.
26. Mk 12:30 (and elsewhere); see also above, 1.42.
27. Ps 51:10.   28. Tb 3:11.
29. Lk 24:11.   30. Acts 7:56.
31. See above, Book 1, n. 159.   32. Cf. Book 1, n. 306.
33. Mt 7:11.   34. Ovid *Metamorphoses* 1.384.

you want to correct your transgressions and recover from depraved works?" Having also risen, they cried out to him with tears: "We are prepared to correct whatever sin we or our fathers committed against the holy one of God and to cease altogether from depraved works."

Then Duke Břetislav, extending his hand over the holy tomb, spoke thus to the crowd of people: "Brothers, extend your right hands similarly to God and heed my words, which I want you to confirm by swearing on your baptism.[35] Let this therefore be my first and greatest decree:[36] that your marriages, which until now you have treated as brothels and common to all, like brute animals,[37] henceforth be legitimate, private, and insoluble, according to the canons. Thus a man should live content with only one wife and a woman with one husband. If a wife should spurn her husband, or a husband his wife, or the quarrel between them boil over to the point of separation, I do not want the violator in this matter—the one unwilling to return to the earlier bond legitimately celebrated—to be reduced to servitude according to the rite of our land. Instead, by the stricture of our immutable decree, whatever his rank, he should be exiled into Hungary. And by no means let it be permitted that he redeem himself with money or return to this land, lest the taint of one small sheep spread though the all of Christ's sheepfold."[38] Bishop Severus said: "Whoever might do otherwise, let him be anathema.[39] Virgins, widows, and adulteress-

35. I owe this interpretation of the more abstract phrase "an oath of your faith" (*vestre fidei sacramento*) to John Van Engen.

36. The legal stipulations that follow, intended to further the Christianization of Czech society, are often called the "Břetislav Decrees" and are sometimes presumed to constitute a text independent of Cosmas's chronicle per se. The provisions here do read like some kind of separate document that Cosmas is quoting, perhaps preserved in the cathedral library. However, the dramatic context and the dialogue format are surely Cosmas's work. See my *Hastening Toward Prague*, 115, 131.

37. Cf. the description of Bohemia's earliest inhabitants in 1.3.

38. Cf. Virgil *Georgics* 3.469.

39. A penalty in canon law by which a person was to be cut off and separated from the Christian community, akin to excommunication but more severe.

es, who are known to have lost their good name, to have corrupted their modesty, and to be considered harlots, are to be punished by this same judgment. For when they have the free choice of marriage, why do they commit adultery and abort their fetuses, which is the worst crime of crimes?" Then the duke spoke, adding: "If a woman truly proclaims that for her part she is not loved equally, but is severely beaten and debased by her husband, let a judgment of God be held between them and let the one who is found guilty pay the penalty in the matter."

"Likewise, concerning those who are accused of homicides, the archpriest will write down their names for the *comes* of that burg and the *comes* will summon them. And if they are rebels [and refuse], he will put them in prison until they perform a fitting penance or, if they deny it, until they are examined by hot iron or blessed water to determine whether they are blameworthy.[40] Regarding fratricides, parricides, killers of priests, and those caught in capital crimes of this sort, the archpriest shall consign them to the *comes* or the duke, or he will eject them from the realm shackled by the hands and around the stomach, so that they might wander the earth as fugitives and wanderers in the likeness of Cain."[41] Bishop Severus said: "Let the duke's just decision be strengthened by anathema. For this reason the sword hangs on the thigh for you dukes, so that you might more often wash your hands in the blood of the sinner."[42]

Again, the duke: "The tavern is the root of all evil[43] and from it proceed thefts, murders, adulteries, and other evils.[44] Whoever keeps one or buys what is prepared there..." "...Let him be anathema," Bishop Severus said. And the duke said: "Let the tavern

40. This, and the "judgment of God" two sentences above, refer to the ordeal, whereby the results of a physical test (such as carrying a hot iron) were taken as evidence of God's verdict upon a person's guilt and therefore as definitive proof in a legal case.

41. Gn 4:12.

42. Ps 57:11.

43. 1 Tm 6:10, though in reference to greed.

44. Mt 15:19, though "the heart" is the source of these evils.

keeper who is apprehended as a violator of this decree be hanged on a stake in the middle of the market and flayed to the point of the herald's nausea. However, his goods should not be confiscated but thrown to the ground, lest someone be sullied by the accursed drink. So also drinkers, if they are caught, shall not leave prison until they each put three hundred coins into the duke's treasury." Bishop Severus said: "What the duke declares, our authority affirms."

Still the duke continued, saying: "We forbid altogether for markets to be open on Sundays, which they should celebrate all the more since they are free to work on the remaining days. If someone should be discovered in any servile work,[45] either on Sundays or on feast days, the accused shall be brought publicly to the church and the archpriest shall take away both the work itself and the draught animal found in the work. The offender will also pay three hundred coins into the duke's treasury. Likewise, those who bury their dead in fields or forests: those so accused shall pay a cow to the archdeacon and three hundred coins to the duke's treasury. Then they should bury the dead anew in a cemetery of the faithful. These are things God hates.[46] For these things, a disgusted Saint Adalbert abandoned us, his flock, and preferred to go teach foreign peoples.[47] We confirm by our oath and yours that we will no longer do these things." Thus spoke the duke.

The bishop, having invoked the name of the Holy Trinity and taken up a hammer, with the rest of the clergy singing seven psalms and other prayers appropriate to this holy office, began gently to destroy the top of the tomb, destroying it all the way to the depths of the holy chamber. When they uncovered the sarcophagus, everyone present at the church was overcome with fragrance of the sweetest odor, such that for three days, as if refreshed by the finest trays, they forgot to refresh themselves with food. Many sick people were also cured through the same orifice [i.e., their nostrils].

45. Lv 23:7, concerning observance of the Sabbath.
46. Zec 8:17.
47. Cf. 1.31.

Then the duke and the bishop and a few of the *comites* looked in and saw that God's saint was entirely unblemished in his face and expression, and in every way whole in body, as if he had celebrated the holy solemnity of mass that same day. The clergy sang *Te Deum laudamus* and the laity *Kyrie eleison*,[48] and their voices resonated into the ether.

Having thus done these things, the duke, tears of joy pouring down[49] his face, prayed thus: "O martyr for Christ, blessed Adalbert, have mercy on us always and everywhere. Look down on us now with your customary piety and have mercy on our sins, and do not disdain to be brought back to your seat in the church of Prague by us, though sinners." It was a wonderful, truly stupendous thing! Although they were unable to touch his tomb three days ago, now the duke and the bishop raised Adalbert's body from the sarcophagus without impediment. Covering it with silk, they placed it on the upper altar so that the commoners could render the offerings they had promised to God and his saint—and on that same day two hundred marks were paid into the lockbox on the altar.

O omnipotent God, turning the world through the ages, you who reign forever, who alone govern all things, nothing is, has been, or will be in the world without your will, good Christ. What mortal could ever believe that this man now crowned with laurels in the celestial realm would permit his body to be returned to this rebellious people[50] whose company he fled, scorning their crimes, while he yet lived. But if we weigh the greater and ancient miracles of God—how the people of Israel crossed the sea on dry ground,[51] how the waters flowed from the dry rock,[52] or how the maker of the world appeared in the world born of the Virgin Mary—we

48. *Te deum laudamus* (We praise you, God) are the first words of a hymn dating at least to the ninth century and a regular part of the medieval liturgy. On the *kyrie*, see Book 1, n. 198.

49. Virgil *Aeneid* 12.64, perhaps.   50. See Book 1, n. 221.

51. Ex 15:19.

52. The story appears in Nm 20:11, but the language here is closer to Ps 77:20.

should not wonder but instead humble ourselves before God,[53] who did and is able to do what he wishes, and ascribe everything to his grace.

God's grace inspiring it, the idea arose in the duke's heart[54] that he might likewise transfer the body of the archbishop of this same burg [Gniezno], named Gaudentius, who by chance was resting in the same church. Gaudentius (as we reported above [1.34]) was the brother of Saint Adalbert not only in the flesh but indeed through a spiritual bond, as well as his inseparable companion in every toil and hardship.[55] Even if Gaudentius did not bear martyrdom bodily with Adalbert, he bore it by suffering with him in spirit. It was impossible that the sword should not pierce his soul[56] as well, when he saw his brother cut to pieces[57] by the spears of pagans and would himself have chosen to be killed too.[58]

It also seemed to the duke and bishop that the relics of the five brothers adjacent to the holy body—of whose life and passion we spoke sufficiently above [1.38]—should similarly be transferred with the greatest diligence. (They were in the same burg, but resting in another church.) What more?

2.5. They came to Bohemia with their entire sacred burden, in prosperity and rejoicing. On the vigil of St. Bartholomew the Apostle [23 August], they camped near the *metropolis* of Prague, around the stream called Rokytnice. There, with day dawning, the clergy and all the common folk came to meet them in procession. The wide field could scarcely hold their long train. For such was the procession: The duke himself and the bishop carried the sweet weight of Adalbert, martyr for Christ, resting it on their shoul-

53. Sir 3:9.
54. Lk 24:38.
55. 2 Cor 11:27. The phrase *individuus comes* (inseparable companion) appears in both Regino (*Chronicon,* 42, 152) and Canaparius (*Vita Adalberti* 3).
56. Ps 104:18.
57. 1 Kgs 15:33.
58. The *vita* of St. Adalbert by John Canaparius mentions his young brother Gaudentius frequently, at Adalbert's side through all his travels, even at the time of his murder by the Prussians (p. 594).

ders; behind them, the abbots bore the relics of the five broth-ers;[59] and then the archpriests rejoiced in the burden of Archbish-op Gaudentius. Twelve chosen priests followed, hardly sustaining the weight of a golden crucifix. (Duke Mieszko[60] had weighed it out in gold of three times his own weight.) In fifth position, they brought three tablets heavy with gold which had been positioned around the altar where the holy body rested. (The larger tablet was five arms in length and ten palms in width, greatly adorned with precious stones and crystals. This line was inscribed on its edge: "This work of gold weighs three hundred pounds.") Finally, they brought huge bells and all the treasures of Poland in more than one hundred wagons. An innumerable crowd of noble men fol-lowed, bound in iron handcuffs, their necks constrained by ropes; among them was led away—alas, wrongfully captured—a partner in the clergy, a priest by office.

O that day, a day to be honored by the Czechs, to be com-mended to memory for all time, to be repeated in sacred myster-ies, to be celebrated by fitting proclamations, to be most devotedly venerated with praises, to be made glad with riches, greatly desired by the weak, pleasing to the poor, glorified by the giving of alms, and adorned by all good pursuits, a day on which a feast added to feasts glitters brightly! O exceedingly lucky *metropolis* Prague, once raised up by a holy duke, now elevated by a blessed bishop, receive the double joy conferred on you by God and through these two olive trees of mercy. In fame you fly beyond the Sarmatians and *Sarigas*.[61] This translation of the blessed martyr of Christ, Adal-bert, occurred on 1 September 1039.

2.6. Despite such prosperity, granted by God, a wicked de-nouncer was not lacking. He reported to the pope[62] that these

59. Cf. 1.38.

60. Again, probably Bolesław Chrobry.

61. Cf. 1.9, where Libuše predicts that Prague will be adorned by two olive trees and names them indirectly as Sts. Václav and Adalbert; see also Book 1, n. 96. Sar-matians were a people of eastern Scythia; who Cosmas means by the *Sarigas* remains uncertain.

62. Presumably Benedict IX (1032–44, 1045, 1047–48).

deeds were done. He made known that the duke and bishop of Bohemia had violated divine decrees and the traditions of the holy fathers. And he [warned] that if the lord pope allowed this to go unpunished, it would subvert the laws of the apostolic see, which ought to be observed throughout the entire world. Immediately, a holy assembly was announced, canons were recited, and sacred scriptures were searched.[63] The duke and the bishop, though absent, were censured for presumption. Some decreed that the duke, deprived of every honor, should spend three years in exile; others judged that the bishop, suspended from every episcopal function, should reside in a monks' cloister for as long as he lived; still others clamored for both to be struck with the sword of anathema.

2.7. Meanwhile, the envoys of the duke and bishop of the Czechs arrived in Rome on their behalf and on behalf of the whole people, bearing mandates more greased with gifts than polished with words of eloquence. When they were given the freedom to speak[64] before the pope and the holy council, they pursued their embassy's purpose with this speech: "O ruler of the Catholic faith and the most holy apostolic see, and O fathers written in the book of life,[65] on whom God conferred the power of judging and of pardoning, have mercy on those who admit to having sinned, spare the penitent and those who ask for forgiveness. For we confess that we did illicit things, contrary to the statutes of the canons, because from such distant regions and given the short space of time, we could not obtain your decree for such a holy endeavor. But whatever it is that we did, you should know, O fathers written in the book of life, you should know, we did it not out of brazenness, but to the great benefit of the Christian religion and with good intention. If this good intention ever fell into vice, O most holy fathers, we are prepared to amend our shameful acts according to your judgment." To this the pope responded with few words: "If he repents, the error is scarcely harmful."

63. Jn 5:39; this whole sentence is modeled on Regino (*Chronicon*, 81).
64. See Book 1, n. 149.
65. Rv 20:15.

Dismissed from the council and expecting to render an account the next day, the day of judgment,[66] the envoys found lodging. That night, the messengers of the duke and bishop, circling, corrupted the cardinals' shrewdness with money, supplanted justice with gold, bought mercy for a price, and eased the judicial sentence with gifts.

On the following day, the envoys again presented themselves to the holy council on the Capitoline. The lord pope opened his holy mouth, full of authority and weighty words and said: "Just as harsher punishment ought to be shown to those obstinate in the sin of impiety, so also we give easy assent to those acknowledging their guilt and desiring penance, and we administer the medicine of mercy to wounds inflicted by the enemy. It is a great sin to seize another's goods, but a greater one not only to rob Christians but in fact to capture them and sell the captives like brute animals. What you perpetrated in Poland, as reported to us through truthful messengers, is altogether abhorrent. Moreover, no one is permitted to transfer a holy body from place to place without our permission; so the canons testify and the decrees of the fathers prohibit it. Divine proclamations order those presumptuous in matters like this to be struck with the sword of anathema. But because you did this either out of ignorance[67] or with good intentions, we order that, for this very brazen and presumptuous act, your duke and bishop should build a monastery sufficiently endowed with all ecclesiastical resources and honors in a suitable place. There they should establish upright persons and offices with clerics serving in the accustomed way. This should be a place where constant service to God is on display forever on behalf of the faithful, both living and dead. In this way, then, the transgression of which you stand accused might be erased in the sight of God."

Much cheered, the envoys departed immediately and reported the pope's commands to the duke. Obeying them as if they were divine commands, the duke built a most lovely monastery in honor

66. Mt 12:36, though there in reference to the Last Judgment.
67. Acts 3:17.

of St. Václav the Martyr in the burg of [Stará] Boleslav,[68] next to the Elbe River, where that same saint once happily achieved martyrdom. There, as can be observed today, a numerous crowd of brothers serves God, and the provostship and basilica are considered very religious.

2.8. 1040. Rumor—than which no worse evil flourishes in the world,[69] which paints with lies and, mixing many things with a few and false things with true, grows by flying—brought word to the ears of Emperor Henry II [III][70] that the Czechs had carried off from Poland a weight of gold and silver a hundredfold more than was true. The emperor then began to seek a pretext against them,[71] a means by which he might snatch away from them the gold that had been mentioned to him. Ordering through investigators that the Czechs send him the silver they seized in Poland down to the last penny and within a set deadline, the emperor otherwise threatened war.

To this the Slavs said: "We have always kept within our law and are still today subject to the command of King Charles and his successors. Our people have never been rebels. We remain, and always will remain, faithful to you in every war—but only if you desire to do us justice. Pippin, the son of King Charles the Great,[72] established this law for us: that we should pay annually to the successors of the emperors 120 choice cows and five hundred marks (we say a 'mark' is two hundred coins of our money). Generation after generation of our countrymen bears witness to this. This we have paid you every year without resistance, and we wish to pay your successors. But if you want to oppress us with any kind of

68. This "monastery" established at Stará Boleslav was, in fact, a collegiate chapter of secular canons.

69. Cf. Virgil Aeneid 4.174.

70. Henry III (1039–56).

71. Regino, Chronicon, 80.

72. Cosmas seems here to have confused the two sons of Charlemagne (768–814) who predeceased him: Pippin (d. 810) and Charles (d. 811). It was Charles, not Pippin, who led campaigns against the Bohemians on his father's behalf in 805 and 806—and must therefore be the one intended here. Riché, Carolingians, 111; cf. also 1.33.

yoke beyond the custom of the law, we are more ready to die than to bear an unaccustomed burden." To which the emperor replied: "It has always been the custom of kings to add something new to previous law. Nor is all law established at one time; rather, a succession of laws grows through the successors of kings. They rule the laws; they are not ruled by them. The law, as they commonly say, has a nose of wax and the king has an iron hand and a long arm, so that he can bend it however he pleases. King Pippin did what he wanted. Unless you do what I want, I will show you how many painted shields I have and my prowess in war."[73]

2.9. Immediately sending letters throughout the entire realm, Emperor Henry gathered a very strong army. He ordered the Saxons to enter Bohemia via the road which leads through Sorbia and whose exit from the forest into this land passes by Chlumec. Their duke at that time was Ekkehard, whom all of Saxony obeyed as much as the king in all things.[74] He was a man of great counsel, endowed with singular skill in arranging the business of the realm and devoted to military affairs since boyhood—but he had never achieved happy successes in war.

The emperor himself camped on the other side of the River Regen. The next day, passing by the castle of Cham, he approached the wings of the forest, which divided Bavaria and Bohemia. Indignant when he realized that the Czechs had blocked the roads through the forest, he hardly kept silent. Striking his head three times, he conceived a wrath worthy of an emperor[75] and let loose a speech with these words: "Although they erect walls higher than the forests, although they raise towers high up to the clouds, still a net is spread in vain before the eyes of those with wings[76] and the Czechs' little sieges will in no way prevail against the Germans. Even if they ascend above the clouds[77] or if they enclose

73. Sallust *War with Jugurtha* 102.11.

74. Margrave Ekkehard II of Meissen (d. 1046). See Gabriele Rupp, *Die Ekkehardiner, Markgrafen von Meißen, und ihre Beziehungen zum Reich und zu den Piasten* (Frankfurt: Peter Lang, 1996), 145–47.

75. Ovid *Metamorphoses* 1.166, of Jove.   76. Prv 1:17.
77. Is 14:14.

themselves among the stars, these things will in no way help that wretched and ruined people." He said this and ordered everyone to rush into the forest.

Leading them himself, he ascended a high mountain situated in the middle of the forest. Sitting on a tripod, he said to the princes of the whole realm standing there: "In this valley hides a depraved band of Czechs, like a field mouse in the refuge of its holes." But his own opinion duped the emperor, for their fortification lay beyond the other mountain. The emperor sent ahead first the margraves, then the more noble armored men, calling each one by name. Then he ordered the foot soldiers to go into battle, promising them victory with these words: "You do not need a laborious battle. Only descend! Surely they will flee from fear, for they will not be able to bear your assault. Away, my falcons, away! Seize the trembling doves by the head. Be like fierce lions and act as wolves—who, when they rush into the sheepfold, have no worry about their numbers and do not have their feast until the whole flock has been slaughtered."

2.10. Immediately, at the king's command, the mailed contingent rushed out. The magnates fought in first position. The front of the army visibly shimmered, like brilliant ice, and as the sun shone on their armor; the foliage of the trees and the peak of the mountain glittered from them.[78] But descending into the valley they found no one, because in this direction and that the forest was thick and places were impenetrable. And as it usually happens in every battle that those behind push those ahead of them unwillingly into the fight, so now the weary magnates were forced by those behind them to climb yet another mountain. Now the tongue stuck to a palate dry[79] from heat and thirst. Strength failed, right arms languished, and panting breaths drew from chests. But they were unable to halt their step. Some threw their mail down on their shields, others stood leaning against the trees vainly seeking a hollow breeze, and others fell down like tree trunks—men

78. 1 Mc 6:39.
79. Cf. Book 1, n. 76.

confused and unaccustomed to marching, unaccustomed to battle like foot soldiers. When they reached the fortification, a great din broke out[80] everywhere, and above the forest an exhalation rose from the exhausted bodies like a cloud. Seeing this, the Czechs hesitated a moment and then, when they understood that the Germans had lost strength, boldly rushed out of the fortification. The invincible sister of Fortune, Bellona,[81] gave them that boldness.

O chance fortune! You are never consistently good and you plunge great men into the depths with your inconstant wheel. See! The iron-shod hoof of leaping horses disfigured the awful faces of fortunate men, ruptured their stomachs and their loins—girded with a belt doubly tinged with scarlet—and tore their intestines and entrails to pieces like a bandage or leg wraps. It is not fitting to say much[82] about the sudden death[83] of so much nobility, nor worthy to put more in writing. So great was the massacre of noble men there that neither in the fields of Emathia,[84] nor in the times of Sulla,[85] nor by some other disease of men, nor ever by an enemy sword was the nobility of the Germans said to have perished at one time.

Meanwhile, the caesar, sitting on the top of the mountain,[86] was deceived by the augury of his own mind. For since he did not judge his own men vanquished by the enemy, when the victors approached, covered in blood, the caesar jumped on the back of his steed, leaned on the mane, and spurred the quadruped's loins. If he had not had the horse ready, in that same hour the Roman emperor would have descended into the netherworld without delay.

2.11. While these things were being done there, the Saxons with Duke Ekkehard (about whom we spoke above [2.9]) entered Bohe-

80. Virgil *Aeneid* 12.756.   81. See Book 1, n. 119.
82. See Book 1, n. 235.   83. *Disticha Catonis* 4.46.
84. Lucan *Pharsalia* 1.1.

85. Cornelius Sulla Felix (168–79 BCE), a Roman patrician closely associated with, even responsible for, a period of rebellion, regional war, and tyrannical rule in the late Republic.

86. Tb 11:5.

mia and, as an enemy, destroyed one small region around the River Bílina. Meanwhile, when their duke heard a perverse rumor that the Slavs had gained a victory over the emperor, he took his stand on the bridge at Hněvin over the River Bílina, very anxious about whether to test fate in war or to return home with considerable disgrace.

Ekkehard preferred to put Duke Břetislav's spirit to the test first. Testing him through messengers, he flattered him with friendly words: "You who rejoice now, having conquered by fighting, if you had conquered by supplication, you would have been a much greater victor. For this reason, I do not want you to praise yourself foolishly, because it is hard for you to kick against the goad.[87] For he who now enters your land with a few men, as if to spare you and have mercy, unless you find his favor in the meantime, will quickly fall upon you with a such a multitude of armies that your springs will not suffice and your little land will scarcely hold them. Then the last state of those men will be worse than the first.[88] So I warn you again and give this advice: lest you lose all that you seem to possess, you should send to the emperor though friends faithful to you not a little of Queen Money[89]—who conquers all, soothes the angry, and reconciles enemies—so that she might intercede for you and gain his favor for you." At this, Duke Břetislav, aroused by anger, spurned the salutary warning and, resting his hand on his hilt, spoke thus: "Tell your Ekkehard: I have enough advice. Do not think you have gained ground by warning. People might style you Saxons 'harder than rocks' [saxa] and, if they are ill-advised men, think you know something. But unless you leave my province in three days without any violence, I will cut off your head with this sword and put your mouth to your backside. What is done in the court of the emperor does not concern me. As long as a sword hangs on the thigh of Břetislav, not milk but more like blood will flow from the side of the emperor." When these words

---

87. Acts 9:5.   88. Lk 11:26.
89. Horace *Epistles* 1.6.37; cf. below, 3.16.

were reported to Duke Ekkehard, although he bore it with great displeasure and was unwilling, he retreated to Saxony in great dishonor—like a wolf who, when he has lost his prey, submits his tail to the tracking dogs and goes back into the forest.

Also, it was reported to Duke Břetislav that *Comes* Prkoš, who was in charge of the burg of Bílina, corrupted by the Saxons' money, did not stand fast against the enemy in guarding the fortress. Instead he had stationed troops where the forests were [already] impassable to the enemy. The duke had put him in charge of the whole contingent from Moravia and three legions sent from Hungary to help. On the spot the angry duke, having gouged out his eyes and cut off his hands and feet, ordered Prkoš thrown into the abyss of the river—in the year of the Lord's incarnation 1041.

2.12. 1042. Emperor Henry, always a magnificent victor, wishing to revenge the destruction of his fine men, entered the land of the Czechs by three roads and laid waste to almost all of it as an enemy. He set fire to many burgs deserted by those unable to defend them. And when he came to the burg of Prague, he fixed his troops before it, on the opposite side, on the little mountain, Šibenice. I found no deed worthy of report there, except that Bishop Severus fled from the burg in the dark of night to the emperor's camp, fearing, I think, to be deprived of the honor of the episcopal see as a rebel against his lord.

Seeing this, Duke Břetislav did not know what he should do; anguish everywhere distressed his mind.[90] Now he was sorry that he had ever fought against the emperor. Now he was sorry that he had spurned the warning of Duke Ekkehard. Now he preferred to fight with entreaties and to conquer with entreaties the man he had once conquered by fighting. So he tried to deflect the terrible anger of the emperor with these words: "The wars you make, Caesar, will have no triumphs.[91] Our land is your treasury; we are yours and wish to be yours. He who rages against his own sub-

90. Virgil *Aeneid* 12.599.
91. Lucan *Pharsalia* 1.12.

jects is known to be more cruel than a cruel enemy. If you look at the strength of your army, we are not of the least importance to you. Why do you show your power against a leaf carried away by the wind?[92] The wind fails, where nothing opposes it. Know what you are: You are now the victor. Now wreath your victorious temples with laurel."[93] Moreover, Břetislav promised him fifteen hundred marks of silver pennies, which was the tribute for the past three years. Immediately, Queen Money[94] quenched the emperor's anger like a remarkable fire when it roils with flame,[95] when anyone pours a great deal of water over it, little by little it floods its spark and, with the waves prevailing, the fire fails. Having accepted the money, he who once invaded this land harshly returned home mildly,[96] with peace agreed upon.

2.13. 1043. There was such a famine in Bohemia that a third of the population died of hunger.

1044. 1045. The monk Gunther died, 9 October.

1046. The monastery in the burg of [Stará] Boleslav was dedicated on 19 March by Severus, the sixth bishop of the church of Prague.

1050. 1051. 1052. Božena, the wife of Duke Oldřich and mother of Břetislav, died.

1053. 1054. The burg of Wrocław and other burgs were returned by Duke Břetislav to the Poles on the condition that they pay five hundred marks of silver and thirty of gold annually both to him and to his successors.

1055. Duke Břetislav—glorious at the summit of virtues, gem of the Czechs, bright light of his ancestors—since he had subjected all of Poland to himself with God's help and was already twice a

92. Jb 13:25.
93. Virgil *Aeneid* 5.538.
94. Cf. Prv 21:14: "A secret present quenches anger." For Queen Money, see n. 89, above.
95. Ovid *Metamorphoses* 4.64.
96. There is a play on opposites here that does not come through in the English, contrasting *immitis* (harshly) with *mitis* (mildly).

victor, now resolved in the third instance to attack Hungary. Going on ahead, while he awaited his army he was struck with a grave
sickness in the burg of Chrudim. As he felt the sickness grow
worse and worse and his body's strength vanish, he called together
those magnates of the land who happened to be present. With
them standing around, he spoke these words: "Because my fates are
calling me[97] and black death flies before my eyes,[98] I want to designate for you and commend to your faith the man who should govern the *res publica* after me. You know that our princely lineage was
reduced down to one, partly by sterility and partly by some dying
at an immature age.[99] Now, as you yourselves see, God has given
me five sons. It does not seem to me useful to divide the realm
of Bohemia among them because every kingdom divided against
itself will be brought to desolation.[100] From the creation of the
world and the beginning of the Roman Empire until today, affection among brothers has been rare,[101] as clear examples bear witness to us: Cain and Abel, Romulus and Remus, and my ancestors
Boleslav and Saint Václav.[102] If you look at what two brothers have
done, what will five do? So much more capable and more powerful
do I consider them, that I predict much worse with a prophetic
mind. Alas, the minds of fathers are always terrified about the uncertain fates of their sons. Whence it must be seen to, in advance,
that after my death no form of discord arises among them for
the sake of obtaining governance of the realm. On account of
this I ask you through the Lord and I call your faith to witness by
an oath, that among my sons and descendants the oldest should
obtain the highest right and throne in the principate, and all his
brothers or others who are born from the ruling tribe should be

97. Virgil *Aeneid* 6.147.

98. Cf. ibid., 6.866: "Death's dark shadow flickers about his head."

99. Regino, *Chronicon*, 116–17.

100. Lk 11:17.

101. Ovid *Metamorphoses* 1:145.

102. Three famous fratricides and their victims, one biblical pair, one pair from
Roman prehistory, and one both Christian and Czech.

under his dominance. Believe me, unless monarchs[103] rule this duchy, the yoke will fall upon you princes and great harm upon the people." He spoke and, in the hands of those present, quitting his corporeal limbs, his breath sought the ether on 10 January.

A great lamentation was immediately made over him.[104] Eloquence would desert Cicero[105] before he could set out all of his merits. How much restraint and how much discernment in divine laws and human judgments this Duke Břetislav had! How generous a giver of alms and how pious a supporter of churches and of widows he was!

2.14. After Břetislav's death, all of the Czech people great and small, by common counsel and like will, chose his firstborn son Spitihněv as their duke, singing *Kyrie eleison*, that sweet song.[106] He was a very good-looking man, with black hair darker than pitch, a long beard, a cheerful face, cheeks whiter than snow and a little red in the middle. What more is there to say? He was a good man, handsome from head to foot.[107] On the first day on which he was enthroned, he did a great and marvelous thing, memorable for all ages, as a memorial to himself: as many as could be found of the German people, whether rich or poor or pilgrim, he ordered all of them banished at once from the land of Bohemia within three days. Not even his mother—the daughter of Otto, named Judith, about whom we spoke above [1.40]—would he allow to remain.

He likewise banished the abbess of St. George, the daughter of Bruno, because she had once earlier offended him with sharp words. For when his father, Břetislav, rebuilt the walls of the whole

103. Literally, from the Greek *monos archein*, one ruler—emphasizing that the Czechs should have only one duke, not many in contention.

104. Cf. Book 1, n. 259.

105. This plays on words using a phrase from Cicero himself, the famously eloquent orator of late republican Rome. The original line reads: "Daylight would desert me if I sought to recount the catalogue of good men overtaken by misfortune, and equally if I were to recall the evil men who prospered." Cicero, *On the Nature of the Gods*, trans. P. G. Walsh (Oxford: Clarendon Press, 1997), 140. Cf. 2.32, 3.60.

106. See Book 1, n. 198.

107. Horace *Epistles* 2.2.4; cf. 2.25, above.

burg of Prague in a circle, and the aforesaid hero held the province of Žatec by his father's grant, he happened to come with his
people to construct a wall around the cloister of St. George. Now,
it was in no way possible to position the wall correctly without
destroying the abbess's oven, which happened to stand there. With
a rope thrown in its midst, others hesitating to do it, the master's son approached. As if making a joke to himself, he ordered
the oven thrown down suddenly into the stream (Brusnice) with a
great guffaw, saying, "The Lady Abbess will not enjoy hot cakes
today." Seeing this, the abbess came out furious from her cloister
and, taking his words very badly, attacked and confounded him
with these ironic words: "What a noble, distinguished, powerful
man, renowned in arms! Much as he stormed great towers and
burgs, now he brings off a famous triumph over an oven. His victorious temples are now wreathed with a golden laurel.[108] Let the
clergy resound with various melodies and bells, because the duke
has thrown down an oven and done a wondrous thing. Ah! It is
shameful to say that he is not ashamed to have done this." The
man stiffened in his body, and his voice choked in his throat.[109]
Indignant, he restrained his rage[110] with a groan.

The duke kept the words of the abbess deep in his heart.[111] After he was enthroned, before he entered the Church of St. George,
he barked to the abbess: "It is more fitting for the clergy to resound with melodies and strike the bells now, when the abbess
has been thrown outside and out of this land, than when her oven
was thrown down. Behold a powerful man, renowned in arms! Not
storming towers or burgs but throwing you out, Abbess, mistress
of that oven, brings about a famous triumph today and wreathes
my temples with laurel." As ordered, the abbess was said to have
been speedily placed on a two-horse cart and, quicker than it could
be said, thrown out of the boundaries of the land.

2.15. After these deeds were carried out, the new duke went

108. See n. 93, above.
110. Lucan *Pharsalia* 9.166.

109. Virgil *Aeneid* 2.774.
111. Virgil *Aeneid* 1.26.

to make arrangements for the new realm of Moravia. His father [Břetislav], dividing it among his sons, had once given half to Vratislav and the other part to Conrad and Otto. (Jaromír, dedicated to studies, was still stretching his wings among scholars.) Duke Spitihněv sent ahead to all the magnates of that land letters in which he called by name three hundred men from all the burgs, those he knew to be better and more noble. He ordered them to meet him at the burg of Chrudim, for the safety of their heads. The men carried out their orders[112] and met their duke already beyond the gate of the guard post in the fields of Hrutov. Angry because they had not met at the appointed place, the duke immediately ordered them seized and sent them to prison in chains, dividing them between individual burgs in Bohemia. He distributed their horses and arms among his men and then took the road to Moravia.

Hearing of this, his brother Vratislav feared him greatly and fled to the regions of Hungary, having left his wife in the burg at Olomouc. King Andrew [of Hungary][113] received him with joy and treated Vratislav honorably as long as he remained with him.

Afterward Duke Spitihněv set in order everything in Moravia at his pleasure. He arranged for his brothers to be with him at court, putting Conrad in charge of hunters and appointing Otto as master of bakers and cooks. His sister-in-law he seized and sent to a certain well-fortified castle called Lštění, committing her to the care of a *comes* named Mstiš. Mstiš did not guard her as befitted such a lady, for every night he shackled her foot to his. Hearing of it, her husband bore it with displeasure; what reward he later gave the *comes* for this brazen act will be made clear in what follows [2.19].

2.16. After one month had passed, with the intervention of Bishop Severus and the magnates, Spitihněv ordered his sister-in-law to return to her husband, giving her safe conduct. Since she was near to giving birth when she made haste to go, this injured

---

112. See Book 1, n. 333.
113. King Andrew of Hungary (1046–60).

the mother and, because it was not possible to remove the immature weight of the fetus, within the space of three days that most
beautiful of women breathed out her spirit.

King Andrew, when he saw his guest Vratislav grieving so long
over her death, consoled the gloomy youth with friendly words:[114]
"O my dear guest, may God keep you safe. Concerning the rest,
cast your burden on the Lord and hope in him, and he will see
that this sorrow is turned quickly into joy.[115] It often happens that
where a man hopes least to benefit, there he gains greater advantage. Be a strong man and do not overstep the bounds in lamenting the death of your wife, as if something novel had happened
to you alone—since it should be known to all men that every human body returns to its origin." He spoke and led his sad guest
with him to the table, where they were refreshed by rich dishes of
food and made joyful by mellow wine. By chance, this king had a
single daughter, named Adelhaid, now ripe for the marriage bed,
very beautiful and desired by many suitors with great hope. When
the guest saw her, he loved her[116] desperately. The good king did
not object, and Vratislav joined with her in matrimony a few days
later.

When Duke Spitihněv heard this, in his wise nature taking care
lest perhaps his brother invade all of Moravia with the Hungarians, he sent messengers to recall Vratislav from Hungary and returned to him the burgs that his father had earlier given him in
Moravia. For Spitihněv was a prudent man at critical moments,
knowing to stretch or relax his bow at the opportune time.[117]

For the common good, as an example for later men to imitate,
I will mention one special practice, worthy of memory, among his
other virtues.[118] Such was always his custom during Lent: spending time in a cloister either of monks or of canons, he made time
for alms, was present at the divine offices, and kept vigils and

114. Virgil *Aeneid* 5.770; cf. Book I, n. 230.
115. This sentence is a combination of Ps 54:23, Sir 2:6, and Jas 4:9 (though in
James, joy turns into sorrow).
116. Gn 34:2.   117. Cf. Horace *Odes* 2.10.19.
118. Cf. Tb 2:12.

prayers. He even went so far as to go through the entire Psalter meditatively, either with his hands extended or with genuflections, before singing matins. Like the monks, he observed silence after compline until prime.[119] As long as the fast lasted, he disposed of ecclesiastical business, but after the meal he handled secular judgments. The episcopal surplice and clerical tunic,[120] which he put on at the beginning of the fast, he wore through all of Lent; on Holy Thursday he gave it to his private chaplain, well and piously reckoning that he who had been a participant in the labor of this period of penance should not go away unrewarded on such a great feast day.

2.17. 1056. 1057. 1058. On 2 August, Břetislav's wife Judith, duchess of the Czechs, died, whom her son Spitihněv had thrown out of his realm. Since she could take revenge no other way against her son for this injury, she married King Peter of the Hungarians as an insult to him and all the Czechs.[121] Her body was later moved by her son, Duke Vratislav, and buried beside her husband Břetislav in the Church of the Holy Martyrs Vitus, Václav, and Adalbert in Prague.[122]

1059. 1060. When Duke Spitihněv came to Prague for the Feast of St. Václav, he saw that the Church of St. Vitus was no longer large and capacious enough for all the people flocking together for the holy festivity. Saint Václav himself had built the rotunda, in which his own body rests, in the likeness of a Roman church.[123]

119. Concerning the liturgical hours, see Book 1, n. 306.

120. The tunic (or tunicle) was a sleeved garment, appropriate to the lowest-ranking subdeacon but also worn by bishops under the dalmatic. The surplice was akin to an alb, but shorter, unbelted, and with full sleeves.

121. This cannot be quite true, since King Peter of Hungary died ca. 1046. However, in 1058, King Andrew's son, Solomon, was crowned king as his successor and betrothed to a daughter of the German king, Henry III, named Judith. Cosmas may be misinterpreting some source about this Judith's marriage and conflating it with another tradition that has Břetislav's widow fleeing to Hungary. Engel, *Realm of St. Stephen*, 30–31.

122. The cathedral church in Prague; see Book 1, n. 8.

123. The "rotunda" was a common layout for churches in the Czech Lands before the twelfth century. Small churches on a circular plan, with semicircular chapels at-

Another little church was attached to it, located almost in the church's portico; in the middle, in a tight space, lay the mausoleum of Saint Adalbert. The duke decided it was best to destroy both churches and construct a single great church for both patrons. He immediately indicated the place for the church in a long circle and laid the foundation. All aglow was the work; the wall rose.[124] But having begun in happiness, in the very next year, it was interrupted by his senseless death.

In the same year [1060], at the time when armies go forth to war,[125] after he had already raised the standards of the army and had gone a day's journey, Duke Spitihněv met a widow, who wailed and wept and kissed his feet.[126] Running after him, she cried: "Lord, avenge me against my adversary."[127] And he said: "I will, when I return from the expedition." And she said: "What if you do not return? Who will you send to avenge me? And why do you neglect the reward you are about to receive from God?" Immediately, at the petition of a single widow, he interrupted the expedition and avenged her against her adversary by a just judgment. What do you say to this, O present-day princes, you who do not answer the cries of so many widows and so many children but, in your puffed-up pride and haughtiness, look down on them? By such bowels of mercy,[128] as we said above, Duke Spitihněv received this nickname for himself: he was called by everyone "father of the clergy, defender of widows." But since we frequently notice that good men are taken from our midst by God's hidden judgment while bad men are left, so this man of such great probity was taken from this light on 28 January 1061, in the sixth year of his rule as duke.

---

tached, they have thick walls, almost no windows, and were painted with interior frescoes. (A number survive to this day.) Archeological research shows that the rotunda church in Prague Castle attributed to St. Václav, which lies underneath the present cathedral, was considerably larger than most.

124. Virgil *Aeneid* 1.436.   125. 2 Kgs 11:1.
126. Cf. Gn 50:1.   127. Lk 18:3.
128. Lk 1:78.

2.18. After Spitihněv's death, his brother Vratislav was raised to the throne, with all the Czechs approving. He immediately divided the realm of Moravia in half between his brothers. He gave Otto the eastern plain, which he himself had earlier held, and which was better suited to hunting and more abundant in fish. He gave to Conrad the western part, which faces the Germans, because Conrad knew the German language, as did Vratislav. That region is flatter and more fertile in fields and fruits.

Meanwhile, with the sun tarrying in the first part of Pisces, the well-endowed youth Jaromír, having heard of the death of this brother Spitihněv, whom he worshipped with love and fear no less than a father, set aside boyish anxiety and returned from his studies, hoping to have some portion of his inheritance in his father's realm. When his brother, Duke Vratislav, perceived him to be aspiring more to the layman's army than to the army of sacred teaching, he reproached Jaromír's impertinence with these words: "I do not, brother, I do not want you to be cut off from the head [of the body] of which you have been made a member and cast into hell by this apostasy. Through divine grace and his wisdom, our father once chose you for sacerdotal rank. He therefore gave you to the study of letters, so that you might be considered a fitting successor to Bishop Severus, if only, God willing, you survived him."

Soon enough, entering the month of March, on the first Sunday—the time when sacred orders were celebrated—Vratislav tonsured Jaromír, even though he was unwilling, forced, and very much resisting it. In the duke's own presence, Jaromír was ordained up to the office of the diaconate; he read the Gospel publicly and, in the usual way, attended the bishop celebrating the Mass.[129] After this, the new deacon—who ought to be called "the apostate" like Julian of antiquity, having wrongly cast aside the shield[130] of the holy army and neglected the grace he received through the laying on of

129. A deacon ranked immediately below a priest. While saying Mass was reserved to priests, deacons were charged with assisting during the service, in particular—as here—with reading the Gospel.
130. Cf. Horace Odes 2.7.10.

hands[131]—put on a warrior's belt[132] and fled with his followers to
the Polish duke, with whom he remained until the death of Bishop
Severus.

2.19. At that time, Mstiš, son of Boris, a man of great boldness,
greater eloquence, and less prudence, although remembering that
Duke Vratislav might consider him suspect because he once held
Vratislav's wife in custody when she was committed to him by his
lord [2.15], nevertheless boldly entered the duke's palace and approached him humbly to make a request. "Through the grace of
your brother," he said, "I have built a church in honor of St. Peter
the Apostle. I humbly beg that you might deign to come to the solemnity of its dedication and, at the same time, make the city joyful[133] by your coming. And I beg that you not look down on my
entreaties." Vratislav, although remembering the injury once done
to his wife, dissembled the anger he held in his heart on account
of his newness [on the throne]. He said: "I will come, I will make
my city joyful, and I will do what the affair and justice demand."
The *comes* did not comprehend the words spoken by the prince.
Giving the duke many thanks, he went away cheerful and prepared
the things necessary for a great feast.

The duke and the bishop arrived. As soon as the church (located in the suburb)[134] was dedicated, the duke ascended into the
burg for a meal. The bishop and the *comes* together reclined at a
table covered with sumptuous food in Mstiš's court, which was in
front of the church. While they were eating a messenger arrived
and said in the ear of the *comes:* "The castellany of the burg is

131. From the beginning of Vratislav's speech through this point in the chapter,
Cosmas has cribbed, sometimes verbatim, from Regino of Prüm's description of the
forcible ordination of Karlomann as deacon by his father (*Chronicon,* 101–2). The reference to Julian "the Apostate" (331–63)—so called because, although he succeeded the
first Christian Roman emperor, Constantine, he supported a return to polytheism—
appears in Regino's entry.

132. Ibid., 96.

133. Ps 45:5. Here and in Vratislav's reply, I have translated *civitas* as "city" rather
than the usual "burg" to convey the ring of the biblical allusion.

134. *Suburbium* in this medieval context indicates a settlement outside, literally below *(sub),* a burg *(urbs).*

withdrawn from you and given to Kojata, son of Všebor," who was at that time first in the ducal palace. To this the *comes* answered: "He is the duke and the lord; let him do with his burg what he pleases. But what my church has today, the duke does not have the power to take away." If he had not fled that night with the advice and help of the bishop, without a doubt he would have lost his eyes—and the foot that he had once shackled to the foot of the duke's wife.

2.20. 1062. On 27 January, Duchess Adelhaid died. She was the mother of Judith and Ludmila, and also of Břetislav II and Vratislav, who was killed in the first flower of youth on 19 November. After the space of almost one year after the death of Duchess Adelhaid, Duke Vratislav took a wife named Svatava, daughter of Kazimierz, duke of the Poles, and sister of Bolesław and Władysław.[135] Vratislav had four free men of good disposition from her: Boleslav, Bořivoj, Vladislav, and Soběslav. Enough will be said about them—and abundantly—in the appropriate places [Book 3], so far as God will grant it.

2.21. 1063. 1067. On 9 December, Severus, the sixth bishop of the church of Prague, departed this world and enjoys a pleasant triumph. He experienced decidedly both adversity and fortune. For once he was captured, chained, and put in prison by Duke Břetislav, and he bore martyrdom both in secret and in the open at the same time.

Almost the entire duration of his episcopate he ruled the bishopric of Bohemia and Moravia as one, undivided, without any opposition or any objection. And he would have ruled it thus, if he had not agreed, overcome by the very urgent demands of Duke Vratislav after the death of Spitihněv, that John be promoted as bishop of Moravia. However, Severus first resolved, under the testimony of many men, something like this (whether as an allod, a fief, or an exchange):[136] that the bishop of Prague should choose

135. Świętosława (d. 1126), daughter of Kazimierz I (1034–58).

136. Cosmas seems here to indicate that while he remembers the details of the arrangement, he is unsure about its legal status: whether the conditions agreed upon were a permanent, proprietary gift (what he calls here "an allod"), a contingent grant

for that bishopric twelve of the more desirable villages in all Bohemia; that he should accept one hundred marks of silver annually from the duke's treasury; and that he should possess in Moravia the court at Sekyrkostel with its appurtenances—as he had before and so also in the future—as well as the village of Slivnice with the market and castle situated there, in the middle of the river named Svratka. The castle is called Podivín after its founder, Podiva, a Jew who was afterward a Catholic. It is said that there had been in Moravia before Severus's time a certain bishop, named Vracen, I think.[137]

How much contention Severus's successor, Jaromír, had with the aforesaid Bishop John over that bishopric will be demonstrated in its place [2.27].

2.22. Then Conrad and Otto, hearing that the bishop of Prague had departed to Christ, sent for and recalled from Poland their brother Jaromír. They ungirded him of his military belt, and he again took a clerical habit and tonsure. Meanwhile, Duke Vratislav, wary of his future and fearing that his brother might conspire against him with the aforesaid brothers if he should become bishop, began quietly to consider[138] how he might be able to defraud Jaromír of the bishopric.

In the duke's court at that time there was a certain chaplain named Lanzo, born of a noble family from Saxony, a personable man and very learned, who had been raised to the provostship of the church of Litoměřice. In his character and life there was nothing contrary to the honor of the episcopate. Because Lanzo had always remained faithful to the duke, the duke took all sorts of pains to make him bishop of Prague.

Meanwhile, Conrad and Otto came from Moravia, bringing their brother Jaromír with them. On his behalf they submissively asked Duke Vratislav to remember their brotherhood, remember

under the auspices of the duke as overlord ("a fief"), or a trade between two independent parties ("an exchange," e.g., of the villages for the silver marks).

137. No bishop of Moravia with this name is known from other sources.

138. See Book 1, n. 331.

their father's arrangement, and remember the oaths by which their father bound the faith of the *comites* to elect Jaromír as their bishop after Severus's death. But Vratislav was a clever man, guileful at feigning and dissembling situations, like a little fox that has not fled away when it has tucked its tail. Keeping one thing locked in his breast, the duke presented something else to his brothers with his mouth. "This is not," he said, "a matter for one man to treat, but requires everyone's public consideration. Since right now the majority of the people and the leaders of the army have meanwhile come out on campaign already, there is nowhere better, I think, for this case to be handled than in the enclosure of this land's guard post. All those elder by birth of this people, the leaders and *comites,* and those better among the clergy will be there. This episcopal election stands in their judgment." The duke did this, so that there—among his warriors, hedged about by arms and fortified by garrisons—he might be able to go against the will of his brothers and raise as bishop the man he wanted, Lanzo. But the twisted intention of the duke was frustrated, because all power is from God[139] and it is not possible for a man to be a bishop who is not predestined or permitted to do so by God.

2.23. What more? They came to the gate of the guard post where one goes into Poland. In a place called Dobenina the duke convened the people and the leaders in an assembly. With his brothers standing at his right and left,[140] the clergy and *comites* sitting in a wide circle, and all the warriors standing behind them, the duke summoned Lanzo. With Lanzo standing in the middle, Duke Vratislav praised and commended him to the people. In a clear voice he spoke as follows: "Your excellent faith, visible to me daily, exacts this from me and compels me to do what I am about to do today, so that our descendents might learn from it how much they ought to be faithful to their lords. Take the ring and staff, be the bridegroom of the church of Prague and the shepherd

139. Cf. Rom 13:1.
140. 3 Kgs 22:19.

of holy sheep."[141] A murmuring arose among the people[142] and no acclamation resounded, as is always the custom during an episcopal election.

Then, taking this as quite intolerable, Kojata, son of Všebor and *comes* of the palace, a man truthful in speech and simple in word, standing at the right hand of the duke's brother Otto, forcefully poked him in the side, saying: "Why do you stand there? Are you like an ass hearing the sound of a lyre?[143] Why do you not help your brother? Do you not see that your brother, the son of a duke, is being repudiated for a stranger and an alien,[144] who came to this land without leg wraps and is now being raised to the throne? And if the duke violates the oath to his father, far be it from us that the ghosts of our parents should render an account before God for this oath and bear the suffering. We acknowledge and will strive as much as possible toward what your father Břetislav constrained us and our fathers to uphold by an oath of faith: that your brother Jaromír is to be bishop after the death of Bishop Severus. Even if your brother displeases you, why do you sully our clergy, not just a little but equally skilled in learning, with this German? Oh, if you had as many bishoprics as you could find chaplains born in this land worthy of a bishopric! Do you think that a foreigner will love us more and desire better for this land than a native? Indeed human nature is such that anyone, wherever his land, not only loves his people more than a foreign people, but would even divert wandering rivers into his country if he could. We prefer, therefore, we prefer that a dog's tail or the dung of an ass be placed on the holy seat rather than Lanzo. Your brother, Spitihněv of blessed memory, who expelled all the Germans from this land in one day, knew differently.[145] The Roman emperor Henry [IV] yet lives and long

141. With the ring and staff, the duke is here attempting to invest Lanzo as bishop, an imperial prerogative; see Book 1, n. 206, and below, n. 146.

142. Cf. Nm 11:1 and Acts 6:1.

143. The only words in Cosmas's chronicle written in Greek letters (ὄνοσ λύρας), they are verbatim from Boethius, *Consolation of Philosophy*, book 1, prose 4.

144. Tb 1:7.

145. Above, 2.14.

may he live; usurping his power, you act against yourself when you give the episcopal ring and staff to a hungry dog.[146] Surely you and your bishop will not go unpunished if Kojata, son of Všebor, lives."

2.24. Then Smil, son of Božen and castellan in the burg of Žatec, together with Kojata, taking Conrad, Otto, and Jaromír by their right hands, said: "Let us go and see whether the tricks and false equity of one man prevails, or whether justice and the wondrous equity of three brothers excels. Comparable age, one will, and the same power links them and the greater abundance of warriors helps them." There arose not a small commotion of people throughout the camp. "Arms, arms," cried some. To everyone this unadvised episcopal election was hateful. Therefore, the larger part of the army seceded to those three lords and made their camp around and within the fortress of Opočno.

Since the other part of the warriors had already proceeded into the forest, the duke, seeing himself almost abandoned and insufficiently safe from his brothers' attack, fled as quickly as he was able, fearing that they would occupy the burg of Prague or of Vyšehrad before him. Vratislav nevertheless sent a messenger to his brothers from the road, saying: "I will do what is to be done, but not on account of the boasting tongue[147] of Kojata, son of Všebor, nor Smil, son of Božen, in whose mouth is honey but in whose heart is bile,[148] and by whose depraved and deceitful advice this has happened. Whom I if I live—but I restrain myself.[149] Very much remembering our father's legacy and his oaths, I will do what jus-

146. The gift of ring and staff constitutes investiture; see Book 1, n. 206. As subordinate to the archbishop of Mainz, bishops of Prague (and Olomouc) were normally invested by the German king before their liturgical consecration as bishops, though they held no temporal lands or authority from him. Kojata is rightly pointing out that Vratislav is endeavoring to usurp an imperial prerogative. See my *Hastening Toward Prague*, 230–31, also 137–41.

147. Ps 11:4.

148. Bruno *Vita Adalberti* 21; for "in whose mouth is honey," cf. Rv 10:9.

149. This threat cut short and the specific words *quos ego*— (whom I) derive from Virgil *Aeneid* 1.135.

tice and fraternal love demands. Only follow me to the burg of Prague."

Upon arriving, they fixed their camp in the fields next to the village of Hostivař and sent to Duke Vratislav [asking] if he wanted to prove his words with deeds. Receiving them peacefully, he elected his brother Jaromír as bishop and, with oaths given and received between them, he dismissed Conrad and Otto in peace to Moravia. But Smil and Kojata, although they had spoken true and just words among the princes, nevertheless if they had not escaped by flight in the night, the duke would have punished them without any hearing as enemies of the *res publica* [i.e., traitors]. This election was carried out in 1068, with the sun entering the twenty-fifth part of Gemini [15 June].

2.25. Without delay, Duke Vratislav sent *Comites* Severus, Alexius, and Markward the German to the emperor, Henry III [IV], with his brother Jaromír, now elected. Arriving on the vigil of St. John the Baptist [23 June], they approached the emperor in the burg of Mainz, doing imperial business there with bishops and princes. Presenting their bishop-elect, they asked on behalf of the duke and the whole populace that he deign to confirm their election by his authority. Agreeing to their request, the emperor—on the third day, that is, on 26 June, a Tuesday—gave him the ring and pastoral staff.[150] And on the next Sunday, 2 July, Jaromír was ordained bishop by the archbishop of Mainz,[151] having changed his name to Gebhard.

That same day, ferrying across the Rhine, the new bishop came up secretly behind a certain warrior of his, William, who was sitting on the bank after the midday meal with his feet hanging down in the riverbed. Unaware that deep water was hidden there, he threw him into the flowing Rhine, saying: "I baptize you anew, William!" Submerged a long time but with his head out of the wa-

---

150. Again, investiture; cf. Book 1, n. 206. According to Bretholz, the dates and the days of the week Cosmas gives here do not match, because in 1068, 26 June should have been a Friday and 2 July a Thursday.

151. Archbishop Siegfried I of Mainz (1060–84).

ter, whirling and catching the waves, William said: "If this is how you baptize, you are very much out of your mind, bishop." If William had not known how to swim well, in one day Bishop Gebhard would have both risen to the episcopate and lost it.

2.26. When Bishop Gebhard arrived in Prague, on the same day that he was seated on the episcopal throne according to custom, he gave his chaplain Mark the provostship[152] of that same church. By the measure of human birth, Mark descended from a noble family of ancestors originating from the German people. He was mighty in wisdom before all the men whom the Czech land then contained. For he was a very good scholar in all the liberal arts, who was able to be called and to be the instructor of many masters, a marvelous interpreter of the divine page, an eminent teacher of the Catholic faith and ecclesiastical law. Whatever religion, whatever regular life, whatever honor there is in this church, he taught and arranged through his prudence. Previously the men there were without a rule, canons in name only, uncultured, unlearned, serving in choir in layman's dress, living as if acephalous or like a beast of two kinds. Instructing them by his words and example[153] and choosing the better from among the many—as if picking flowers from a meadow—with divine help the wise man, Mark, ordained twenty-five brothers, giving them the habit of religion and an equal measure of food and drink according to a rule.[154] But

152. The provost was head of the cathedral chapter, the body of canons who assisted the bishop and also served the bishop's parish.

153. Cosmas here echoes the famous injunction to teach by word and example *(docere verbo et exemplo)*, which echoes Gregory the Great's *Pastoral Care* as well as the New Testament. See Caroline Walker Bynum, *Docere verbo et exemplo: An Aspect of Twelfth-Century Spirituality,* Harvard Theological Studies 31 (Missoula, Mont.: Scholars Press, 1979), esp. 15.

154. What Cosmas is describing here is the institution of a reform among the canons serving at the cathedral. Before Mark's provostship, their life was "irregular," meaning without a rule; "acephalous," headless, thus presumably without clear leadership; a beast of two kinds, like a centaur, neither lay nor clergy, as reflected in their dress. Mark not only established a rule to govern the canons' lives, including the provision of appropriate clothing, he fixed their number at twenty-five and established a standard distribution of their shared income. Obviously, from what follows, this did

often, either through the negligence of servants or by some excuse of the masters, the brothers' prebends were interrupted and therefore they often badgered Mark with their complaints. Wishing to please them fully[155] and assigning the fourth part of their tithe to himself, he divided the three other parts among the brothers, so that each brother would have—without interruption—thirty measures of wheat and the same of oats annually, as well as four pennies per week for meat.

Concerning his actions pleasing to God, more worth reporting could be said, but it is better that I remain silent about them than to appear to have said a few things out of many.[156] After thirty years of ruling the provostship of this church, on 14 November this provost of blessed memory departed from these shadows to the pleasant places of everlasting light.[157] Mark is now in the heavenly kingdom, about to receive the blessed interest on the talent he invested.[158]

But behold, while we discussed our stipends, we have digressed by a roundabout way far from the work begun. Now let us return to those things we promised above. Let us see what cause brought about such great conflict between two angelic men. O greed and worldly ambition, execrable plague and enemy of humankind, you even assail God's priests by your craft!

1069.

2.27. 1070. On 8 June, Bishop Gebhard consecrated his church in the new court called Zerčice.

1071. 1072. 1073. After Bishop Gebhard saw that his labor had been spent in vain[159] because neither by entreaties, with gifts, or through friends was he able to persuade his brother Vratislav to

---

not go easily or without quibbling. And there is notably no mention here of clerical celibacy or the sharing of common quarters. Mark seems particularly to have earned Cosmas's respect and admiration for his role in elevating the quality of education at the cathedral.

155. Col 1:10.
157. Cf. 1 Pt 2:9.
159. Lv 26:20.

156. Virgil Aeneid 3.377.
158. Cf. Mt 25:27–28.

accept an exchange from him, expel Bishop John, and again unite both bishoprics, he changed, like Prometheus, into the form of another shape.[160] "Since indeed," he said, "imploring for three years or more now, I am not able to achieve what I want, I will do what I am able and, with God as a witness, I will either unite them or lose both bishoprics."

Without delay, he arranged to go to his court at Sekyrkostel in Moravia. Turning off the road, he went to the burg of Olomouc, as if to visit his brother [Otto] but eventually and secretly to harm Bishop John. Receiving him as an agreeable guest, John said: "Oh, if I had known of your coming, I would have prepared an episcopal repast for you." Gebhard, like a lioness[161] driven by hunger, stared at him for a long time with flashing eyes and then responded: "The time to take food is some other time; some other kind of business is to be done now. But let us go," he said. "It is necessary for us to enter a private place to talk." Then Bishop John, ignorant of the future, led him into his bedchamber. You would see it no differently if a gentle lamb were leading a ravening wolf into his stall, voluntarily offering himself[162] for slaughter.

There, when Jaromír saw before the bed a half-eaten cheese, a sprig of thyme, and an onion on a plate with a toasted morsel of bread[163] (which were perhaps left over from the bishop's meal the day before), he said, very indignant, as if he had discovered some great fault worthy of the cross: "Why do you live sparingly? Whom are you sparing, O wretch and beggar? By Hercules! It is not fitting for a bishop to live sparingly." What then? Forgetting the holy order, forgetting brotherhood, not remembering humanity, as a leopard seizes a rabbit or a lion a little lamb, so Jaromír furiously grabbed his host with both hands, lifted his brother bishop

160. Cosmas here confuses Prometheus, the mythic figure sentenced to eternal torture for giving humans fire, with Proteus, the shape-shifting minor sea god described at length in Virgil *Georgics* 4.387–529.

161. Key words in this passage seem to be drawn from Ovid *Metamorphoses* 13.542–47.

162. Heb 9:25.

163. Gn 18:5.

up high by the hair, and threw him to the ground like a bundle of hay. Immediately, of those ready for this criminal act, one man sat on his neck, another on his feet, and a third said, smiling while he beat the bishop: "Learn to suffer, child of one hundred years,[164] invader of others' flocks." But while the humble monk was flogged he sang "Miserere mei, Deus," just as he usually did in the cloister. For the wicked man observing all this, who laughed at no one unless he saw him doing evil, there came great laughter and applause.

Just as when sometimes a brave warrior boldly invades the enemy's camp at night and attacks them as an enemy while they are sleeping, then flees quickly lest he be captured by them, so Bishop Jaromír, having dishonored his brother bishop, left the burg sweetened with the bile of his own impropriety and went to that court of his [Sekyrkostel] to which he had earlier promised to go.

2.28. This was the first cause, the kindling, and the beginning of all the discord that later arose between those two columns of the church. Bishop John, having sustained such a great injury, immediately sent his messenger to Duke Vratislav and troubled him with complaints of this sort: "If you look with equanimity at the insult done to me by your brother Gebhard out of inhumanity, you create danger, since everyone knows this to be your injury not mine. How did I fail or how did I merit this, I who did nothing unless it pleased you? Behold! I, although unworthy, nevertheless called 'bishop' through your grace, beaten by the herald's whips to the point of nausea, would prefer never to have reached the episcopal summit. Certainly either return me to my abbot, however late, or, taking this insult with equanimity, break with me and send me or my messenger to the apostolic see." Having heard this, Duke Vratislav was inflamed with great zeal and could not keep himself from tears at so great a turn of affairs. Immediately a contingent of warriors was sent for Bishop John, so that he might be able to come talk with the duke without endangering his life. For the

164. Is 65:20.

duke feared that his brother Jaromír might remove him from their midst[165] by ambush.

In the chapel of Bishop John, there was a cleric named Hagno, a German man, a servant of philosophy and a pupil of Ciceronian eloquence. The duke summoned Hagno, bound him with many promises, and entrusted to him much concerning his brother Gebhard, much concerning the injury done to Bishop John, and much on the state of the church, both in writing and in speech, in order to report it to the pope. When Hagno took to the road, passing through Regensburg, by a sinister omen he lodged at the house of a certain *cives* named Gumpold, who was a warrior of Bishop Gebhard's, holding a benefice from him of thirty silver marks per year. After the meal, between drinks, Gumpold asked—as a host is accustomed to do of a guest—who he was, where he came from, and what the purpose of his trip was. He elicited it from Hagno with a crafty mind and when he realized that he was carrying out a mission against Bishop Gebhard, Gumpold could not bear for this denunciation to be brought against his lord. The next day he sent robbers after Hagno in order to obstruct the purpose of his journey with some kind of trouble. Apprehending him on the road, they took his money, cut off his nose and, with swords pressed to his throat, threatened death unless he turned back. Fearing to lose his life, however disfigured now, Hagno returned to his bishop in Moravia.

2.29. The duke's great indignation soon grew from a great to a greater one. A Roman embassy was again decided upon but with more careful counsel and safer assistance on the road. In the duke's chapel there was a certain priest Peter, born to his father Podiva, excelling in the provostship of St. George's, exceeding others in the literature of wisdom, and knowing both the German and the Roman languages equally well. The duke sent him to Rome with a *comes* named Preda, son of Byš, and not without ample money. He made known to both of them the first and the most recent injuries committed by his brother against himself and Bishop John,

165. 1 Cor 5:1.

enclosed in a written summary, so that they might report them to the pope's ears. So that they might be able to make a safer journey, he committed them to the count palatine of the Roman emperor named Rapoto,[166] asking with considerable humility that the envoys travel to Rome and return under his safe conduct. For Rapoto was a count of such great power that through continuous places all the way to Rome he had his own villages or estates, or warriors loyal to him in castles. On behalf of the Duke Vratislav, he also received 150 marks of silver annually as a benefice.

When the envoys came to Rome by his safe conduct, they presented to the pope [Gregory VII] letters smeared with two hundred marks. When they were recited before everyone by a notary, the Roman pontiff asked the envoys if they could prove by their own words what the letters declared.[167] They said, "It would be very inappropriate for us to offer one thing in letters and something else in speech." Then the man who occupied the second seat after the pope, advising everyone who was present at the meeting, decided that such a scandal ought to be eradicated from the church by papal command. Rudolf, plenipotentiary and counselor to Pope Gregory,[168] was immediately sent to Bohemia so that, if things were as had been reported to the supreme pontiff,[169] he might correct errors, reprove the disobedient, upbraid unbelievers, and strike the negligent with anathema in the pope's place. If any matters should prove beyond this means of correction, Rudolf should defer on those and compel them to come before the higher audience of the apostolic see.

2.30. When the pope's emissary arrived [in Bohemia], he found

166. Rapoto of Cham (d. 1080). He was never the count palatine, a title assumed only by his son, Rapoto II (d.1099), after 1082–83; cf. below, 2.49 and 3.2.

167. Regino, *Chronicon*, 83.

168. Pope Gregory VII (1073–85). Letters preserved in the papal register name *two* papal legates sent to Bohemia in 1073, Bernard and Gregory. *Codex diplomaticus et epistolaris regni bohemiae*, vol. 1, ed. Gustav Friedrich (Prague: Sumptibus Comitiorum Regni Bohemiae, 1907) (hereafter CDB), no. 62, pp. 63–64.

169. Here Cosmas combines borrowings from two separate passages in Regino's *Chronicon* (66 and 82), the first of which includes the word *apocrisarius* (plenipotentiary).

Duke Vratislav in the burg of Prague. Offering him apostolic blessing and the status of an adoptive son of the universal father, Rudolf wielded as great authority and power as if the supreme pontiff himself were present.[170] Then he ordered the duke to convene at a holy synod all the princes of the land, together with abbots, provosts of churches, and Bishop John of Moravia. Summoned by name once, then twice, Bishop Gebhard refused to come and, finally, is said to have given a response of this sort: "According to the statutes of the canons, valid episcopal dignity, and justice, I will not come to your assembly unless my master, the metropolitan [archbishop] of Mainz, is there and a crowd of other fellow bishops is present also."[171] For he knew that there he might fall into a snare, retribution, and a stumbling block.[172] The Roman emissary, seeing himself despised and dishonored, moved by anger, suspended Gebhard from every priestly function and deprived him of the episcopal dignity.

Hearing this, not only the canons but indeed all the clergy throughout their chapels cut up their stoles[173] and denuded their altars (as on Good Friday). Not a small wrinkle furrowed the brow[174] of Mother Church because the priestly offices were silent. If their pastor's original honor and rank were not restored to him, the whole clergy preferred to lose their own rank forever. Seeing a great uproar among the people, the cardinal, compelled by necessity, returned the bishop his priestly office alone.[175] And he constrained both [Gebhard and John] by the ban, if each bishop did not give a reckoning to the Roman pontiff concerning the charges leveled [against him] in that same year.[176]

170. Again, ibid., 66.
171. A legal gambit, asserting his legitimate rights according to canon law. A surviving letter from Archbishop Siegfried of Mainz to Pope Gregory VII, probably dating to September 1073, makes a similar argument on Bishop Gebhard's behalf (CDB no. 63, p. 66).
172. Ps 68:23, in combination with Sir 9:3.
173. The stole was a narrow strip of cloth worn as a mark of rank by clerics.
174. Ovid Metamorphoses 3.276.
175. In other words, his status as priest but not as bishop.
176. Letters from Gregory VII to Bishop Gebhard (whom he always calls Jaromír)

Without delay the aforesaid bishops went to Rome and offered their letters to the pope. After these letters had been read aloud but with their case neither admitted, rejected, nor discussed, they were ordered to go to their lodgings until they were summoned back to a general synod on a set day.[177]

2.31. In those days the most powerful lady had come to Rome: Matilda, who governed all of Lombardy together with Burgundy after the death of her father, Boniface, and had power over 120 bishops, whether to be elected and enthroned or removed.[178] The whole senatorial order was arranged according to her will, as if she were their own lord, and Pope Gregory himself handled both divine and human business through her, because she was a most wise counselor and the greatest supporter of the Roman church in all its troubles and needs. Descending from her lineage through his mother's blood, Bishop Gebhard had a connection to her.[179] When he reported this about himself so that the aforesaid lady would acknowledge that he was her relative, she began very much to honor him, to commend him to the lord pope, and to treat him honorably so far as she was able, as if he was her brother.

Bishop Gebhard would certainly have lost his good name and honor, together with his rank, if she had not been at Rome. With her intervening and wearying the pope with many entreaties, peace was made between the aforesaid bishops on the condition that they live in peace content with their own bishoprics and that they should not return again to the apostolic see to receive judgment on this same case until ten years [had passed]. And thus through Pope Gregory, by Matilda's doing, Bishop Gebhard was restored

---

and Duke Vratislav, dated 31 January 1074, confirm that both bishops were ordered to come to Rome and that Jaromír was restored to his priestly, but not to his episcopal, office. CDB nos. 65–66, pp. 68–70.

177. Regino, *Chronicon*, 83.

178. Matilda (1046–1115), margravine of Tuscany and countess of Canossa, who indeed held vast estates in Lombardy and was Pope Gregory VII's most powerful supporter. Her father, Boniface, died in 1052.

179. Presumably through his mother, Judith of Schweinfurt, though no specific connection can be traced.

to his original rank and honor in the year 1074, the sun entering the fifteenth part of Virgo [August]. Also at Matilda's behest, the lord pope gave letters to the Czechs' envoys, in which he ordered and commanded the duke to receive his brother honorably, obey his pastor in all things like a father,[180] and live in peace with God's blessing.[181]

2.32. Since this mention of Matilda occurs to us, I will report one thing this woman did manfully—briefly, so that I not produce disgust in the reader. The aforesaid girl, always the victor in many wars, led an unmarried life after her father's death and ruled alone the very large kingdom of Lombardy. It therefore seemed to the princes, counts, and bishops of the land that they should persuade her to take a husband, so that the royal dignity, lacking an heir, might not perish at the same time as offspring. Acceding to their counsel, she sent letters to the Duke of Swabia, named Welf,[182] containing much in these few words: "Not from feminine fickleness or brazenness but for the advantage of my entire kingdom, I direct these letters to you. When you receive them, receive me and the kingdom of all Lombardy. I will give you so many burgs, so many castles, so many famous palaces, and quite

180. Cf. Col 3:20.

181. A letter of Gregory VII, dated 16 April 1074, states that in Rome Bishop Gebhard denied under oath that he had assaulted Bishop John or ordered his servants to do so. The pope therefore dropped the charges and restored Gebhard to his episcopal rank (CDB no. 70, p. 73). Given that Bishop John had not also come to Rome, however, Gregory postponed a final decision in the case until both bishops could present their positions before him personally, and ordered that John be allowed to retain his office and territory in the meantime (CDB no. 70, pp. 73–74). Five months later, on 22 September, Gregory wrote letters to Gebhard, John, and Duke Vratislav, chastising Gebhard for lying to his fellow Czechs about the decision reached in Rome and taking possession of a castle in Moravia, probably Podivín, which he ordered returned (CDB nos. 71–73, pp. 74–77).

182. Duke Welf V (1101–20) of *Bavaria*. In 1089, when the wedding took place, Matilda was forty-three years old and Welf was eighteen. Although the pair did ultimately separate, it was not until 1095. Stefan Weinfurter, *The Salian Century: Main Currents in an Age of Transition*, trans. Barbara Bowlus (Philadelphia: University of Pennsylvania Press, 1999), 161–62.

unlimited gold and silver. Above all this you will have a famous name, if you make yourself dear to me. Nevertheless, do not judge me by this boldness of speech, because now I approach you first with this address. For it is permissible for both the masculine and the feminine sex to seek after legitimate marriage. Nor is there any difference whether a man or a woman touches the outer reaches of love first, so long as an insoluble marriage results. Nor should it be otherwise than with the consent of both. Farewell." What Duke Welf responded to this, or by what rationale he consented to her proposal, or how many armed thousands Lady Matilda sent ahead to receive the duke at the borders of Lombardy, or how honorably she received him, or with how many provisions she held a party—if any one wishes to know of it, daylight would desert him[183] before he could read through it all. Let King Assuerus, who had a magnificent party with his warriors for 120 days, yield in provisions.[184] Let the queen of Saba and the wondrous table and royal foods of Solomon yield.[185] For all that there, here was a hundred times more.

What more? Night came, they entered her chamber, they placed themselves together on a deep coverlet, and Duke Welf lay with the virgin Matilda without Venus.[186] There, among and after everything, amid such things as did happen, Duke Welf said: "O Lady, what did you want of me? Why did you summon me? In order to make a laughingstock of me and subject me to the hissing of the people and shaking of the head?[187] You confound yourself more, if you wish to confound me. Surely either by your order or through your handmaids something evil hides either in your clothes or in your sheets. Believe me, if I was of a frigid nature, I would never have responded to your will."

Since on the first and second night the duke had been exposed

183. Cf. above, n. 105.   184. Est 1:3.
185. 3 Kgs 10:4.
186. That is, without their having sex. The implication from what follows is that Welf was impotent.
187. Ps 43:15.

to the lady, on the third day she led him alone into the bedchamber, placed a three-legged stool in the middle and a dining table above, and showed herself naked as she came from her mother's womb. "Behold!" she said. "Whatever has been hidden I lay it all before you. Nor is there any place where some evil might hide." Then he stood with his ears drooping like an ass with a nasty disposition,[188] or like a butcher who stands in the meat market sharpening his knife over a skinned fat cow, desiring to disembowel it. Next, the woman sat a long time upon the table like a goose when it makes itself a nest, turning its tail here and there, but in vain. Finally the nude woman, indignant, arose and took the collar of the half-alive man in her left hand and, spitting in her right hand, gave him a great slap. Then she threw him outside, saying: "Go far from here, monster, so that you might not pollute our kingdom. You are viler than a worm, viler than discarded seaweed.[189] If you appear before me tomorrow, you will die a bad death." Thus disgraced, Duke Welf fled and told all his men of his disgrace into eternity. It suffices to have said these things briefly, which I rather ought not to have said!

2.33. It happened that, when Bishop Gebhard was returning from the burg of Rome, as many magnates as were his followers, rejoicing very much on his return, ran to meet him as he came out of the forest. While he was relating to them with pleasure the deeds that were done in Rome and how much he relied upon the influence of Lady Matilda, he said playfully to one of them, named Beleč, whom he loved above the rest: "Look what a beard I'm bringing back." And, stroking it with his hand, he said, "Surely it is worthy of an emperor." But Beleč said: "All that you praise, Lord, pleases me. But I would have praised it more if you had brought a changed spirit back with the beard. O, if you would change that, you would be in peace from now on."

2.34. I do not wish to be silent about what we happened to hear

---

188. Horace *Satires* 1.9.20 (cf. Boyce's translation, p. 74).
189. Virgil *Eclogues* 7.42; cf. Book 1, n. 270.

and see in that same year, while still in school.[190] One day, while I was ruminating on my little Psalms, standing in the crypt of the holy martyrs, Cosmas and Damian,[191] a certain man came in, carrying a wax taper and a filament of silver, with which he had measured out the limbs of his own body, following his vision's command. Approaching me, he said: "Hey, my good boy, show me where lies Saint Radim, the brother of Saint Adalbert."[192] I said to him: "The man you call a saint has not yet been canonized by the pope. We still celebrate his mass like that for all the dead." Then he said: "I do not know about such things, but one thing I do know: that when I was put in a subterranean prison in the burg of Cracow for three years—spending my life in those narrow confines, where there was only one small window up high, through which they rarely offered bread or water—one day a man appeared before me whose clothes were white as snow and whose face glittered like the sun.[193] I remember this much. Then suddenly I was in terror. And then, as if waking from a bad dream, I felt myself to be standing in front of the burg. The man who appeared to me in prison, standing next to me, said: 'Go to Prague. Do not fear anyone. Entering the Church of St. Vitus, bestow your gift on my tomb in the crypt of the holy martyrs, Cosmas and Damian. I am Radim, the brother of Saint Adalbert.' He said this to me and then immediately vanished from my sight.[194] Behold: this hair and the gauntness of my visage bear witness that the things reported to you are true." (In addition, the caretakers of the church often saw visions in that same crypt, when they tended the candle which is lit there at night.)

190. Scholars agree that this incident cannot have occurred at the point at which is it inserted in the chronicle. There is a gap in the numbering of years here, between 1073 and 1083, but even circa 1073, Cosmas, born circa 1046, would have been twenty-seven years old, not a young boy still learning his "little Psalms."

191. The crypt of the cathedral church in Prague.

192. Radim was the given name of Gaudentius, St. Adalbert's brother and the first archbishop of Gniezno. Cf. 1.34 and 2.4.

193. Mt 17:2.

194. See Book 1, n. 84.

2.35. I do not think it ought to be omitted that Duke Vratislav and his brothers, Conrad and Otto, went to war against Leopold, the son of Lutz, the Austrian margrave.[195] But first we should see how such great enmity arose between Leopold and Conrad, *dyarch* of Moravia,[196] for previously they had always been friends to one another.

Since no forest, mountains, or other obstacle delimits the boundaries of the two provinces but a little river called Dýje, flowing through a flat place, scarcely divides them, always at night bad men from both sides took booty for themselves in turn, thieving, seizing cattle, laying waste to villages. Just as a little spark often ignites a large fire, so these lords (of whom we spoke) came to their great ruin from these little things, because they were unwilling to extinguish the noxious tinder. For Conrad had frequently sent to the margrave about how the war ought to be restrained in some way but Leopold, puffed up with pride, had disdained his words. Therefore, Conrad humbly went to his brother Vratislav, duke of the Czechs, asking him for help against the Germans' arrogance. Although he did not distrust his own men, Vratislav nevertheless hired to help him one detachment of choice warriors from the bishop of Regensburg, for a price.[197]

The duke did not conceal his coming from the margrave. Sending one of his satraps, speaking in a way to mean the opposite, he ordered Leopold to prepare a great feast for him and promised a contingent of Mars would quickly come to that very party. The margrave became cheerful at this news and ordered everyone, from swineherd to cowherd, to be armed with every appearance of iron, from awl to goad, and ready for battle. Duke Vratislav came with

195. Margrave Leopold II of Austria (1075–95), whose father was *Ernst* (1055–75); see Lechner, *Babenberger.*

196. A term based on the Greek, akin to "monarch," to indicate the ruler of a half-territory. There was otherwise no distinctive title for the subordinate rulers of Moravia; they were styled "duke" just as their overlord, the duke of Bohemia, was. See my *Hastening Toward Prague,* 194.

197. The bishop of Regensburg at this time was Otto (1061–89).

the Bohemians and also the Germans who were the bishop of Regensburg's men; from the other direction, Otto and Conrad joined together with their men, that is, all the warriors there were in the whole of Moravia.

When from a distance the margrave saw them meet up in a level field, he arranged his own men in the shape of a wooden wedge and bolstered their spirits with words of advice of this sort: "O warriors, whose strength I have tested sufficiently through many battles of fortune, fear not those runaway shadows. I very much grieve for them because the field lies open to them for flight. For I know they do not dare go to battle with you. Do you not see that fear drives them into one mass, since the paralysis of their powers holds them back? There is no outward appearance of arms there. They are sheep, I think, and food for wolves. Why do you stand there, O rapacious wolves and fierce lion cubs?[198] Attack the flocks of sheep and tear asunder their bodies, which stand bloodless, about to fall before they see war and quickly about to feed our kites and vultures. O Hell, how many victims we will give you today! Open your workshops to receive the souls of the Czechs. For I know that to God and his saints they are hateful, men without mercy,[199] who entered this land in order to ravage not only our goods but our wives and their children—may God drive that far away. And if it happens that any one of you dies, this one death is more blessed than every other death because it is sweet to die for the fatherland."[200] He was about to say more but his words were cut short by the attack of the Czechs.

Duke Vratislav, when he saw that the enemy would not cede the field, ordered the Germans to attack the right wing of the army and arranged for his brothers, Conrad and Otto, to fight against the left wing. He himself, where the enemies' line was most closely pressed, ordered his army to descend against the very face of Mars[201] and to fight it out with their adversaries by meeting on

198. Acts 20:29 ("savage wolves") and Ps 103:21 ("young lions").
199. Cf. Rom 1:30–31.
200. Horace Odes 3.2.13.
201. Lucan Pharsalia 7.200 (cf. loose translation, p. 176).

foot. Quicker than it was said, leaping from their horses and giving a cry of exhortation, just as a flame let loose in a dry haystack
rages and consumes everything in a moment, so they pounded
their adversaries' troops with iron and threw them to the ground.
Of such a great multitude, there was hardly one man remaining,
who escaped with the margrave himself. And so the lion cubs fed
the flocks of sheep. Having lost few of their own, the Czechs
brought a notable triumph back from the eastern plain. In this
slaughter were killed Stan with his brother, Radim; Hrdoň, son of
Janek; Dobrohost, son of Hyneš; and not so very many others—on
12 May 1082.

2.36. 1083. 1084. 1085. On 25 December Judith died, the wife of
Władysław, duke of the Poles,[202] and the daughter of Vratislav, duke
of the Czechs. Since she was sterile, she always mortified herself, offering a live sacrifice to God with tears. Being free with alms, she
helped widows and orphans. Scattering gold and silver very liberally
throughout monasteries, she commended herself to the prayers of
priests so that, through the approval of the saints, she might obtain
by divine grace the offspring that nature had denied. Meanwhile, she
sent her chaplain, named Peter, who brought her vow to the tomb
of Saint Giles[203] as well as other small presents for the abbot and his
brothers, so that God might heed her request through their interces-
sion. Peter went immediately to carry out his lady's orders (since he
wanted to return home already). The abbot is said to have spoken
thus to him, with a quasi-prophetic mouth: "Go with God's blessing
and tell your lady: 'Hope in God and do not doubt your faith at all,
because you will conceive and bear a son.'[204] There is no one who
did not obtain what he faithfully asked Saint Giles. I fear that by
chance we offend God when we weary him with prayers against fate.
Yet sometimes God, through Saint Giles's merits, grants to those
petitioning our patron what nature forbids." When this had been

202. Duke Władysław I Herman (1079–1102), the son of Kazimierz I (cf. 2.2).

203. The monastery of St.-Giles is located in Provence.

204. This sentences combines different verses of the Bible: Sir 2:6 ("hope in
God"), followed by Mt 21:21 ("have faith and do not doubt") and Lk 1:31 (of Jesus,
"you will conceive in your womb and bear a son").

reported to his lady, she conceived in her time. She died at the first cock's crow on the third day after she had borne a son (on 25 December, as noted above). Later, at his baptism, her son was called by the name of his paternal uncle: Bolesław.[205]

2.37. 1086. With the august Emperor Henry III [IV] ordering it and carrying it out, a great synod was celebrated in the burg of Mainz. With four archbishops and twelve bishops (whose names we will tell later) in residence there, together with abbots of monasteries and the rest of the faithful, they confirmed in writing many decrees concerning the status of the holy church. At this assembly, with all the leading men of the empire—dukes, margraves, satraps, and bishops—agreeing and praising it, the caesar set Vratislav, duke of the Czechs, over both Bohemia and Poland.[206] Placing the royal crown on his head with his own hand, Henry ordered the archbishop of Trier, named Egilbert,[207] to anoint him king in his seat, the *metropolis* of Prague, and place the diadem on his head.

At this same council, Bishop Gebhard of Prague produced written documents of his ancient complaint concerning the aforesaid Moravian bishop, John. Although John had already departed this world that same year, taking care nevertheless for the future, the aforesaid Bishop Gebhard, acting through friends, beat on the emperor's ear so another bishop might not find himself in the same position. He unrolled before everyone the privilege from Bishop Adalbert, his predecessor, confirmed by both Pope Benedict and Emperor Otto I.[208] Moved by the entreaties of Duke Vratislav, the brother of Bishop Gebhard, and on the advice of Archbishop Wezilo of Mainz[209] and other good men, the emperor, who supported justice, added a new privilege of almost the same tenor

205. Bolesław III (b. 1086, duke 1102–38). Essentially the same story appears in the anonymous *Deeds of the Polish Princes* (105–9).

206. These two sentences borrow from Regino, *Chronicon*, 143.

207. Archbishop Egilbert of Trier (1079–1101).

208. This clearly does not refer to the papal letter Cosmas reproduces in 1.22 but rather to the document embedded—and confirmed—in the imperial privilege that follows.

209. Archbishop Wezilo of Mainz (1084–88).

as the old one. He confirmed it with his imperial sign, as will be shown in the following. We do not consider it superfluous if we insert the form of this privilege here in our work. It contained this text or something like it:[210]

In the name of the holy and indivisible Trinity. Henry III, with divine mercy supporting him, august emperor of the Romans. We know it to befit the royal title and imperial dignity for us, helping to benefit of God's churches everywhere, to ward off their damage and injury wherever necessary. Therefore, we wish it to be known to all those faithful to God and our realm, both present and future, how our faithful Bishop Gebhard of Prague has often to his confrères and fellow bishops as well as the rest of our princes and most recently to us complained that the bishopric of Prague, which was established from the beginning singular and whole throughout the duchy of Bohemia and Moravia, having been confirmed as such by both Pope Benedict and Emperor Otto I, was later with the consent of his predecessors and by the power of tyranny alone divided and diminished by the enthronement of a new bishop within his boundaries. At Mainz, before legates of the apostolic see, and with us and many of the leading men of our realm present, he raised the same complaint. By Archbishops Wezilo of Mainz, Sigewin of Cologne, Egilbert of Trier, and Liemar of Bremen, Bishops Dietrich of Verdun, Conrad of Utrecht, Ulrich of Eichstatt, Otto of Regensburg, and with the assent of the laymen Duke Vratislav of the Czechs and his brother Conrad, Duke Frederick, Duke Lutold, Count Palatine Rapoto, and all those gathered there, it was judged that the original diocese within the full extent of its borders pertains to the see of Prague. Its boundaries to the west are these: Tuhošt, which extends to the middle of the River Chub, Sedlec and Lučané and Děčané, Litoměřice, and Lemuzi to the

---

210. No original of this document survives. A late eleventh-century copy is preserved at Munich that is neither clearly genuine nor clearly forged, but the language of which matches the text here almost exactly. *Die Urkunden Heinrichs IV,* vol. 2, ed. D. von Gladiss, Monumenta Germaniae Historica, Diplomata 6 (Vienna: Böhlau, 1959), 515–17. The main variants are the spelling of proper nouns. The Munich copy also includes a line after the *signum:* "Herimann the chancellor, in place of Wezilo the archchancellor, also signed it," as well as the notation, after the dating clause, "done in *Regensburg,* in the name of Christ, happily amen."

middle of the forest which delimits Bohemia. From there to the north, these are the boundaries: Pšované, Charvati, and the other Charvati, Slezané, Třebované, Bobřané, and Dědošané to the middle of the forest where the boundaries meet the Milčané.[211] To the east, it has these rivers as boundaries: namely, the Bug and the Styr with the burg of Cracow and the province whose name is Wag, with all the regions pertaining to the aforesaid burg, i.e., Cracow. Expanded, it proceeds to the boundaries of the Hungarians, up to the mountains whose name is Tatra. Then, in that area that looks to the south, having added the region of Moravia up to the River Wag and to the middle of the forest whose name is More, that same diocese extends to the mountain by which Bavaria is bounded.[212] And so, with us mediating and the common vote of the princes favoring it, it was ordered that Duke Vratislav of Bohemia and his brother, Conrad, should return to the aforesaid bishop of Prague, their brother, the diocese requested in its entirety and reendow it by judicial order. Accordingly, rationally persuaded by the request of this same bishop, we confirm for him and his successors the reintegration of the diocese of Prague by proclamation of our imperial authority and fix it inviolably, decreeing that no person of any condition and no society of men should later presume to alienate from the church of Prague any rights within the aforesaid boundaries. In order that the authority of this reintegration and confirmation remain firm and unchanged for all time, we ordered this charter drawn up and sealed with the impression of our seal, confirming it by our own hand, as it appears below. Given on 29 April 1086, in the eighth indiction, in the twenty-second year of Lord Henry's reign as king, and his third as emperor (see figure 2).[213]

211. These names of peoples (as indicated by the -ané suffix) were already archaic at the time the document was issued; they were either part of an original document being reconfirmed here or, more likely, included in a forgery specifically to suggest its antiquity. On the Lučané, mentioned here, see 1.10, above.

212. The territory described here is vast, encompassing not only Bohemia and Moravia but much of southern Poland, including Cracow. Note too that Vratislav is acclaimed as king of Bohemia and of Poland. These aggrandizing claims by both king and bishop to southern Poland seem never to have been enforced or recognized in practice.

213. Henry IV was accustomed to sign documents in his own hand: "I Henry, king by grace of God, third august emperor of the Romans, subscribed [to this]." He

FIGURE 2. Seal of Henry III

The sign of Lord Henry III, august emperor of the Romans.

I saw the caesar write this sign himself with his own hands on the privilege of the Prague episcopate.

2.38. Likewise in the same year, with Emperor Henry mandating it and Archbishop Wezilo of Mainz[214] intervening through the papal legates who were present at the same council, Lord Pope Clement[215] corroborated by his privilege the bishopric of Prague with the aforesaid boundaries. (Bishop Gebhard was also urgently asking and suggesting it through his chaplain named Albinus, whom he had sent with the papal legates from Mainz to Rome on this same matter.)

In the same year, on 9 June, Duke Otto of Moravia, the brother of Duke Vratislav of Bohemia, died.

---

would also make his special sign, or *signum*, in the form of a monogram of his name and titles. Sometimes the *signum* alone was used, accompanied by language indicating that the emperor himself signed the document. For this reason Cosmas emphasizes witnessing the emperor's handwritten monogram and faithfully reproduces it here. (This version of the *signum* appears in most, if not all, of the surviving manuscripts of Cosmas's chronicle.) See Harry Bresslau, *Handbuch der Urkundenlehre für Deutschland und Italien*, vol. 2 (Berlin: De Gruyter, 1958), 180–83.

214. Archbishop Wezilo of Mainz (1084–88).

215. Clement III, the imperial "antipope" (1080, 1084–1100).

Meanwhile, Archbishop Egilbert of Trier, obeying the emperor's orders, came to the *metropolis* of Prague on 15 June. Among the holy solemnities of the Mass, he anointed Vratislav, dressed in royal bands, as king and placed a diadem on both his head and that of his wife Svatava, wrapped in a royal robe—with the clergy and all the satraps crying out three times: "Life, health, and victory to Vratislav, Czech king as well as Polish king, great and peaceable, crowned by God."²¹⁶ On the third day after this, enriched with an immense weight of gold and silver and endowed with other gifts and presents (in accordance with royal grandeur), the archbishop went home happy and with great honor.

2.39. 1087. King Vratislav gathered an army and entered Sorbia,²¹⁷ which Emperor Henry had once given him to hold in perpetuity. While he was rebuilding a certain castle near the burg of Meissen, named Gvozdec, he sent two contingents of chosen warriors with his son Břetislav—at the urging of others—to take revenge for an injury once done to him. At a time some days back, while Vratislav was returning from the emperor's court, it happened that he spent the night at a certain very large village named Kyleb. There, at night, a quarrel arose between his men and the citizens. Two brothers— first among the magnates,²¹⁸ enormous columns of the fatherland, men bright with the light of virtues, Načerat and Bznata, sons of *Comes* Taz—were killed by the villagers. Thus [later in 1087], at the king's command men were sent straightaway [to Kyleb], hurrying day and night. At daybreak on the third day, they invaded the aforesaid village with a great assault and took away all the goods. They despoiled both the citizens and their wives down to their san-

216. The first part of this sentence borrows words from Regino's account of the coronation of Pippin in 753 (*Chronicon*, 45), while the acclamation is modeled on Regino's report of Charlemagne's coronation as Roman emperor by Pope Leo (62).

217. See Book 1, n. 142.

218. The wordplay gets lost in translation: Cosmas's *primi inter primates* essentially means "first among those already first," or "first among the first rank of men," since the word "primates" (usually rendered "leaders" or, here, "magnates") derives from *primus* (first).

dal thongs,[219] overturned their buildings from the foundations and burned them with fire, and then took to the road unharmed, carrying off their horses and cattle too.

Come midday, while they were crossing a certain river, the lord's son Břetislav, when he reached the pleasant parts of the river, ordered his shield bearers to go on ahead with the spoils and invited the men braver in war to have a meal with him there. Because there was a great heat wave, the duke's son, panting from excessive heat, cooled himself off a little[220] by swimming in the water after the meal. *Comes* Alexius sent to him and ordered: "Not here." He said, "You swim in the Vltava or in your Ohře. Toss off restraints,[221] for you bear the treasures of brave men." To this the youth replied: "It is natural for old men always to tremble at the motion of the air[222] and, in spite of its proximity to them, to fear fate more than young men do." When this was reported to Alexius, he said: "Let God make it so that this might now be inevitable fortune's opportunity—though with a favorable outcome—whereby young men might see whether old men or they themselves fear fate more." While the aforesaid *comes* was saying this, behold, more than twenty horsemen appeared, sent from the Saxons as if provoked by a trumpet (just as a mongoose, wishing to strangle its enemy viper, provokes it from the shade with its tail).[223] When our men saw them, those fools, more daring than smart—with Alexius very much arguing against it, forbidding it, and calling them back—rushed into their fates in pursuit of their enemies. The iron legion of Saxons immediately jumped from their ambushes and not one of our men who pursued the enemy escaped.

Those who had remained in camp saw a ball of dirt rise into the sky as if from a whirlwind. Although even the most courageous men are accustomed to be thrown into confusion by a sudden and unexpected calamity during battle, nevertheless they snatched up

219. Lk 3:16 and Is 5:27.
221. See Book 1, n. 121.
223. Cf. Lucan *Pharsalia* 4.724–29.
220. Regino, *Chronicon*, 92.
222. See Book 1, n. 279.

their arms very quickly and boldly met the enemy. Battle was engaged with the greatest vigor. The clash of arms and the cries of the men rose up to the clouds.²²⁴ Lances were broken in the first encounter, so they took to the sword²²⁵—until, with God carrying the work, the Saxons were turned to flight. Our men had the victory but it was a very bloody one. Because the warriors of the second rank had already gone ahead with the booty, in this battle only nobles were killed: Alexius, his son-in-law Ratibor, Braniš with his brother Slava, and many others. Comes Předa barely escaped death, having lost his foot. The duke's son was wounded under his right thumb; if the head of the sword in his hand had not blocked the blow, he would have lost his whole hand. This slaughter was committed on 2 July.²²⁶

2.40. 1088. In the same times in which these deeds were reported, there was a certain warrior, who had the name Beneda, a high-spirited youth with an exceptional body, such that he was the equal of Hector in beauty and Turnus in arms.²²⁷ He was the son of Jurata, whose first ancestor was Taz. Having offended the king then (I do not know for what reason),²²⁸ he fled to Poland, where he was made a warrior of Lady Judith, wife of Duke Władysław.²²⁹ Returning from Poland after two years had passed, Beneda approached Wiprecht, King Vratislav's son-in-law,²³⁰ asking that he

224. This sentence is a combination of Lucan *Pharsalia* 1:569 ("clash of weapons"), Virgil (see Book 1, n. 122), and Isaiah (see Book 2, n. 77).

225. Sallust *War with Catiline* 60.2.

226. Much of this paragraph is copied from Regino, *Chronicon*, mostly from p. 92, but also including phrases on pp. 107 and 112.

227. A line of verse, the first part of which comes from Ovid *Metamorphoses* 12.77, for Hector, and the second part from Virgil *Aeneid* 11.910, for Turnus. Hector was the great Trojan champion, the son of Priam; in the *Aeneid*, Turnus was Aeneas's most formidable opponent.

228. The beginning of the chapter, up to this point midsentence, consists of six lines of verse.

229. Cf. 2.36.

230. Count Wiprecht II of Groitzsch (d. 1124), who married Vratislav's daughter Judith in 1098 (below, 3.7). For a brief summary of his life and career, see Alfred Haverkamp, *Medieval Germany, 1056–1273*, trans. Helga Braun and Richard Mortimer (Oxford: Oxford University Press, 1988), 201–2, also 175.

might be able to return him to his lord's original favor by his good word. But since this Wiprecht was a man very discerning in all matters (who also did not wish to offend his father-in-law in any way), he advised Beneda that he would be safer in the meantime with the bishop of Meissen, named Benno,[231] and to secure him as his intercessor.

Meanwhile, it happened that King Vratislav again entered Sorbia with his army, where he moved the aforesaid castle of Gvozdec to another, stronger location. Since the king knew Beneda to be in the burg of Meissen, he sent for him with the message that he might come to him under a pledge of faith. When the king saw that he was coming right away, he began to consider how he might capture him by deception. After many words promiscuously spoken and some conveniently fabricated, the king took Beneda fraudulently by his right hand and led him outside the camp with him, as if planning to speak to him privately there. Then the king saw the golden hilt and head of the sword with which the warrior was girded (among the various things he wanted from Beneda, this sword was particularly valuable). "Even if you put a millstone on your helmet," he said, "I will cut both head and body in half to the thigh in one blow with that sword." With deception the king marveled at and praised the sword, and asked that Beneda show it to him. Suspecting nothing evil, he gave the unsheathed sword into the king's hand. Snatching it and shaking it in his hand, the king said: "What are you going to do now, you son of a woman desirous beyond her husband?" To the nearby chamberlain, Vitus Želibořic,[232] a man worse than the worst, the only person there with him, Vratislav said: "Seize him! Seize him and tie him to a tall horse." But since audacious deeds are always unsafe against audacious men, the audacious warrior [Beneda] quickly snatched the sword from the chamberlain's thigh by its hilt and cut his loins in half. Kicking at the ground, [Vitus] lay there half-alive. Though Beneda could have run away, the brave warrior did not

231. Bishop Benno I of Meissen (1066–1106).
232. This is the regular Czech form for a patronymic; thus, "son of Želibor."

flee. But like Hercules around the Lernaean Hydra,[233] springing up and springing back three times, he wounded the king for a while with his lowly sword but nevertheless received no blow[234] from the duke's [i.e., the king's] right hand—until people rushed from camp at the clamor. One of them, Kukata, flew at Beneda first before all the others and intercepted the warrior rushing at him with a broad hunting spear, like a forest pig. Then the king, as if he could revenge himself against the dead man, ordered him tied by the feet to the tail of a horse and dragged here and there through the thistles.

2.41. 1089. 1090. That ancient serpent, enemy of humankind, who never sleeps but always disturbs the quiet,[235] could not bear for the brothers—namely, King Vratislav and Bishop Gebhard—to live at peace any longer. He vexed the one with empty glory and ambition and stirred up the other with arrogance and puffed-up pride, so that neither one believed the other, nor was one able to get the upper hand against the other. This one did not want to consider his brother his equal; the other did not want to be considered less than his brother. This one wanted to be in charge; the other did not want to be subordinate. One wanted to rule like a king and be above all others; the other did not want to obey [the king's] commands but to acknowledge an obligation to the emperor alone, from whom he received the episcopate. They sometimes disagreed with each other in such vigorous wrath that the king would not have the bishop crown him on feast days. Compelled by this necessity [i.e., in order to be crowned by a bishop on feast days], as well as ambition, and not by reason but by tyranny alone, the king again enthroned his chaplain, named Vecel, as bishop in Moravian territory. Having done this openly, he made himself notorious, not only for having spurned what he himself had approved before the emperor and his bishops, namely, that both bishoprics be one, but also for having violated the privilege of Pope Clement, which confirmed the boundaries of the bishopric [2.37].

233. The many-headed Hydra was killed by Hercules in his second great labor.
234. Ovid *Metamorphoses* 12.374.
235. Cf. Rv 20:1. The word here, *chelidrus*, probably comes from Sedulius *Paschale Carmen* 3.190.

In order to deplore to the pope this injustice committed against the church, Bishop Gebhard was about to go to Rome. But having taken counsel with his familiars he went first to his old friend Ladislas, the Hungarian king.[236] Disclosing to him the damage done to his church, he asked for help on the road to Rome—alas, not knowing that fate was already nearby, hanging over him. For on the very first day that he went to the king, Gebhard fell into considerable vexation of body. Since he was near the burg of Esztergom, the king sent for him there by ship, committing his care to the bishop of that burg.[237] Alas, he endured such pain for six days that, prevented by tears,[238] I cannot express it in words. With evening approaching on the seventh day, 26 June,[239] that gem of priests, light of all Czechs, celebrated in his doctrine, the pious Bishop Gebhard, departed this world. May he live in Christ. Concerning his life and character the spirit is moved to say much,[240] but the thoughts in my mind fail.[241] Nevertheless it is lawful to say those few things which we saw ourselves.[242]

2.42. In Lent the following was his custom. Always wearing a hairshirt underneath while dressed in episcopal garb on top (but dressed in sackcloth at night), Gebhard entered the church secretly and, prostrated on the tile of the floor, he persevered in prayer for a long time—until the ground on which he lay was drenched in an abundant shower of tears. Rising from there to the feast to be performed, he first ruminated on the Psalms. As many wretches as he found before the church, he supplied their want through an abundance[243] of good work (he did this having finished the Psalter). After matins, he divided forty quarters of bread among the poor, and the same amount of fish or other food. With the day

236. King Ladislas I (1077–95).

237. Perhaps Archbishop Acha (1085–93?); the sources for the see of Esztergom make it difficult to determine a precise chronology.

238. Sedulius *Paschale Carmen* 5.95; also cf. Ovid *Metamorphoses* 9.328.

239. I am here condensing a more elaborate dating, rendered in verse.

240. See Book 1, n. 356.

241. Virgil *Aeneid* 12.914 (cf. West's prose translation, 331).

242. This chapter concludes with ten lines of verse.

243. 2 Cor 8:14.

now approaching the fourth hour, he washed the feet of twelve pilgrims (the number of the apostles) and he divided among them twelve pennies. At the hour for the midday meal, having placed them in a heated room or house, he himself served up necessities in abundance and he blessed the food and drink for them with his right hand. From there he went to his public table and fed forty of the needy together with himself.

Similarly, at his see in Prague, he established that forty paupers be fed daily and clothed twice annually from their sandal thongs[244] to the straps of their caps. The many visiting and poor clerics who arrived he bound with copious grants so that, remaining with him for all of Lent, they might read the Psalter for both the living and the dead. At particular solemnities of the Mass, he also arranged for three pennies to be given to however many were in the chapel on the day celebrated. On all Sundays he bestowed twelve silver coins on the box of holy relics, and on apostolic feasts and other greater solemnities two hundred. If you desire, O wise reader, to know how generous he was: he never wore an episcopal surplice[245] for a whole year, but gave to his chaplains the winter one at Easter and the summer one on the Feast of St. Václav [28 September]. You should know him to have been likewise generous in the rest of his gifts.

After Gebhard's death, on 4 March 1091, Cosmas was elected bishop both by the king and by the whole clergy and people of the Czechs—but with the august Emperor Henry III [IV] doing imperial business in Lombardy at that time.

2.43. In the same year, on 17 April, on Thursday of the second week of Easter, the monastery of the holy martyrs Vitus, Václav, and Adalbert in the burg of Prague was destroyed by fire.[246]

In the same year, King Vratislav was very angry at his brother Conrad because Conrad, remembering their mutual affection, favored the party of the sons of his brother Otto, namely, Svatopluk

244. See above, n. 219.
245. See above, n. 120.
246. The cathedral church in Prague; see Book 1, n. 8.

and Ottík,[247] who had been expelled from their paternal inheritance when the king gave Olomouc and other burgs to his son Boleslav. Not long afterward, on 11 August, this was prevented by Boleslav's untimely death there, in the aforesaid burg of Olomouc.

As long as they lived, those three brothers, Jaromír, Otto, and Conrad, were so of one mind that the king was unable to estrange them by any wiles. Just as a lion is said to be frightened by three young bullocks standing with their horns together, so the king never dared to attack his brothers. Later, when he saw that Conrad was alone after the death of his brothers, wholly deprived of fraternal help, Vratislav entered Moravia with an army in order to expel him also from that province, which had come to him by lot and inheritance and by right through paternal grant.[248]

The king came to the burg named Brno. There, with the magnates of the land standing around him, he arranged a siege in a circle. While they were designating the places where each *comes* would fix his tents, the bailiff Zderad, like the crafty man he was, obliquely giving a sign to the king with his eyes, pointed out the youth Břetislav among the satraps standing before his father. Then he uttered a call to disorder: "Since indeed your son, O Lord King, plays and swims freely in the river in summer, if it pleases your majesty, let him put his tents, with his followers, on this side of the burg near the river." He spoke in this way because once, in Saxon parts, when the aforesaid youth swam in the river at midday, the enemy rushed from the other side and attacked them (as we mentioned above [2.39]). The youth fixed this speech deep in his heart[249] and felt no less pain than if a poisoned arrow had wounded his heart. He went away sad to his camp and did not take food until the stars rose in the night.

But, under the darkness of night, a band of his men having been

247. The standard Czech masculine diminutive suffix (*-ík*), appended here to Otto's name.

248. Regino, *Chronicon*, 90; though "by lot and inheritance" comes originally from Est 13:17 and Dt 32:9.

249. Cf., perhaps, Sallust *War with Jugurtha* 11.7.

summoned, he laid bare the wounding of his heart, taking counsel on how he could take revenge on the evil bailiff. That same night he also sent to his uncle Conrad, explaining the dishonor to him and by whom it was committed, and sought advice on what needed to be done. Then Conrad said: "If you know who you are, do not be afraid to quench the fire scorching me no less than you. It is not praiseworthy to disregard it." For it had not been concealed from Conrad that the king did all things on the advice of Zderad. When the messenger reported his uncle's words to Břetislav, everyone supported, agreed with, and praised duke Conrad's pronouncement as if it was given to them by God,[250] since they themselves had first counseled the same thing. What more? Everything set in motion that night would be carried out in the morning.

2.44. With day dawning, Břetislav sent to the aforesaid bailiff, demanding that he enter into private discussion with him, wherever he pleased. Suspecting no evil, with only *Comes* Držimír as his companion, the two went alone. Having seen them from afar, when they were a stone's throw away,[251] the youth leapt forth from among his men to meet them. He had given his warriors the signal that, when he threw his glove against Zderad's chest, they should do what they had promised to do. Then, upbraiding Zderad with a few of the things by which he had often offended him, Břetislav said: "The faith I promised you: behold, I renounce it." Turning his horse away, he threw his glove in his face. No differently than when an angry lion raises its mane and, lowering its tail, striking its face with the bald part that is at the end of its tail, and pricking its rear with the goad that is under its tail,[252] is said to attack everything that opposes it, so, on the spot, three ardent, armed youths leapt

250. This seems to be an allusion to Livy *Ab urbe condita*. 54.3—concerning Tarquinius.

251. Lk 22:41.

252. Cf., as a possible inspiration, Lucan *Pharsalia* 1.208: "A lion has sighted a nearby foe; he crouches down, hesitant, while he rouses his anger; and soon, when he has whipped himself up with his savage tail, with mane erect and a throaty grumble from gaping jaws, he lets out a roar."

forth from the army. Nozislav and his brother Držikraj, the sons of Lubomír, and a third, Borša, son of Olen, lifted Zderad, fleeing in vain, high in the air on their three lances and threw him to the ground like a bundle of hay. They trampled him with the feet of their horses, wounded him again and again, and fixed his body to the ground with a spear. By such a death, from the pinnacle of the wheel, false fortune threw down her friend Zderad on 11 July.

Comes Držimír, pale with fright, flew to the camp and announced to the king what had been done. The king alone grieved and wept; everyone else praised the youth, though they did not dare praise him openly. Břetislav moved his camp a short distance apart, beyond one little mountain. The greater part of the army and the stronger in war followed him.

2.45. Meanwhile Conrad's wife, named Wirpirk,[253] one among the number of prudent women, entered the king's camp without her husband knowing it. When she had been announced to the king, he convened his magnates in a circle. Commanded to appear, she stood before the king with copious tears pouring down[254] her face and with sobs interrupting her words. Finally, struggling for voice, she spoke thus: "Hardly worthy to be called your sister-in-law, pious king, I do not come now brazenly but as a supplicant at your knees." And she fell on her face and adored the king.[255] Commanded to rise, she stood and said: "You will find no reason, my lord king, for war in these parts. You bring back no victory from this battle.[256] You commit a war worse than civil.[257] If you see us and our goods as booty for your warriors, you turn your spears against yourself since you despoil with bloody rapine your own brother, to whom you ought to be a guardian. He who attacks his

253. This is clearly a German name, perhaps Werberga, but an unusual one; she cannot, however, be identified from other sources.

254. See above, n. 49.

255. Rv 7:11.

256. Wirpirk's speech here harks back to Břetislav I's remarks to Emperor Henry III; cf. 2.12.

257. Lucan *Pharsalia* 1.1.

own people goes against God. For whatever spoils you seek to possess here, far away within your own borders, I can show you better in the middle of your realm. You will never grow more rich nor be more glorified than in the suburb of Prague and the village of Vyšehrad. There are the Jews most filled with gold and silver, there the richest merchants from every land, there the wealthiest money changers, there the market in which the abundant spoils are more abundant than your warriors. But if it pleases you to see how Troy burned,[258] nowhere will you seem more like raging Vulcan[259] than when you see each aforesaid burg burning. Indeed, you say, 'those things are mine.' These things you lay waste as an enemy, whose do you consider them to be? Are we and our goods not yours?

"However, if you sharpen your thunderbolts only against your brother's throat, let it not be that you are considered another Cain. Without violating your favor, he preferred to wander than to incriminate you with fratricide. Greece lay open to your brother, Dalmatia lay open.[260] Accept instead the things he sent you, not as your brother but as if your servant." And she produced tongs and a bundle of twigs from her cloak. "If a brother sinned against his brother, correct him.[261] This land, which is yours, you should instead entrust to him."

She spoke and so touched the king's heart[262] and moved the hearts of the princes[263] that no one was able to hold back tears. The king ordered her to his side so that she might be seated, but before Wirpirk sat, she said, "If I have found favor with you,[264] I ask still one more request and I ask that you not refuse me.[265] For a son's great sin a little bit of a father's punishment is sufficient." Then the king said, "I know what you are about. Go instead and

---

258. Virgil *Aeneid* 2.581 (lines considered spurious but circulated as part of the *Aeneid* in the Middle Ages).

259. Cf. Virgil *Aeneid* 5.662; on Vulcan, see Book 1, n. 105.

260. Presumably these are places suggestive of exile, beyond the borders of Hungary or the empire.

261. Lk 17:3.

262. Jer 3:18.

263. Jb 12:24.

264. Gn 18:3.

265. 3 Kgs 2:16.

bring my brother and son freely to me for the holy kiss[266] and in a bond of peace,"[267] and he kissed her. The king very much feared that his brother and his son would conspire against him. When they had come to the king by the arrangement of Lady Wirpirk, giving them the kiss of peace, the king said to his son: "My son, if you do well, it will be better for no one than you yourself; but if you do not do well, your sin will be lurking at the door."[268]

2.46. After this, understanding that his father had made peace with him not from his heart but out of necessity, Břetislav withdrew to the region around the burg of Hradec with all those who had crossed over into his army. There he tarried in vain, waiting on the uncertain vicissitude of fortune. For as many as followed him, no one dared return to his own home. They greatly feared that the king, whom they had offended, would send them captured and in chains or punish them with a capital sentence.

The king, seeing that he was not able to do what he wanted, namely, revenge his anger upon his son and his followers, summoned his brother Conrad, gathered the elders of the land, and confirmed by the oath of all the *comites* that his brother Conrad would obtain the throne and duchy of Bohemia after his own death. Then the king, strengthened by the counsel and aid of his brother, began to scheme openly how to take revenge upon his son.

This was not concealed from Břetislav. Without delay more than three thousand strong men had flocked to him. Moving quickly, they made their camp along the Rokytnice, ready to engage the king in battle the next day. Břetislav sent a messenger ahead to his father, saying: "Behold, here I am, he whom you were about to seek afar. What you were about to do later, do today."

How a revelation worthy of God's work occurred in the early part of that same night should not be passed over in silence. For even if we lay out the deeds of men to the extent of our knowl-

266. Rom 16:16, 1 Cor 16:20, etc.
267. Eph 4:3.
268. Gn 4:7, spoken to Cain before the murder of Abel.

edge, it is unworthy for us to be silent concerning the great works of God that we have seen.[269]

2.47. On the aforesaid night, while these things we just said were being done among the princes, our patrons Saint Václav and Saint Adalbert visited those in prison and, by their most blessed condescension, liberated those worn down by great suffering in the following way. First they tore out the front doorposts along with the gate. Next, with their rods they broke the iron back door of the prison itself as well as the post to which the feet of the condemned men were cruelly bound. Then they threw the broken pieces outside. Suddenly a pious voice resounded in the ears of the condemned, saying: "Until now our approval has been absent from you and this fatherland, because you have been unworthy of God's grace—on account of this worse than civil war[270] these princes are waging between Bohemia and Moravia. But since God's grace and mercy and regard are for his saints and his chosen ones, and we are directed where that grace has cast its regard, our approving presence surely cannot be present anywhere he has not first been mercifully present. Sure now of God's mercy, therefore get up, rush to the church, and proclaim that we, Saint Václav and Saint Adalbert, expressly freed you and brought peace to everyone." Immediately, as if roused from a deep sleep, [the prisoners] were released from their chains and, with the guards still sleeping, went free and carried out these orders.

On the very same day another miracle shone forth: as the above revelation of the holy martyrs declared, the king's brother Conrad arranged for peace between the king and his son. For earlier they were in such discord that each was suspicious of the other—the father that he be deprived of the throne, the son that he be seized by his father—and they greatly feared each other. Those of similar age as that young man and the greater part of the magnates, swifter of hand and stronger in war, accompanied the son. Yet Bishop Cosmas and the provosts of the churches and all the magnates of

269. Ex 14:13.
270. See above, n. 257.

the land older in age and more useful in counsel, together with a whole army of common folk, supported the father and held him in great affection. Indeed in that storm, the worst crime since the founding of Prague would have been committed,[271] if the most blessed Václav's holy condescension and omnipotent God's great pity had not arranged every move of the princes and the people toward the king's wish.

2.48. Seeing this, the *comites* who remained in camp sent to Břetislav, saying: "Even if you believe your father and so return to your original state of favor with him, we will never believe him because we know him to have a very shrewd cleverness. We fear his friendship more than his enmity. Like a bear, he will not allow the slightest blow to go unavenged. Thus he will never cease from revenge until he has dismissed avenged all the acts by which we offended him, down to every iota. You should therefore either send us away to some land with your favor, or seek higher palaces somewhere with us. We are prepared to serve no one other than you as our lord." Seeing this—and because just as a warrior without arms lacks his office, so too a duke without warriors has only the title of a duke—Břetislav preferred to seek his bread with them abroad than to have peace with his father at home and be alone without a warrior.

Without delay, having gathered all their cattle and servants, more than two thousand warriors went with Duke Břetislav to the Hungarian king. King Ladislas, acknowledging Břetislav as his relative,[272] received him favorably and granted to his warriors a place to live which is called Banov, next to the castle named Trenčin. The place was situated in the midst of forests and mountains, and so was quite suitable and excellent for hunting. By the king's order, nourishment and the rest of nature's provisions were supplied them from neighboring regions. The king kept Břetislav himself, together with a few men, in the delights of the royal hall with him.

271. Sallust *War with Catiline* 18.8, verbatim, but substituting Prague for Rome.

272. Břetislav's mother, Adelhaid, was the daughter of King Andrew of Hungary, the uncle of King Ladislas I.

2.49. In the same year, with King Vratislav arranging it, Cosmas, elected to the church of Prague, and Andrew, likewise elected to the see of Olomouc, came to Mantua by the safe conduct of Count Palatine Rapoto.[273] They were presented to the august emperor Henry III [IV] in the beginning of the year 1092, on 1 January. On the 4th of the same month, with the aforesaid Rapoto acting as mediator, the handsome caesar sat in the palace of Mantua surrounded by not a few of the episcopal and comital order on both sides, with the aforesaid bishops-elect positioned in the middle, and opened his handsome lips, after being silent for some time. He said: "Our faithful friend, the Czech king Vratislav, sent these brothers to us so that we might confirm their election according to canonical and papal law and by our authority. I do not want to make this decision without your consent." Then the bishop of Münster,[274] who was returning from Jerusalem at that time, rose. Leaning on the table where the staffs, episcopal rings, and reliquaries of the saints lay, he said: "It is very dangerous for a few to destroy what has been confirmed by the sanction of many.[275] Many of us bishops were present, also many princes of the Roman Empire, and papal legates too, when you confirmed by your privilege that both bishoprics, i.e., Bohemia and Moravia, would remain united and whole as they had been in the beginning." To this the emperor replied: "I will do what my friend asks of me without delay; I will discuss all this at a later time." Giving them their pastoral staffs, he immediately espoused them [Cosmas and Andrew] to their respective churches with rings. These things having been carried out, both bishops were ordered to go to Verona and wait there until all the royal business was done and Count Palatine Rapoto could lead them back to their fatherland with him.

273. Rapoto II (d. 1099), count palatine of Bavaria and the son of Rapoto of Cham, mentioned in 2.29. Jürgen Dendorfer, *Adelige Gruppenbildung und Königsherrschaft: Die Grafen von Sulzbach und ihr Beziehungsgeflecht im 12. Jahrhundert* (Munich: Kommission für Bayerische Landesgeschichte, 2004), 80.
274. Bishop Erpho of Münster (1084–97).
275. Cf. Sallust *War with Jugurtha* 8.2: "It was dangerous to buy from the few what belonged to the many."

2.50. Meanwhile, an inauspicious rumor struck our ears[276] that King Vratislav had departed to Christ on 14 January and that his brother Conrad has succeeded to the principate. Conrad immediately sent a courier to the emperor. Promising him money, he asked him to nullify the election of the bishops (which we just mentioned). But the emperor, considering justice more than acceding to the iniquity of money, said: "I have done what I have done. I cannot change my action." The messenger, named Viklin, went away sad because he had not obtained what he sought on the duke's behalf.

By the emperor's order, the bishops [Cosmas and Andrew] tarried in Verona until the beginning of Lent, awaiting the return and safe conduct of the aforesaid Count Rapoto. Afterward, arriving in Prague on Palm Sunday, there were received honorably by the clergy and people. On Wednesday that same week, they approached Duke Conrad in the burg of Boleslav.[277] Having now changed his mind, the duke received [the bishops] favorably and celebrated Easter with them in the burg of Vyšehrad.

In that very same Easter week, around 1 April, a huge snow fell and the cold mixed with ice terrified [people] to a degree that rarely occurred in the midst of winter.

We do not have much to write about the deeds of Duke Conrad because he lost his life after seven months and eighteen days, on 6 September, in the same year in which he assumed the duchy.

Břetislav the Younger succeeded him. Approaching the burg of Prague with happy choirs of both girls and boys positioned at various crossroads, singing to pipes and drums, and with the bells ringing throughout the churches, the common folk joyfully received him. Together with the clergy and a magnificent procession, Bishop Cosmas himself took Duke Břetislav the Younger through the gate of the burg and led him to the throne before the Church

276. Virgil *Aeneid* 5.503, though Cosmas has misread or misremembered *aures* (ears) for Virgil's *auras* (breezes). Notice that this remark also suggests that Cosmas was himself in Verona with the bishops.

277. There is no sure way to know whether Stará (Old) Boleslav or Mladá (Young) Boleslav is meant.

of St. Mary.[278] There he was enthroned by all the *comites* and satraps according to the rite of this land on 14 September.

2.51. In that same year on 20 September, a Thursday, there was an eclipse of the sun after midday.[279]

Coming to this land on 1 October, a certain pseudo-bishop named Robert said he had ruled the church of Cavaillon in Gascony for many years. Since one of our brothers [in the cathedral chapter at Prague], named Osel but also known as Asinus, recognized him and asserted that Robert had performed episcopal functions once, when they traveled together through Hungary on the road to Jerusalem, Duke Břetislav and Bishop-elect Cosmas[280] received him with joy and allowed him to perform the rounds as a bishop. What more? He consecrated many churches, ordained many clerics in the month of March, and exorcised the most sacred chrism on Holy Thursday.[281]

At Easter a certain cleric, aware of his [Robert's] very great misdeed (I do not know who), came to him and secretly made himself known. It is a wondrous thing that neither the duke nor the bishop-elect was able to get Robert to remain there even a short while—since in the very week of Easter he took the road toward Saxony in haste. Afterward, when it was made known that

278. An older rotunda church no longer standing but the subject of archeological excavation; it stood in the small first courtyard of Prague Castle, whereas the cathedral, ducal palace, and monastery of St. George are in the next, larger courtyard. The Church of St. Mary was one of the oldest churches in Bohemia, associated with St. Václav.

279. According to Bretholz, the dates here do not accord with the year 1092, when 20 September was a Monday.

280. Although Cosmas has previously referred to Cosmas and Andrew as "bishops" of Prague and Olomouc, here he properly calls Cosmas "bishop-elect." Although invested with the ring and staff by the emperor, neither Cosmas nor Andrew had yet been ordained by the archbishop of Mainz. As a consequence, they were still unable to perform religious functions exclusive to bishops—which helps explain the duke and bishop's eagerness to accept the episcopal imposter Robert.

281. Chrism is a mixture of olive oil and balsam that, once consecrated, was used as part of various liturgical ceremonies, including the consecration of priests and churches and the anointment of kings. Note that all the liturgical ceremonies mentioned here can be performed only by bishops, hence the difficulties that follow.

he had been a pseudo-bishop, they sent one of the Latins, named Constantius, to Gascony. The bishop of Cavaillon, named Desiderius,[282] replied by letters through Constantius that that church had never had a bishop named Robert. They sent also to Pope Clement, consulting his authority: what needed to be done in such a great crisis of affairs?[283] In reply, he ordered them to reconsecrate wholly the churches, but not to rebaptize those baptized by the pseudo-bishop's chrism, only to confirm them. Similarly, they should not reordain those ordained, but only stand among the ordinands and, at the ordination, let them receive benediction through the laying on of hands alone. And thus the wounds made by the enemy upon mother church were cured by the antidote of justice, with Pope Clement III overseeing the status of the Catholic faith and with Jesus Christ our Lord ruling all things with the Father and the Holy Spirit forever. Amen.

> Halt your step,[284] Muse,[285]
> You indulge these chronicles enough.
> The poem finished,
> Say farewell, friendly reader.[286]

Here ends Book 2 of the Chronicles of the Czechs.

282. Bishop Desiderius of Cavaillon (1082–95).

283. Cf. Virgil *Aeneid* 1.204.

284. See Book 1, n. 18.

285. One of a set of goddesses, the Muses, credited in ancient times with artistic inspiration.

286. Ovid, *Tristia* 3.1.2, trans. Arthur Leslie Wheeler, 2d ed. (Cambridge, Mass.: Harvard University Press, 1988), 101.

✠ BOOK THREE

Here begins the Apology of the same Dean mentioned above to the Third Book of the very same work

With God's piety supporting me, I have now fulfilled the promises I consider myself to have made you, reader.[1] Remembering a few things among many concerning exploits, causes, and times past, I have now brought my narrative's history up to the time of Duke Břetislav the Younger. But why I have now decided to delay this pressing work, this work of value, is not irrelevant.

Concerning present-day men and times it is more beneficial for us to remain completely silent than to speak the truth, because the truth always makes us unpopular and we incur loss by it. But if we were to write differently than the way things were, deviating from the truth, we would stand accused of flattery and lies—since their causes are known to almost everyone.[2] Men of this time, denuded of virtues, seek to dress themselves only in praise; their greatest madness is to wish to be decorated with favors rather than to do what is worthy of favor. But it was not so among men of old. Although they were most worthy of praise, they nevertheless fled

1. This first sentence consists of two lines of verse, which borrow from Valerius Flaccus, *Argonautica* 7.518, in *Valerius Flaccus*, trans. J. H. Mozley (Cambridge, Mass.: Harvard University Press, 1934).

2. These two sentences are lifted, with modifications, from Regino's entry for 892, where he too comments on what it means for a historian to write about contemporary events (*Chronicon*, 139). Several other words and phrases from this entry appear elsewhere in the Apologia. However, the declaration that "the truth makes you unpopular" (*veritas odium parit*) comes from Terence (*Woman of Andros* 68) and does not appear in Regino. Cosmas has folded it in, as a kind of riff on Regino's word *odium*.

the praise modern men seek. What was a disgrace to those men is considered an honor by these. If we were transparently to describe with a pen their actions—some of which were not done with God—without a doubt we would not escape offending some of those still living. These are new men and yes men, who have no other response to the duke's voice ready in their mouths than: "Yes, lord," [one says]; another, "Yes it is, lord"; and a third, "Yes, do it, lord."[3] But once it was not so. For the duke himself especially cultivated the man who set his shield against iniquity by reason of justice and suppressed with one word of truth[4] bad counselors and those deviating from the path of equity.[5] There are no such men now, or few; and if they exist, so long as they keep silent, it is as if they do not exist. For it is the same vice or judgment to have silenced the truth or assented to falsehood. Thus it seems to us much safer to narrate a dream, to which no one bears witness, than to write the deeds of present-day men. For that reason we leave it for later men to explain their exploits more expansively. Nevertheless, lest someone blame us for passing over them untouched, we will take the trouble to note a few things summarily.

3.1. The new Duke Břetislav—the "younger" but mature in age and more mature in attitude—worthily celebrated the Feast of Saint Václav, his patron, according to the rite of this land and with all the obligatory ceremonies, in the burg of Prague. With his satraps and *comites* he hosted a great three-day feast. There, when he perceived how much the church might profit from certain things by virtue of his newness, he established those things for the benefit of this land. Just as previously, in the first campaign [*tirocinium*][6] of his youth, he put every hope in God's protection alone, so now,

---

3. This echoes Libuše's remarks in 1.5.

4. Jas 1:18 and 2 Tm 2:15 *(verbum veritas)*.

5. Ammianus 22.10.2, in *Ammianus Marcellinus,* trans. J. C. Rolfe (Cambridge, Mass.: Harvard University Press, 1937).

6. This play on the word *tiro* harks back to 1.12. Cosmas is also specifically referring to Břetislav's break with his father and his withdrawal to Trenčín with his followers, described in 2.48.

burning with great zeal for the Christian religion at the beginning
of his rule, he expelled all the magicians, prophets, and soothsay-
ers from the midst of his realm. He also eradicated and consumed
with fire the trees and meadows which the base commoners[7] worshipped in many places. So also the superstitious practices which
the villagers, still half-pagan,[8] observed on the third or fourth day
of Pentecost, offering libations over springs, offering sacrifices,
and making offerings to demons;[9] the burials they made in forests
and fields; the plays they performed according to the pagan rite
at crossroads and crossroad temples as if for the suppression of
spirits; and the profane jests, which they performed over the dead,
rousing useless ghosts, wearing masks on their faces, and reveling.
The good duke exterminated these abominations and other sacri-
leges, so they might no longer persist among the people of God.
Because he always worshipped the only true God[10] with a pure
heart[11] and possessed zeal for him, this pleased all the lovers of
God.

He was an admirable prince, a duke welcome in camp, and an
unconquerable warrior in arms. However often he invaded Poland,
he always returned with a great triumph. In 1093, the first year of
his reign, he destroyed that place with such frequent raids that,
from the castle Ryczyn to the burg of Głogów, not a single man
lived on this side of the Oder outside the one fortress at Niemcza.
Nor did he cease from plundering until, with great supplication,
Prince Władysław of Poland[12] had paid the tribute for the past
and current years down to the last penny. The sum of this payment was one thousand marks of silver and sixty of gold. This
duke [Władysław] gave the burgs around there, which pertained to
the province of Kłodzko, to his son, Bolesław.[13] He then entrusted
him to Duke Břetislav by giving him his hand and by a promise of

7. See Book 1, n. 78.
8. For these words and the previous sentence, cf. 1.4 and n. 55.
9. Cf. Lv 17:7.   10. Jn 17:3.
11. 2 Tm 2:22.   12. See Book 2, n. 202.
13. Bolesław III "Wrymouth," born 1086, duke of Poland (1102–38).

fidelity that Bolesław, by obeying his uncle, would hold the province given to him by his father in peace. Duke Władysław himself gave his oath that the tribute previously established by Duke Břetislav in exchange for peace—five hundred marks of silver and thirty marks of gold, annually—would be paid at a set time.

3.2. 1094. With Emperor Henry III [IV] still across the Alps in Lombardy doing imperial business, a general synod of all the bishops and princes of the Roman Empire was ordered for the middle of Lent in the burg of Mainz. Duke Břetislav sent Bishops-elect Cosmas and Andrew there, putting them in the hands of the aforementioned Count Palatine Rapoto [2.49] and asking that they be offered to the archbishop of Mainz for ordination. With Rapoto intervening on their behalf and testifying before the archbishop and the entire synod that their election had previously been approved before the emperor at Mantua,[14] Bishops Cosmas and Andreas were ordained by Bishop Ruthard of Mainz[15] on 12 March, with the praise of all the suffragans.

3.3. In the same year there was a great mortality of men, especially in German regions. When the aforesaid bishops were returning from Mainz, while they were passing through a certain village named Hamberg, they were not able to enter the parish church (located outside the village) to hear Mass because, although it was quite large, the whole floor—every spot—was filled with cadavers. Similarly, in the burg of Kager, there was not a house which did not have three or four dead bodies. Passing through there, we spent the night in the middle of a field near the burg.

In September the same year, Duke Břetislav married a certain matron from Bavaria, named Liutgard, the sister of Count Albert.[16]

14. Cf. 2.49.
15. Archbishop of Mainz (1089–1109).
16. The sister of Albert I (d. 1146), count of Bogen, across the Bavarian-Bohemian border northwest of Passau. See František Kubů, "Die Grafen von Bogen in Böhmen," in *Die Anfänge der Grafen von Bogen-Windberg: Studientagung zum 850. Todestag des Grafen Albert I, 17.–18. Januar 1997*, ed. Thomas Handgrätinger (Windberg: Poppe-Verlag, 1999), 129.

In the same year and by the order of this same duke, on 27 September, Bishop Cosmas consecrated the altar of St. Vitus the Martyr (because the monastery itself was not yet completed).[17]

3.4. 1095. On the northern plain, a redness appeared in the sky for many nights.

1096. On 14 April, on the orders of the most glorious Duke Břetislav, the monastery of the holy martyrs Vitus, Václav, and Adalbert was consecrated by Bishop Cosmas.

That same year, there was such a great commotion among the people—indeed a divine compunction—for going to Jerusalem that very few peasants remained in the burgs and villages in German regions and, especially, in eastern Francia [i.e., France].[18] Since, on account of the size of the army, they could not all take one road at the same time, some of them passed through our land. With God permitting it, they attacked the Jews and baptized them against their will, killing those who objected. Seeing that these things were being done against the statutes of canon law, Bishop Cosmas, led by zeal for justice, tried in vain to prevent them from being baptized unwillingly. But he did not have anyone to help him. For Duke Břetislav was in Poland at that time, with his whole army, beyond the banks of the River Nysa. Having destroyed their castle called Bardo, he built a much stronger castle further down on the same river, on a high crag, whence it takes its name, Kamieniec [kamień, stone]. The Jews, after not many days, cast off the yoke of Christ,[19] spurned the grace of baptism and the salvation of the Catholic faith, and again submitted their necks to the yoke[20] of Mosaic law. It was possible to ascribe this to the negligence of the bishop and the prelates of the church.

17. The main altar in Prague cathedral was dedicated to St. Vitus. Cf. 2.43 for the fire of 1091 that compelled the church's reconstruction. Cf. Book 1, n. 295, concerning a comparable use of *monasterium* in reference to a cathedral church.

18. The First Crusade of 1096. Similar anti-Semitic incidents were reported elsewhere in the empire, particularly in the Rhineland. Afterward, by imperial edict, Jews forcibly converted to Christianity were allowed to return to Judaism, although canon law normally prohibited such "apostasy" after baptism under any circumstances.

19. Cf. Mt 11:29.

20. Sir 51:34.

Having built the aforesaid castle, Kamieniec, but before he left there, Duke Břetislav took hold of Mutina, son of Božej, his right-hand man and intimate counselor, and accused him of many deeds by which he had often offended him. He said: "If I was not afraid to offend God, I would gouge out your eyes as you deserve. But I do not want to do that, because it is a great sin to destroy what God's fingers have wrought[21] in man." Permitting him the company of two warriors, Břetislav banished Mutina from his sight and his side. Sending word to Bohemia, he ordered all Mutina's property confiscated. When he returned, without delay the duke sent a retinue to take hold of Mutina's relative Božej, son of Čáč. He had always considered the Vršovici kin [natio] hateful, because he knew them to be very proud and deceitful. Since they were to take hold of him immediately, as was ordered, Božej embarked on a ship with his wife and two children and went into exile in Sorbia. From there he fled to Poland, where he found his brother[22] Mutina. The duke of Poland received them quite well.

3.5. 1097. Summoning Oldřich, son of Conrad, Duke Břetislav ordered him seized and sent to prison at Kłodzko.

1098. It was reported to Duke Břetislav that some of the Jews, having fled into exile, secretly took their wealth away with them, partly to Poland and partly to Hungary. Thus the duke, very angry, sent his chamberlain with some warriors to polish them from head to toe.[23] Arriving there, the chamberlain summoned the Jewish elders and said the following to them: "O Ishmaelite people born from the sons of prostitutes,[24] the duke commands that you answer for yourselves: why did you flee and why did you freely diminish the royal treasures acquired? Whatever things are mine

21. Is 17:8.
22. Cosmas probably does not mean "brother" literally, having just said two sentences back that Božej and Mutina were relatives. Such usage of *frater* to indicate a close relationship between men of similar age from the same kindred is common for Přemyslids; see n. 60.
23. Cf. Book 1, n. 203; also 1.36.
24. Cosmas has *manzer*, but he is surely referring to the *mamzer* from Dt 23:2: "A mamzer, that is to say, one born of a prostitute, shall not enter into the church of the Lord."

are all mine. None of your goods or riches come from Solomon. Proscribed by Caesar Vespasian for one coin thrice ten, thus were you scattered across the globe.[25] You came skinny, you should go skinny to wherever you want.[26] As God is my witness, that you were baptized was accomplished not with me commanding it but the Lord. That you have again relapsed into Judaism, Bishop Cosmas should have seen, whence he should have done something about it." When the chamberlain had said this on the duke's behalf, his men, rushing in immediately, turned their houses upside down, took their treasures, and found whatever furniture seemed the best. They left them nothing, not even a grain of corn, except what pertained to the victim alone. O how much money was taken from the wretched Jews that day! So many riches from the burning of Troy were not collected on the Euboean shore.[27]

3.6. In the same year, on 10 December, Bishop Cosmas departed to Christ. He was a humble bishop, simple, patient, and very merciful. He bore with equanimity whatever injuries might be done to him by any man. He was a pious supporter of those who acknowledged their faults, an attentive listener to widows, a swift helper of orphans, and—remembering his ultimate fate—a prompt performer of funerals.

3.7. After Cosmas's death, Duke Břetislav, having the care of souls and weighing carefully the power bestowed on him by God to choose the church's bridegroom—full of anxiety and ever watchful, but keeping his mind silently to himself—began to inspect the mores of his clerics and to examine the life and conversation of those individuals among whom he would raise one to the most powerful pinnacle of sacerdotal rank. Although he himself knew what there was in each of his clerics, nonetheless he remembered the words of Solomon: "Do everything with counsel, son."[28]

25. Virgil *Aeneid* 1.602.
26. Cf. Horace *Epistles* 1.7.33.
27. The phrase "on the Euboean shore" is lifted from Virgil *Aeneid* 9.710, though the context has nothing to do with treasures.
28. Cf. Sir 32:24.

Thus he summoned Wiprecht, his brother-in-law through his sister,[29] a wise man, well versed and shrewd in such matters, and said to him: "In the days of my father, King Vratislav, you were always first among his friends at court. You have observed the ways and life of the Czechs. You have come to know not only all the laymen but even the clergy inside and out. I want your advice now to choose a bishop." To this the hero responded in his own words, not inappropriately: "At the time when your father the king still flourished," Wiprecht said, "he valued my counsel. Now men of such character live, who consider themselves to be something when they are nothing, and whom the counsel of no one pleases except what they themselves know. But you know better. And you know that in this holy matter, those who consider the benefit of the holy church ought to be free of anger and hatred, of mercy and friendship. For where these things stand in the way, human opinion deceives the mind.[30] Friendship does not bind me to anyone, nor does it overthrow mercy, stir up hatred, or ignite ire. For which reason, I should speak less before you about what the order of justice demands. A man named Hermann, known better to you than to us, is now your chaplain, as he was your father's. He was always constant in the king's service, faithful in the matters entrusted to him, a trustworthy executor of embassies to be carried out, chaste, sober, humble and kind, not violent, not ambitious, not haughty, and—what is the primary virtue in a cleric—he is especially learned. And insofar as one looks to human opinion, he is perceived to be a good man and brought to perfection[31] if this one thing is not held against him: that he is a foreigner."[32] The duke, astonished at the unanimity of his own will and Wiprecht's, said: "Your heart and mine hardly think differently. Because he is a foreigner, this will

29. Wiprecht II of Groitzsch; see Book 2, n. 230.
30. Adapted from Sallust *War with Catiline* 51.1–2: "All men who deliberate upon difficult questions ought to be free from hatred and friendship, anger and pity. When these feelings stand in the way the mind cannot easily discern the truth."
31. See Book 1, n. 9.
32. See 3.49, where Cosmas notes as part of Hermann's obituary that he was originally from Utrecht.

profit the church more. His kin will not exhaust it, the care of his freemen will not burden it, a crowd of his relatives will not despoil it. Whatever he brings from wherever he comes from, his bride and mother church will have the whole of it. Therefore I order that he be bishop of Prague."

Without delay all the magnates of the land and provosts of the church were convened at the duke's pleasure in the burg of [Stará] Boleslav. With the acclamation of all the clergy and the support of the people, Hermann, deacon by rank, raised to the provostship of [Stará] Boleslav,[33] was called unwillingly to the higher honor of the episcopate. This election took place on 28 February 1099.

3.8. Because Emperor Henry III [IV] celebrated Easter at Regensburg that year, Duke Břetislav was ordered to come there with his bishop-elect. After celebrating Easter at Vyšehrad, the Czechs arrived in Regensburg on the third day after the octave of Easter. Since the duke had sent expensive gifts ahead to both the emperor and his satraps before the holiday, he had so many friends at court that almost three thousand men came to meet him and thus led him into the burg with great honor. On the first request, the emperor confirmed the Czechs' election and gave Hermann the episcopal ring and staff.[34]

Břetislav also obtained by entreaties before the emperor, that Henry would give a banner to his brother Bořivoj and designate him to all the Czechs who had come with him, so that they would raise him to the throne after Břetislav's death.

3.9. In the same year, coming to Moravia with his army, Duke Břetislav rebuilt the castle of Podivín and returned it to Bishop Hermann's power, as it had been previously. He also celebrated Pentecost there, in the village of Slivnice.

From there he went to meet King Coloman of Hungary[35] in the

---

33. Although Cosmas does not distinguish specifically, this must be *Stará* Boleslav, rather than Mladá Boleslav, because only in Stará Boleslav did a collegiate chapter of canons exist at this time, of which Hermann might have been provost.

34. Investiture; see Book 1, n. 206.

35. King of Hungary (1095–1116).

field called Lučsko. They said many things publicly, each in turn, to the pleasure of both parties. With huge gifts exchanged mutually between them, they renewed their age-old bonds of friendship and peace and confirmed them with oaths.

Duke Břetislav sent his bishop-elect Hermann, a deacon, to be ordained there by Archbishop Seraphim.[36] Arriving at his see in the burg of Esztergom at the time when holy orders are celebrated, he ordained Hermann a priest on 11 June and similarly raised me, although unworthy, to the same rank.

After the council was held, on his return the duke set up camp next to the burg of Brno: for he was very angry with the sons of his uncle Conrad, Oldřich and Lutold. Fleeing from his face,[37] they shut themselves up in protected fortresses and handed over the rest of their burgs to him, asking that he not lay waste to the land as an enemy. Meanwhile, Duke Břetislav distributed garrisons throughout the burgs handed over to him, entrusted them to his brother Bořivoj, and returned to Bohemia. The sons of Otto, Svatopluk and Otto, together with their mother Eufemia, remained very obedient to the duke and faithful.[38]

That same year Duke Břetislav invited Bolesław, a kinsman of his through a sister,[39] to a feast that was set to take place in the burg of Žatec. There, with the approval of all the magnates of Bohemia, Bolesław was made his uncle's sword bearer. Sending him home af-

36. Seraphim of Esztergom (d. 1104); when he began his term as archbishop remains uncertain. Hermann is here being raised in rank from deacon to priest, but not consecrated bishop, since that right pertains to the archbishop of Mainz. Why his ordination was handled separately, after his investiture but not as part of his consecration, and why Archbishop Seraphim should have been involved, are both unclear.

37. Ps 67:2.

38. Břetislav II, the first duke of a new generation of Přemyslids (see the genealogical chart), is here rearranging the governance of Moravia, ostensibly as a consequence of bad relations with his cousins. The larger issue, recurrent in Book 3, concerns whether the heirs of Conrad of Brno and Otto I of Olomouc retained a hereditary claim to rule their fathers' territories in Moravia, or whether the reigning duke of Bohemia had the right to appoint others to these positions. See my *Hastening Toward Prague*, 99, 195–96, as well as Cosmas's direct comment on the problem, 3.34.

39. Bolesław's mother, Judith, was Břetislav's sister; cf. 2.36.

ter the holiday, Břetislav gave him as a gift and established that, in exchange for fulfilling the office of sword bearer, he would always receive one hundred marks of silver and ten gold talents annually from the tribute paid by his father, Władysław.[40]

3.10. 1100. Having found out for certain from some people that the emperor wanted to celebrate Easter at Mainz, Duke Břetislav thought it best to send his bishop-elect Hermann there. Thus Hermann might bring his presents to the emperor and also receive the blessing he anticipated from his master. Trusting him to Wiprecht, who likewise had to be present at the emperor's palace, Břetislav asked that Wiprecht support all of his business at the opportune time. But Archbishop Ruthard, charged with the simoniac heresy, had left Mainz at that time and tarried in Saxony. Therefore, at the emperor's command and with approval of all the suffragans of the church of Mainz, Hermann was ordained bishop on 18 April, in the octave of Easter, by Cardinal Robert, Pope Clement's plenipotentiary,[41] who happened to be there.

3.11. In the same year a wondrous miracle, memorable throughout the ages, was deemed worthy to be revealed by divine grace through the merits of the most holy martyr, Ludmila; we describe it to your charity as we saw it ourselves. The lady Abbess Windelmuth [of St. George], devoted handmaiden of God, took the Church of St. Peter the Apostle, located on land of the same monastery over which she ruled but ruined from the foundation on account of old age, and rebuilt it, bringing it back to perfection. Since the abbess had succeeded in getting the bishop to consecrate the church, when she gathered the relics of the saints into a pyx,[42] as was customary, she offered the bishop a strip of cloth one palm wide, which she had taken from the headdress of Saint Ludmila, and asked that he likewise place it in the pyx among the other relics. The bishop, as if indignant, then said: "Be quiet, lady, about her sanctity;

---

40. Cf. 3.1.

41. Bishop Robert of Faenza (c. 1086–1104).

42. Normally, "pyx" refers to the small box used for the consecrated Eucharist (for instance, to transport it for distribution to the sick); here, however, Cosmas seems to be referring to a reliquary, presumably also a box.

let the old woman rest in peace!"[43] To this the abbess responded: "Lord, do not say such things. God does many great things[44] daily through her merits." Immediately, at the bishop's order, a large pan full of burning coals was brought in; having invoked the name of the Holy Trinity, he threw the strip of cloth into the coals spitting flames. It was a wondrous thing: a little smoke and small flame burst up around the cloth, but scarcely damaged it. And this too was of note, to the increase of this great miracle: on account of the great heat, the cloth could not be removed from the flames for a long time; nevertheless, when it was removed, it was seen to be whole and strong, as if it had been woven that very day. Thus the miracle was rendered manifest to the bishop as well as to all of us. Shocked, we shed tears of joy and gave thanks to Christ. The church was dedicated in honor of St. Peter the Apostle on 3 October.

3.12. On 18 October of the same year, Bořivoj, the brother of Duke Břetislav, married Gerberga, the sister of the Austrian margrave Leopold,[45] providing a very sumptuous feast in the burg of Znojmo.

In those days Lutold, the son of Conrad, having been let into the castle of Raabs by Gottfried's grant, committed many injuries against Bořivoj, laying waste to his villages on various nights and then taking refuge in the castle. Very indignant therefore, Duke Břetislav again gathered an army and moved his tents to Moravia, wishing to avenge his brother's injury. But first he sent to Gottfried, protesting to him on the basis of their bond of old friendship. He also announced that Gottfried should expel Lutold from his castle within the very hour, or without delay he would send Lutold back to Gottfried vanquished. Since this was not kept secret from Lutold, he seized the castle by force with his men, having driven the castellans outside by deception. With the envoys that had been sent to him, Gottfried met the duke next to the burg

43. Cf. Lk 2:29.
44. Cf. Book 1, n. 288.
45. Sister of Leopold III (1095–1136); she died in 1142. Lechner, *Babenberger.*

of Vranov and declared before all that Lutold was faithless and an enemy of the *res publica*, the castle having been entrusted to him on friendly terms. He asked the duke's help in immediately storming it as an enemy. Not refusing his request, the duke moved his army around the perimeter of the burg. There, for six weeks, day and night, battle was engaged with the greatest vigor, until famine, which outfights strong burgs,[46] prevailed in the castle. Conquered by it and broken by war, Lutold fled, having slipped away at night, secretly and nearly alone. He left his warriors behind there; come morning, they handed the castle and themselves over to the duke. Meanwhile, while this battle was taking place, Paul, the son of Markward and Vladislav's tutor, died, struck by an arrow. Also Dobeš, son of Lstimír, was killed while he performed his turn on the nightly watch. These two men having been lost and the burg returned to Gottfried, the duke returned as a victor to Bohemia with his men.

3.13. With Christ's nativity approaching, Duke Břetislav was staying in the village of Ztibečná to hunt. One day, in the midst of the midday meal, the duke is reported to have said to a certain hunter, who was seated not far from him, at the fourth table: "Hey Kukata! Do you think I don't know who among you seeks to kill me?"[47] And the hunter, since he was a man impetuous in his words, exclaimed, "Indeed he should be quickly killed, who contrives such things—may God divert him entirely, nor let your eye spare him."[48] To this the duke said: "Ah, good man! No one is permitted to avoid his unavoidable fate."[49]

The next day he went hunting, having heard Mass in the morning, since it was the vigil of St. Thomas the Apostle. When he returned that night, servants ran to meet him outside the village with lanterns and torches.[50] Next, Lork, an impious thief sent

46. Lucan *Pharsalia* 4.410.   47. Jn 7:20.
48. Dt 13:8.
49. Curtius Rufus *Historiae* 4.6.17, in *Quintus Curtius*, ed. and trans. John C. Rolfe, 2 vols. (Cambridge, Mass.: Harvard University Press, 1956).
50. Jn 18:3, where the reference is specifically to Judas meeting Jesus in the garden "with lanterns and torches."

by the devil, burst from his hiding place, girded with a sword. As powerfully as he was able, he struck the duke in the groin with a hunting spear. The duke fell in the middle of the mud no differently than if bright Lucifer had fallen from high heaven.[51] A mourning crowd of his men flew to him immediately and, having extracted the spear, lifted the half-dead duke.

That minister of Satan, Lork, while he hastened in flight through the dark night, was thrown headlong with his horse into a cistern made by a torrent of rain rushing down. It is unclear whether he took his sword from its sheath by his own hand or whether it slipped. But it cut through the middle of his belly so that all his internal organs flowed out. There was commotion throughout the village, with some leaping on horses, others running here and there with weapons, tracking the contriver of such an evil deed. Soon one man found him half-alive and, although Lork had a wound sufficient for death, nevertheless he cut off his head, saying: "You will not go innocent to the dark shadows of the underworld. And remember to tell the son-in-law of Ceres of my deeds."[52]

But the duke, although placed in such pain and grief, did not release his spirit either that night or the next day, nor cease from God's praises, now offering tearful penitence, now confessing his sins both to Bishop Hermann and to others of God's priests. He ordered the tribute that was brought from Poland at that time, as well as whatever was found in his treasury, distributed to monasteries through the bishop's hands. When he had disposed of all the things which were to be disposed for the sake of his soul, "Give," he said, "to my little son[53] my trumpet and javelin; it is not for me to give him other things, which God has put in his own power."[54] After cock's crow on the following night, 22 December, in the hands of priests like a good athlete of God, he separated

51. Is 14:12.
52. Two lines of verse, deriving from Virgil *Aeneid* 2.547, but compressed and modified. For the "son-in-law of Ceres," cf. Book 1, n. 109.
53. Also named Břetislav; cf. 3.38.
54. Acts 1:7.

the double substance of man into its beginnings [body and soul]. Without a doubt, we believe that the heavenly consort has already received him or is about to do so.

One of the clergy, following his bier[55] as far as the tomb, repeated a lament of this sort, saying: "Soul of Břetislav, *Sabaoth Adonai,* may he live free of *thanaton,* Břetislav *ischyros."*[56] It was a wondrous thing: by his weeping in this way, he moved the clergy and the people to weep, so that, although you were weeping, you wished to weep more. Duke Břetislav was buried with the greatest lamentation of his men in the cemetery of the Church of St. Václav, outside, in front of the door, on the left—as he himself had arranged. His sister, Ludmila, devoted handmaid of God, built a chapel with bowed arches above the vaults in honor of St. Thomas the Apostle. She also established that mass would be celebrated there daily on behalf of the dead.

The report immediately spread abroad among the people[57] that the duke was killed on the advice of Božej and Mutina, whom Břetislav had earlier expelled from his realm. It is customary for some people to debate whether the one who gave the advice is more guilty, or the one who agreed to act upon it. While the truth of the matter is that both are guilty, nevertheless he who advised homicide is more guilty, because he incriminated both himself and another man. Therefore you who gave the advice that he should be killed, you killed Břetislav!

The bishop and the *comites* immediately sent an emissary to Moravia in haste, to Duke Bořivoj, to say that he should hurry to receive the duchy of all Bohemia once granted to him by the caesar. Coming in haste, he was enthroned on the very day of Christmas, with everyone supporting it. Then Cyllenia wiped out altogether

55. 2 Kgs 3:31.

56. The inclusion of two Hebrew words for God (*Sabaoth,* Lord of Hosts; *Adonai,* Lord), as well as of the Greek words for "death" *(thanaton)* and "strong" *(ischyros),* as part of Břetislav's dirge is probably a rhetorical flourish on Cosmas's part, meant to elevate the lament for the murdered duke and perhaps even inspire the reader to weep.

57. Ru 1:19.

whatever tracks she had left barely imprinted in Bohemia, when, hating the earth, she sought out heaven.[58] For it was justice among the Czechs that the eldest among their princes always succeeded to the principate.

3.14. 1101. Oldřich and Lutold, the sons of Conrad, repossessed their burgs, after expelling from Moravia the garrisons that Bořivoj had left behind there as a guard when he left.

Similarly Božej and Mutina returned from Poland.[59] Duke Bořivoj, not from his heart but on account of the need of the times, granted them his grace. They received the burgs they had earlier held: Božej, Žatec and Mutina, Litoměřice.

3.15. In the same year, Oldřich went to the emperor in Regensburg, beseeched him with entreaties through friends and wearied him with huge promises, so that Henry might restore to him the duchy of Bohemia, unjustly seized by his younger brother Bořivoj.[60] Having accepted money from him, the caesar gave him the insignia of the duchy and a banner; but he placed the pretense of electing the duke in the judgment of the Czechs.

Sending as his emissary a very well spoken man named Neuša, the son of Dobřemil, Oldřich accused his brother Bořivoj, goaded the magnates, and threatened them. He asserted himself to be

58. The last clause cites Ovid *Metamorphoses* 1.150; however, the lines report that "the maiden Astraea, last of the immortals, abandoned the blood-soaked earth." The first part of the sentence derives from Virgil *Georgics* 1.473: "as she departed from the earth, Justice left the last imprint of her feet." I have not been able to trace the source or reason for Cosmas's "Cyllenia" (feminine); normally, Cyllenius (masculine) is a byname of Mercury, born on Mt. Cyllene in Arcadia, who figures in neither of these passages. The original line from Virgil, however, makes clear Cosmas's meaning: that *Justice* fled Bohemia after Bořivoj's enthronement. This also explains the next sentence, which refers to "justice among the Czechs" and the normal rule of succession; cf. 2.13. The omission of Ovid's "blood-soaked" might be meant, paradoxically, to emphasize the bloodshed to come.

59. Cf. 3.4.

60. Bořivoj was Oldřich's cousin, not his brother. However, throughout this chapter, Cosmas uses this designation deliberately and not by mistake, as it was common in Czech sources to call Přemyslids of the same generation "brothers," especially with regard to claims to the throne. See my *Hastening Toward Prague,* 101.

older in age, owed [the throne] according to the custom of the country, and unjustly supplanted by his younger brother. Thus he requested the honor of the princely seat. Although he had a just cause, nevertheless, you catch the tail in vain when you let go of the horns. Just so, Oldřich tried too late to expel his brother, already confirmed on the throne, from the realm. After his emissary reported back, Oldřich understood that neither would his brother cede the throne nor would the magnates acquiesce to his advice.

So this alone he obtained by his entreaties [at the imperial court]: that, by the emperor's leave, it would be lawful to invade by force the province owed to him. Men strenuous in warlike matters soon joined him in the war tent: Sighard, count of Burghausen; his brother Ulrich, the bishop of Freising; and his brother-in-law through his sister, named Frederick.[61] Oldřich inflamed their spirits to war, assuring them of mountains of gold[62] and promising that all the elders of Bohemia were his supporters. Meanwhile, wherever he was able, he acquired not a few Germans to help him: on account of their stupidity, they thought that in Bohemia great quantities of gold and silver[63] would be scattered and laying out on the streets.[64] Assembled together in the month of August, Oldřich entered Bohemian parts with his brother Lutold, but under an unlucky omen.

Bořivoj, having gathered an army and racing to meet them, set up camp atop two hills next to the fortress of Malín, ready to go to war with them the next day. The Germans made their camp not far away, on the other side of the River Vyspliše. Thus each army could be seen by the other. The Germans, after they understood the

61. Count Sighard X of Tengling-Burghausen (d. 1104); Bishop *Henry* of Freising (1098–37), his brother; and their *brother*, Count Frederick II of Tengling (d. ca. 1120). Notice that, unaccountably, Cosmas has quite muddled the names and relationships of these three very powerful Bavarian noblemen. For a genealogical chart, see Karl Brunner, *907–1156: Herzogtümer und Marken, vom Ungarnsturm bis ins 12. Jahrhundert* (Vienna: Überreuter, 1994), 86; also Brandmüller, *Handbuch der bayerischen Kirchengeschichte*, 1208.

62. Terence *Phormio* 68: "promising him a mountain of gold" (though Cosmas has substituted another verb so that he can move "promising" to the next phrase).

63. Dt 17:17.

64. Cf. Rv 21:21 and Zec 9:3.

unanimous steadfastness of the Czechs to be with Bořivoj, said to
Oldřich: "Where are those elders of Bohemia you said were your
supporters? Well have you lied to the detriment of your own head.
You deceived us and led us into great danger." They wanted to turn
back but were unable: behind them on the same road, Svatopluk
and his brother Otto, leading two contingents, were coming to aid
Bořivoj. What were [Oldřich and the Germans] to do? Pressed on
all sides by such narrowness, they hurried at night in disgraceful
flight on the narrow road and the extremely tight footpath which
went through the forest to Habry.[65] There the bishop of Freising
lost his sacred vessels. There, on account of the difficult road, the
army threw away every bundle with useful things. Come morning,
the arriving Czechs, missing the enemy, seized their spoils.

At that time Bořivoj and Svatopluk were in accord and of one
mind toward each other. I will say a few things about how discord
arose between them (repeating a little of the above as a beginning).

3.16. 1102. Duke Władysław of Poland, having two sons—one
born of a concubine, named Zbigniew, and another, named Bolesław,
born of Judith, the daughter of King Vratislav—divided his realm in
half between them.[66] But, according to the Lord's word, every kingdom divided against itself will be brought to desolation and house
upon house will fall[67]—or, as is commonly said, two cats cannot be
held in the same sack at the same time.

Just so, in 1103, after the death of his father, Zbigniew took
up arms against his brother and, promising money, allied Duke
Bořivoj with himself for assistance. Bořivoj immediately sent for
Svatopluk in Moravia and, gathering together, they set up camp
next to the fortress of Ryczyn. Hearing of this, Bolesław sent his
tutor, Skarbimir,[68] and asked Duke Bořivoj to remember their

65. Southwest of Malín.

66. The protracted struggle for control of Poland after Władysław's death in 1102
is described in great detail in the anonymous *Deeds of the Princes of the Poles*, 158–209.
Zbigniew was finally ousted from power in 1106 and died sometime after 1114.

67. Lk 11:17.

68. Cf. *Deeds of the Princes of the Poles* (173 and frequently elsewhere), where he is described as "count palatine." In 1117 he would lead a rebellion against Bolesław. Gieysztor, *Medieval Poland*, 79.

affinity: he said that he was a nearer kinsman [than Zbigniew] through Bořivoj's sister Judith. Moreover, he had in readiness ten sacks filled with a thousand marks. O Money, queen[69] of all evil, friend of deceit, enemy and foe of faithfulness, you hinder justice and subvert proper judgment! Corrupted by you, Hrabiše and Protiven, Duke Bořivoj's counselors, compelled the duke himself to renounce the faith promised to Zbigniew. Having accepted the money, Bořivoj immediately returned home. Because he did not give him even a penny, Svatopluk, very indignant and burning with anger, is said to have declared when departing: "I will put out my fire by destruction."[70]

3.17. 1104. John was elected bishop of Moravia.[71]

In the same year, Svatopluk sent to Bohemia seekers of wickedness, denouncers of justice, sowers of discord, and authors of every evil art,[72] who were able to arm for battle brothers of one mind.[73] With these men going around to almost all the burgs of Bohemia, they corrupted some with money, others they bound with rewards or promises. Those whom they knew to be desirous of a change,[74] or deprived of offices, or fickle and inconstant in spirit, they joined to the party of Duke Svatopluk with all their tricks.

After these things were thus accomplished, in 1105, with the sun tarrying in the tenth part of Libra, Svatopluk entered Bohemia with his retinue and met these contingents of perfidious men. Some of them expected that they would receive him within the walls of the burg of Prague, having opened the gates. But earlier that same day, coming at dawn, Duke Bořivoj occupied the burg, positioned a strong garrison within it and, entrusting it to Bishop Hermann, took himself to Vyšehrad with his men.

69. Cf. Book 2, n. 89; also 2.12.

70. Sallust *War with Catiline* 31.9.

71. Cosmas is notably laconic here, whereas he usually gives a fuller description of the deaths and elections of bishops of Prague. More important, it is likely that he has omitted to mention two other bishops, Henry I and Peter I, who apparently occupied the see of Olomouc after the death of Bishop Andrew in 1096. See Table 2.

72. 2 Mc 7:31.   73. Virgil *Aeneid* 7.335.

74. Sallust *War with Jugurtha* 19.1.

Behold, Svatopluk appeared in the field with six legions in good order, beautifully equipped. Although uncertain and a little doubtful because no one came to meet him from the burg, he stood firm. Immediately crossing the Vltava within the village called Buben, he and his men approached the burg but found the gates closed and warriors strongly resisting atop the walls. Shamefully disgraced there by a certain servant girl standing atop the walls, they retreated by the same road. They fixed their tents between both burgs (in the place where there is a market on Saturday) thinking that their coconspirators would flock to them that night from either burg.

Come morning, when they had not done so, Svatopluk convened the company and spoke to them in this way: "Although now there is no time for me to give a prolix speech, nevertheless I will say a few words for my conduct,[75] lest I seem to anyone to fear the moment of death. Death is best suited to the timid and cowardly, those to whom this wretched life is considered sweet. But to a strong man, to suffer death in battle is sweeter than liquid nectar.[76] I debated with myself once whether it was better to acquire[77] bread and honor or to meet death[78] honorably by fighting. For you, however, this death alone is to be guarded against now: that none of you, captured, hands bound behind your back,[79] and made a spectacle[80] by the enemy—like an ox to the slaughter[81]—fall to the ax, executed. There is one victory for the vanquished, one memory worthy of praise: that a bloodless victory not come to pass for the enemy."[82] He had spoken and, turning immediately on the road to Moravia with his retinue, said this to *Comes* Vacek: "O

75. Virgil *Aeneid* 4.337.

76. This is a paraphrase of the *Aeneid*, 2.317, cited verbatim below, 3.36 and n. 184. "Liquid nectar," however, derives from Virgil *Georgics* 4.164.

77. There is wordplay here with *potiri* (acquire) and *potiori* (better), which is impossible to capture in the English.

78. Part of a line from Virgil cited in full below, 3.22 and n. 92.

79. Virgil *Aeneid* 2.57.   80. 1 Cor 4:9.

81. Prv 7:22.

82. These sentences expand upon Sallust *War with Catiline* 58.21: "Do not be captured and slaughtered like cattle, but fighting like heroes, leave the enemy a bloody and tearful victory."

wretched work of fortune, by which I am now forced to dwell on the ground like an owl, I who had seemed to rise up like an eagle[83] almost to the clouds." Vacek said to him: "Let this adversity not break you, my lord, more quickly than happier prosperity follows. For the sun's brightness too shines more after rain clouds.[84] Such is the vicissitude of all things in the world."

At their departure, Duke Bořivoj followed with his men. But although he had more than seven times the warriors, nonetheless he did not dare engage [his own men] in battle because he feared their perfidy, i.e., that they would abandon their camps and transfer themselves to the enemies' army. From a distance, he followed [Svatopluk and his men] as far as the entrance of the forest.

3.18. 1106. With the devil, author of discord, sowing discord[85] throughout the globe, there were certain of his coworkers, leading men among the Germans, who, seducing the son of the emperor, King Henry IV [V],[86] persuaded him to take up arms against his father. Fleeing from the face of his son, the emperor fortified himself in the burg of Regensburg with a few armed men and sent for Duke Bořivoj to come to his aid with an army. Coming without delay, the Czechs made their camps not far from Regensburg, along the Regen River. On the other side of the same river were the camps of the emperor's son. Then those who seemed to be the caesar's supporters, first Margrave Leopold of Austria went home with his men, having slipped into flight at night, and then Margraves Diepold and Berengar crossed over to the camp of the younger King Henry.[87] Seeing themselves abandoned on all sides, the Czechs hastened at once into flight at night, as quickly as they were able.

Seeing this, the emperor abandoned Regensburg and, crossing

83. Jer 49:22.
84. Cf. Ovid *Metamorphoses* 5.570; cf. 1.10.
85. See n. 165.
86. Henry V (1106–25).
87. Margrave Diepold III of Cham-Vohburg-Nabburg (1102–12) and Count Berengar I of Sulzbach (1099–1125); see Weinfurter, *Salian Century*, 164. The Austrian margrave is, again, Leopold III (1095–1136), whose sister was Bořivoj's wife; cf. 3.12.

the southern plain, entered Bohemia by the road which goes to Netolice. Receiving him honorably, Duke Bořivoj gave him safe conduct through his land in the direction of Saxony, as the caesar himself had arranged, leading him to his brother-in-law Wiprecht. From that point, crossing both Saxony and the Rhine, he came to Liège. There, not many days later, he lost the empire with his life, on 8 August.

3.19. That same year, Svatopluk summoned those who had followed him from Bohemia and sought their advice about what needed to be done in this business begun. Then Budivoj, son of Chřen, older than the rest and better spoken, a man even tempered in prosperity and adversity, experienced in such affairs from a young age and full of tricks, made these exhortations: "Varied is the outcome in battle:[88] now these, now those prevail in war. Yet we, brothers, have not yet fought to the point of shedding blood.[89] We have not yet made a bridge to the throne with our heads. We are about to make such a bridge, surely, if destiny compels it to be made. Since one comes to the lofty summits of honor not always by arms but more often through deception, having now laid down arms, let us use deception. By such arts, Troy was captured by the Argives in the tenth year. And Prudentius says in the *Psychomachia:* 'It makes no difference whether the palm of victory comes by arms or by deception.'"[90]

Without delay, another crafty Sinon[91] (as I might have said) was sent to Bohemia, furnished with various deceptions: the nephew of Hapata. Ready for any fortune,[92] he did not fear the event

88. 2 Kgs 11:25.

89. Heb 12:4.

90. Prudentius *Psychomachia* 550, in *Prudentius,* 1:317.

91. As explained two sentences below, Sinon is the name of the man who persuaded the Trojans to allow the famous equestrian statue inside their walls by pretending to desert from the Greek army and then released the soldiers from its hollow belly—especially in the Virgilian tradition most familiar to Cosmas (*Aeneid* 2). The Argives mentioned here are another name for the Mycenaean opponents of the Trojans, so called after Argos, one of the chief cities of Agamemnon's kingdom.

92. Virgil *Aeneid* 2.61; fittingly this phrase appears in precisely the passage in which Sinon is preparing to offer the horse to the Trojans.

of death; a manly name is fittingly applied to him, since he acted manfully. For just as by his lies Sinon once led the armed Argives within the walls of Troy, shut up in the horse, so too through the lying fictions of this man, Bohemia was laid open to be conquered by Duke Svatopluk. When he came to Duke Bořivoj, falling down on his knees,[93] he washed the duke's feet with feigned tears.[94] Ordered to rise, he said such words: "O wretched me! I barely hid myself in flight and barely escaped the villainous hands[95] of the impious Svatopluk. If he had captured me, without doubt he would have torn out my eyes. Since I do not know any other way to avenge myself against him, O omnipotent God, it is no sin for me to reveal his secrets. It is no sin for me to make known all those who are his familiars in this land."[96] And so, mixing falsehoods with truth, he accused Svatopluk of many shameful things, and, so that he might be believed more, he confirmed his words with oaths.

Through such snares and craft,[97] Duke Bořivoj, a good and simple man, was deceived. Much believing these lies, he heedlessly cut the strong branches[98] on which he himself sat and leaned, and on which hung his honor, and thus fell from his lofty height.[99] For he had often wanted to seize his faithful friends, Božej and Mutina, and punish them as enemies of the *res publica*. Because he had counselors, Hrabiše and Protiven, who were full of cracks, his wish was not hidden from the aforesaid *comites*.

Božej and Mutina immediately transferred themselves to Bořivoj's

93. Mt 17:14.   94. Cf. Lk 7:38.
95. Silius Italicus *Punica* 9.567.

96. Through the repetition of this simple phrase, *fas mihi*, Cosmas alludes again to Sinon, who gives himself a similar allowance as a feint to persuade the Trojans to accept the horse. Cf. Virgil *Aeneid* 2157 (see also West's prose translation, 34): "It is no sin for me to break my sacred oaths of allegiance to the Greeks. It is no sin for me to hate these men and bring all their secrets out into the open."

97. Virgil *Aeneid* 2.195. Note that the context for these words is relevant to Cosmas's point here: "The trap was laid. These were the arts of the liar Sinon, and we believed it all. Cunning and false tears had overcome the men . . ." (West's prose translation, 35).

98. Cf. Dn 4:11 and 17.
99. Virgil *Aeneid* 2.290.

brother, Vladislav. Howling and raging, they now gave him the goad to rage more at his natural brother, Bořivoj. Vladislav now renounced his faith, fraternity, and friendship to Bořivoj. And he openly sent the brother of William, named Pulo, for Svatopluk in Moravia. Upon Svatopluk's arrival, Vladislav and the rest of the *comites*—alas senseless,[100] like enemies to themselves and enemies of their fatherland—to their own ruin led into the sheepfold a rabid wolf,[101] who would tear not only the sheep to pieces but the enclosures themselves. Therefore Bořivoj, mild as a sheep, was deprived of the realm and Svatopluk, more savage than a tiger, more ferocious than a lion, was enthroned on 14 May 1107.

3.20. No sooner had this new deed been done in Bohemia than neighboring peoples marveled and predicted worse for the Czechs in the future, with the prognostications of an empty mind. Hence the sons of Cassandra[102] in Hungary rejoiced, whence those in Poland, worthless rags, gave thanks with uncircumcised lips[103]—because while these [Czech] princes were restless among themselves, they had rest.

Many of the *comites*, those foreigners whom Bořivoj himself had made *comites*, attended him and went with him to Poland. Seeing what they had done, Soběslav, the third born after Bořivoj, now a youth of good disposition, followed his brother to Poland.

At this same time, King Henry IV [V] happened to be in Saxony. Bořivoj hurried to him and lamented his injury. So that Henry might restore to him the duchy of Bohemia, taken unjustly, Bořivoj promised to give him a great quantity of gold and silver[104] in the future. Sending one of his satraps right away, the king commanded Svatopluk, in a few words: "By the crown on my head, I command and order you to come to me without delay. If you are late in coming, without doubt, I will quickly visit you and your Prague in

---

100. Gal 3:1.

101. A common image for Cosmas: cf. 1.13, 2.9, and below, 3.23.

102. The daughter of Priam of Troy, endowed with prophetic powers by Apollo but often unheeded.

103. Ex 6:12.

104. Cf. above, n. 62.

justice and in judgment." Svatopluk immediately gathered an army. When they arrived at the entrance to the forest, near the fortress of Chlumec, he convened his leaders and satraps. Svatopluk put forward his brother Otto, saying to them: "I will go alone and, to the danger of my head,[105] investigate the double-edged mind of the king. You wait here on the dubious outcomes of uncertain events. For the rest, may omnipotent God go before and follow up your deeds."[106] Taking a few men with him, he went heedlessly, about to fall into an open trap. O the foolish wisdom of the man,[107] the foolhardy courage of the duke! He went hardly ignorant of what the king was about to do to him, corrupted by gold and greedy as hell. When Svatopluk arrived, the king ordered him thrust into prison without any hearing. Summoning those who had come to him, Henry gave Duke Bořivoj to them so that, leading him back to Prague, they might raise him again to the princely throne.

Returning with him, on the third day they camped next to the castle of Donin. Hearing this, Otto said to his men, "Why do we wait here? What we feared has now come to pass and what we were afraid of has occurred. Let's go and see the new duke, and see if the king's right arm defends him from our lance." Otto arranged six legions from his chosen warriors: they crossed the mountains at night and attacked Bořivoj's camp at dawn. But Bořivoj, prescient, slipped into flight and hid—because a certain fugitive from Otto's camp had secretly alerted him.

3.21. Bishop Hermann, a prudent and just man, positioned between the various misfortunes of both dukes as if between Scylla and Charybdis,[108] fled to his friend, Bishop Otto of Bamberg,[109] lest he seem to follow either insecure party.

---

105. 1 Par 12:19.   106. Ps 58:11 combined with Ps 22:6.
107. Cf. 1 Cor 1:20.

108. Perils made famous in the Odyssey: Scylla, the voracious polycephalous monster on the cliff, and Charybdis, the violent whirlpool no ship could escape. Opposite each other across a narrow strait, they together constituted obstacles almost impossible for sailors to navigate and survive. As with so much else, Cosmas's knowledge probably derives from Virgil (*Aeneid* 3.684).

109. Otto I of Bamberg (1102–39); cf. 3.58 and n. 283.

Bořivoj, although he did not obtain what he sought, neverthe-less paid the king the money he had promised. Since all men, how-ever they find themselves, are great or small, as things turn out to be, behold the duke of great name, placed in the custody of one of the smallest men, obeyed his commands and was harassed by humiliating reproaches. Ah! How many cares Bořivoj turned over within his heart![110] How often the tried to appease the king's anger through those first in the palace! But since an empty hand knocks at the king's door in vain[111] but a greased hand breaks the hard-est steel, he promised the king ten thousand marks of silver. Ah, what will a man not give with a sword threatening his neck? Who, found in difficulty, would not cheerfully give whatever he had in exchange for himself? If a king demanded one hundred thousand talents from someone, there would be nothing more stupid than if he did not promise mountains of gold[112] in exchange for his life.

The king, accepting his oath of faith as grace in this matter, re-leased Bořivoj and sent with him one of his followers, who would receive the designated money. When Bořivoj came to Prague, he immediately plundered the holy sanctuaries, collected women's or-naments, and scraped together whatever in Bohemia glittered of gold or silver—and he scarcely gathered seven thousand marks. He gave the king his brother Otto[113] as a hostage for the remainder. Bishop Hermann, arriving in Prague, similarly presented the duke 120 marks of fine gold[114] from the endowment of the holy church. Also five *pallia* of the same church, with fringes, were placed among Jews in Regensburg as surety for five hundred marks of silver.[115] To

110. Virgil *Aeneid* 5.702.

111. Cf. Propertius *Elegies* 4.5.47, ed. and trans. G. P. Goold (Cambridge, Mass.: Harvard University Press, 1990): "Let your janitor be awake to those that give: if someone knocks empty-handed, let him be deaf and continue sleeping on the bar that bolts the door."

112. Cf. 3.15 and n. 62.

113. As usual, Cosmas has used "brother" to designate Přemyslids of the same generation, though Otto was actually Bořivoj's cousin.

114. 2 Par 3:5; the unusual word here is *obrizi,* modifying gold.

115. Cf. Book 1, n. 293, for an explanation of *pallia.* Here they have been offered as collateral for a loan.

be sure, there was no abbot, no provost, no cleric, no layman, no Jew, no merchant, no money changer, no minstrel, who did not unwillingly give something to the duke from his storehouse. But after a few days, Otto slipped into flight and returned to his brother from the king's court—which very much displeased the king.

3.22. 1108. As it often happens where two, a man and woman, sleep in one bed, a third is quickly begotten who might become a man, so the wife of the noble Duke Svatopluk bore and hung from her breasts a tender child.[116] After five months, King Henry sent for him and raised him from the sacred font of baptism and called him by his own name, Henry.[117] Sending the boy back to his father, King Henry sent the whole debt, namely, three thousand talents, to his fellow father[118] Svatopluk, and ordered that he prepare to go with him on campaign against the cruelty of the Hungarians. At the request of certain Germans, he intended to revenge there the murder of crusaders, some of whom that people had put to the sword as a consequence of their bloodthirstiness, others of whom they reduced to servitude.

In September, while Duke Svatopluk tarried with the king in Pannonia next to the burg of Pozsony,[119] with the Poles Bořivoj invaded Bohemia as an enemy. They were put to flight by Vacek and Mutina with garrisons from the fortification that was firmly positioned across the border from Poland. For on his departure, Duke Svatopluk had entrusted every care to these two men and put them above everyone else in order to guard Bohemia. Since Vacek had seen his comrade, Mutina, not fight zealously or resist the enemy manfully on his fortification, certain from this incident that Bořivoj had entered Bohemia by Mutina's counsel, he secret-

116. Sedulius *Paschale Carmen* 1.113.

117. No son of Svatopluk named Henry appears in any other sources. However, Svatopluk's son Václav would control Olomouc from 1126 until his death in 1130; that may be the boy mentioned here, who may not have used his baptismal name. Cf. my *Hastening Toward Prague*, 214–15.

118. See Book 1, n. 158.

119. Today's Bratislava, the capital of Slovakia, then part of Hungary, for which reason I have retained the Hungarian name (which is also closer to Cosmas's "Possen").

ly sent one of his warriors right away to make all this known to Svatopluk.

Vacek furnished another warrior with deceptions and sent him—ready either to work these deceptions or to meet death[120]—to Duke Bořivoj's camp. Coming to the aforesaid Duke Bořivoj, he pretended that he had fled from the camp of Duke Svatopluk. He announced that Svatopluk had already returned from Hungary. And he confirmed by an oath of his faith that Svatopluk was about to fight them in the morning. Terrified by these lies, [Bořivoj and his forces] returned to Poland that same night.

Hearing of these things, King Henry is said to have told his fellow father Svatopluk: "Unless you take revenge against these Poles for your injuries, you will always be considered viler than discarded seaweed."[121]

Meanwhile, Svatopluk, absent himself and inflamed with anger, ground his teeth at the absent Mutina, flashed his eyes, and sighed deeply. He could hardly wait for the day when he might pour out his anger upon him.[122] He reckoned it worthless if he punished Mutina alone. He bound himself with an oath to ominous promises: that by the sword he would put out that whole generation like a lamp.[123] Because he always had some of them in his train before his eyes, he felt pain in his heart but, in his face, he showed himself cheerful to everyone.

Later, Vacek and Mutina met Svatopluk, arriving at the very exit of the forest, next to the fortress of Litomyšl. It was announced three times that day to Mutina by his friends that, unless he fled, without doubt he would lose either his life or his eyes. But since his fate already bore down on him, the words of his friends seemed to him an idle tale.[124] "The man is not strong," he said, "who fears the fate of death."

3.23. As they entered the castle of Vráclav, after the full light of morning, Svatopluk summoned all the magnates to a meeting.

120. Cf. above, n. 92.
122. Ps 78:6.
124. Cf. Book 2, n. 29.

121. Cf. Book 1, n. 270.
123. Jb 21:17.

When they had gathered into one, like a lion emerging from his cage, standing in the theater roaring, with his mane erect, expecting a meal, so Svatopluk, entering the hall, sat in the middle before the block of an oven. Burning with anger more than the oven (which was kindled with a sevenfold flame), looking around at everyone and regarding Mutina with sharp eyes, he opened his indignant lips and spoke:[125] "O hateful clan and offspring odious to the gods! O vile sons of the Vršovici, familiar enemies[126] of our stock [*genus*]! How could I ever cut out of my memory that you made sport over my great-grandfather Jaromír on Mt. Veliz, and that you have always made laughingstocks of us?[127] How could I forget, that by a malicious trick you and your brother Božej killed my brother Břetislav, who was like an extraordinary star in the whole world of dukes?[128] Did my brother Bořivoj deserve it, that he reigned under your power and was obedient to you in all things as if your own purchased property? But through pride inborn to you, you did not sustain the duke's moderation. And as for me, you disturbed me with your customary craftiness, until, acquiescing to your depraved advice, sinning, I sinned greatly against my brother Bořivoj, since I deprived him of the throne. This is the one thing that pains me and will pain me forever. Even still, even so, hear, O my magnates, what this son of iniquity and source of all impiety, what this Mutina has done! Recently, when I was going with you on campaign, I left him as protector and ruler of this land, second after me. But that good man, pretending that he was going hunting, was not afraid to go to Poland at night, to the fortress of Świń, in order to take counsel with his uncle Němoj about how to expel me from the throne."

A disorderly murmuring arose. Their assent kindled the spirit of the duke, burning with anger, so that it burned more and more. Then the duke went outside, giving a look to the lictor[129] standing nearby—his accomplice in this enterprise. At once he attacked

<hr/>

125. Ovid *Metamorphoses* 1.181.   126. Cf. Book 1, n. 266.
127. Cf. 1.34.   128. Cf. 2.13.

129. This is an unusual, anachronistic word. By it, I think Cosmas is indicating some kind of ducal official, rather than one of the high-ranking men in the assembly.

Mutina, who had feared nothing of the sort. O the marvelous patience of the *comes!* For two blows he sat unmovable; when he tried to rise at the third, he suffered capital punishment.

In the same hour and in that very hall, Vnislav, Domaša, and the two sons of Mutina were captured. One man, Neuša, who was from another kin [*natio*] but nevertheless a great familiar of Mutina, seeing what was happening, fled. He would have gotten away, fleeing through the orchards outside the burg, if his red tunic had not rendered him visible. Captured, he was deprived of his eyes and his penis on the spot.

And just as often happens when a bloody wolf attacks a sheep in the sheepfold, he rages, kills, and does not calm his frenzy nor cease from slaughter before all the sheep are killed[130]—so Svatopluk, having forgotten one man's slaughter, burned in anger and ordered that everyone of that kin, without regard for age, should suffer capital punishment without any delay of time. With the army of *comites* standing nearby, he said: "Whoever does not shrink to fulfill my commands, a heavy mass of gold will be given to him. Whoever kills Božej and his son, let him receive a hundredfold[131] and possess their inheritance." No less quickly than the winds flew out when their king, Aeolus, pierced with his spear through the side of the mountain[132] under which they were held imprisoned, the magnates Vacula, Hermann, Krása, and many others leapt on their horses and flew on the swift course of fate to Božej and his sons. The rest ran in different directions and tracked them throughout the land, in order to remove that whole clan from their midst.

3.24. Meanwhile, Božej was in the village of Libice, alas, unaware of his fate. While he sat with his wife and son at the midday meal, a boy stood by, who said: "Behold, Lord, many men come running, hurrying through the field without order." But Božej said: "They are returning from campaign. Let them come to us with

130. Cf. 2.9.
131. Mt 19:29.
132. Virgil *Aeneid* 1.81; Cosmas's verbal borrowings are drawn from two lines in the middle of several stanzas relating the story of Aeolus.

God's blessing." While these things were said, behold, grim Krása opened his mouth and said, with his unsheathed sword flashing: "Come out, scoundrel! Come out, you who, wrongly counseled, killed my relative, Thomas, without cause during Lent." Rising, Božej's son Bořut said: "What are you doing, brothers? If we are commanded to be seized, we can be seized without arms or tumult." Heedless, he took a sword down to the hilt through the middle of his belly. Without delay, his father took the sword, still dripping with his son's blood, to the throat.[133] But those invaders, like those who storm burgs, snatched away immense treasures. As Cato says: "What took a long time to acquire will be given away in a short time."[134] From such riches not one rag was left to cover the bodies. Without coffins or funeral rites Božej and his son Bořut were thrown naked into a ditch, like cattle, on 27 October.

It was not permitted for me to know how many heads were given to death from that clan, because they were not killed on one day or in one place. Some, led into the market, were slaughtered like brute animals;[135] others were beheaded on Petřín hill; and many were murdered in the streets[136] or in private. What should I say about the death of Mutina's sons, whose death seemed crueler than any death? They were little boys of good disposition, with faces worth looking at, lovable in appearance, of the like that no skilled craftsman would be able to express in white ivory, nor a painter on a wall. We saw them pitifully dragged into the market, frequently crying out: "Mother! Mother!" when the bloody butcher killed them both under his arm with a small knife, like piglets. Everyone scattered, striking their breasts,[137] in order not to see the butcher performing such a cruel misdeed.

The rest who survived from that clan concealed themselves by

133. Ibid., 10.907, where a father chooses to welcome the sword after the death of his son.

134. *Disticha Catonis* 2.17, verbatim from the second line of the two-line *distich*: "Seek to spend in moderation. When expenses abound, / what took a long time to acquire will be given away in a short time."

135. Regino, *Chronicon*, 118.   136. 1 Mc 2:9.

137. Virgil *Aeneid* 12:155.

flight, some to Poland, others fleeing to Pannonia. Although we have ample material for writing about their destruction and separation, let us return to the chronicle where we digressed a bit,[138] lest we seem to be setting out a tragedy, like a song for a goat.[139]

3.25. This took place after King Henry had returned from the burg of Pozsony, having lifted the siege. Not long afterward, King Coloman of Hungary, wishing to revenge the injuries done to him by Duke Svatopluk, entered Moravia and began to lay waste to it as an enemy. For at the time when King Henry, intent upon military arms, surrounded the burg of Pozsony from every side with a siege, the aforesaid duke with his Czechs, whatever there was on this side of the River Wag, they left nothing unburned—from Trenčin as far as where the Wag flows into the Danube. Often, whenever the duke seized lookouts and spies sent by the Hungarian king, he also deprived them of nose and sight. Likewise, one day, the aforesaid king sent more than one thousand men from chosen warriors in the direction of Pozsony, in order to either capture the guard searching for fodder by ambush or attack the incautious Germans at night. Duke Svatopluk, knowing in advance where they hid among the reeds, attacked suddenly. He ordered everyone to a man, like fish caught in a large thrown net,[140] some killed and others hung on a horse-shaped rack. He granted life to a few, having received much money.

When Duke Svatopluk heard that King Coloman had entered Moravia because of these deeds and others like them with which he had afflicted the Hungarians, he hastily gathered an army from both Bohemia and Moravia. While hastening through the forest in the dark night, impatient to come upon the enemy secretly and engage them in battle in the morning, among so many thousands of warriors hastening with him—an amazing thing—a cut branch

138. Cicero *Nature of the Gods* 3.60.

139. Cosmas is here referring to the origins of ancient Greek tragedy in a song sung for the prize of a goat, which is reflected in the word's etymology. Cf. Isidore *Etymologies* 7.7.5, citing Horace *Ars poetica* 220; either of these may be Cosmas's source.

140. Cf. Mt 12:47.

badly overhanging was thrust forcefully into the pupil of the eye of the duke himself. With his eye almost torn out at the same time as the twig, the army returned home sorrowful, carrying the duke half-alive, on 12 November.

3.26. 1109. On 14 February, since a great cold shivered and all the waters were very much frozen, Duke Svatopluk, now healed from the wound to his torn-out eye, immediately gathered an army again. Hastening for three uninterrupted days and three nights, he entered Hungary. With none of them knowing about it, he approached the burg of Nitra from an unexpected direction with an army. He would have rushed inside if the sentinels, who are always standing guard there, had not closed the gates. After plundering and burning its suburb, they met people returning, fleeing to the aforesaid burg, on the march in chariots and on horses. Duke Svatopluk and his army gathered them in the field like bundles of hay, burned their villages, and thoroughly laid waste to that whole region—and then returned home cheerful, laden with an abundance of cattle and other things.

3.27. In the same year the most excellent King Henry, remembering his anger and displeasure at the duke of Poland, named Bolesław, and remembering also the promise he promised his fellow father[141] Svatopluk at the burg of Pozsony (as we reported above [3.22]), took the road through Saxony. He led with him Bavarians, Alemanni, eastern Franks, and those from around the Rhine below Cologne up to the western boundaries of the empire. Nor were the Saxons, harder than rocks,[142] missing, with their long spears. After the Czechs joined them, they entered Poland in the month of September.

After they arranged a siege around its first fortress, Glogów, they laid waste to Poland on both sides of the River Oder, from the aforesaid fortress to the castle of Ryczyn, and then returned to camp again with much booty.[143] Since the king had now ar-

141. Cf. Book 1, n. 158.
142. For the same phrase, cf. 2.11.
143. For a previous campaign in the same region, cf. 3.1.

ranged things there so that he could dismiss Duke Svatopluk and his army in the morning, they drew out the whole day with royal business until nightfall.

Meanwhile, a certain warrior, bolder than the boldest men, was present in the camp. As we heard from people telling it afterward, he was sent by John, son of Čsta from the Vršovici clan. He was ready either[144] to acquire his share of fame from bold deeds, or to lose this life at the same time as a duke's death. He stood under a spreading beech[145] along the road which led to the royal court, watching the duke's return as he returned from the king's court. Now at the first twilight of the night, when he saw the duke accompanied by a huge train of compliant warriors, he spurred his horse and slowly mixed himself into the middle of the army. He hurled a javelin with all the effort of his strength between the duke's shoulder blades, and so pierced him through the midriff with death-dealing iron.[146] As soon as he touched the ground, Svatopluk breathed out his spirit—namely, on 21 September.

Not without grief the crowd lifted his lifeless body and lamented. Weeping, they brought it back to his camp. In camp there was a great commotion throughout the night. Wandering here and there, the common folk fled and returned again, until Burchard, sent from the king, barely checked their uncertain movement.

Come morning, the king arrived to grieve for his fellow father. He granted to all the Czechs present that they should elect as their duke whomever they wanted from the sons of their princes. Then, as he was mourning, Vacek asked with tears welling up[147] that they choose Otto, the brother of the murdered prince, as their duke. The king instantly praised him, and throughout the camp the foolish people cried *Kyrie eleison* three times.[148]

Without delay and with only a few knowing, Dětříšek, son of Buza, ran at full speed and at dawn on the fourth day led to Prague Otto, whom Vacek and everyone from Moravia bustled to

---

144. Cf. n. 92, above.   145. Virgil *Eclogues* 1.1.
146. Ovid *Metamorphoses* 6.251, verbatim.   147. Virgil *Aeneid* 3.492.
148. Cf. Book 1, n. 198.

raise to the summit of the princely seat. Since they tried to bring it about without the consent of the Bohemians and the bishop, their audacity was frustrated, and the oaths given earlier in the midst of council were recited. For when they enthroned Svatopluk as duke, all the Bohemians had confirmed with oaths that after his death Vladislav, if he lived, would be raised to the throne.

3.28. Amid such movements of the people, the counsel of Bishop Hermann and *Comes* Fabian, who held the castellany of the burg of Vyšehrad—men who surpassed the rest in both rank and wisdom—prevailed. With all their effort they brought it about: that the oaths would be considered inviolate; and that, with everyone agreeing, Vladislav would obtain the right of the principate by the law they adopted. He was raised to the throne with the sun tarrying in the ninth part of Libra [25 September]. Concerning his virtues and glory, it seems to me that I should be silent in the meantime, while he abides in this life, so that we neither fall into flattery nor, when we write less in his praise, fall into the offense of disparagement. For this reason a certain man warns: "Praise the duke's virtue, but after the duration of his life."[149]

When Bořivoj heard that his younger brother Vladislav had obtained the throne of the realm after the death of Svatopluk, coming down from Poland without delay, he went to Sorbia, to Wiprecht, his brother-in-law through this sister. Relying on Wiprecht's counsel and aid, and also on the promised support of certain perfidious men of ours, he entered the burg of Prague with day dawning on the vigil of the Lord's Nativity and no one resisted him—alas, to the ruin and impoverishment of many.

3.29. At this unexpected turn of events, the townsmen were afraid, most disturbed and uncertain which party they should follow amid these sudden accidents of fortune. Many, whose lot was more fortunate, left their belongings with their dear offspring in the burg, fled, and could not decide which camp to follow. Many,

149. This sounds like it should be a coyly unattributed citation from authority, but if so, I cannot determine its source.

eager for change,[150] rejoiced, ran riot, and behaved insolently toward those fleeing—since they despoiled their goods with Duke
Bořivoj's permission. But Bishop Hermann, apprehended in his
palace, as if hedged in by enemies, was kept safe, shut up by his
own peaceful men—for they knew that he would gladly have run
away, if he was able to do so.

Among the wavering fears of the people, Fabian, castellan of
Vyšehrad (to which he had returned), uncertain, preferred to hear
about rather than to see the heinous things at hand. Departing
from the burg committed to him, having left communal affairs behind, he had a care for himself alone. Conquered by melancholy,
standing, he said these many words: "Woe to you, Bohemia! Not
so very large, still you are communal and subject to many lords.
Now there are twenty little lords from the master's lineage and of
the manly sex, if I am not mistaken. For this reason Lucan, the
clear-sighted poet, is said to have said: 'Power increased too much
burdens not the lord but the people. Whatever folly dukes commit, the common folk pay for.'"[151] Fabian spoke and then, having
left the burg of Vyšehrad behind (as was said above), he tarried in
the villages in its vicinity, doubtful of the uncertainty of fortune.

Meanwhile, talk, swifter than the wind or a thunderbolt,[152]
filled all the burgs with diverse rumors[153] and throughout the land
there was a great commotion among the people. There were many
in whom the good arts were lacking, who rejoiced in the change in
things, who wandered here and there in villages and laid waste to
them, while they awaited the uncertain events of fortune. But there
were others, in whom there was a loftier mind and a purer faith,
who headed for the princely seat in the burg of Prague. What did

150. Sallust *War with Catiline* 28.4 (p. 49, where the translation is rather loose: "ripe
for revolution").

151. The first sentence is modified from Lucan *Pharsalia* 3.150: "A slave's poverty
grieves not the slave but his master"; cf. 1.33, where Cosmas cites Lucan's words verbatim. The second sentence is not from Lucan but is adapted from Horace *Epistles*
1.2.14: "Whatever folly their kings commit the Achaeans must pay for."

152. Virgil *Aeneid* 5.319.

153. Ibid., 7.549.

they do? Scarcely ignorant they rushed into an open pit and willy-nilly they engaged Duke Bořivoj in the game of fate.[154] Receiving them courteously, he bound them by oaths and many promises. Entrusting them to *Comes* Hrabiše, that same day Bořivoj moved himself with others to the safer walls of the burg of Vyšehrad. In the morning, at prime, on the very day of the feast, Bořivoj returned to Prague and was received with a great procession of clergy. He heard mass there and returned to the aforesaid burg, Vyšehrad.

3.30. That same night, Svatopluk's brother Otto and *Comes* Vacek came from the castle at Hradec with three contingents of warriors and made their camp along the Rokytnice stream. Come morning, they attacked the fortress at Vyšehrad and blocked all the roads on every side with guards, so that no one was able to go in or out to help Bořivoj.

Duke Vladislav had previously arranged to celebrate Christmas in the aforesaid burg, Hradec. But, summoned in the meantime by King Henry, he had be present at a royal synod in Regensburg on the octave of Christmas. So he ordered *Comes* Vacek to assist Otto, whom he had invited to the feast, to set the festivities in motion as assiduously as possible. Hurrying on account of the king's order, the duke himself remained for two feast days in the burg at Plzeň with the rest of the *comites*. But on the third day, when he realized what was happening in the burg of Prague, he put off and disregarded the king's orders. On the Feast of St. John the Apostle and Evangelist, he flew toward the walls of the aforesaid burg with those men who had been with him in his court. But Vladislav found the gates closed. He saw men armed[155] and ready to fight with him. To those standing on the high ramparts,[156] he began saying: "I come to you as a peaceable man.[157] Recognize me and open the gates to your lord." When no one responded to the duke's words, very angry and much threatened by them, he turned to cross the Brusnice stream.

154. Cf. Lucan *Pharsalia* 6.7.   155. Virgil *Aeneid* 2.485.
156. Ibid., 9.664.   157. Cf. Gn 42:11.

When he ascended the brow of the hill,[158] he saw from a distance a long line of armed men in the field. Among them, Václav, son of Wiprecht,[159] was coming to aid Bořivoj. Vladislav sent one of his satraps to discover whether they came in opposition or were peaceable. When each had recognized the other in turn (through an intermediary), the aforesaid youth became very frightened and wheeled his step around no differently than if he had trod upon a hardy serpent hiding in the brambles.[160] Calling his men together in one company, Václav said: "No place lies open to us for flight or to hide those of us unwilling to enter into the game of battle. Make it only so that they do not wage this battle with impunity." He spoke, and they unfurled a banner and cried out to Saint Mary to aid them. But the duke, through his inborn goodness, always detesting civil wars and caring little for them and their noise, wanted to pass them by.

3.31. Then Dětříšek, son of Buza, fomenter of evil, inciter of crime, said: "If the injuries done to you by men less worthy do not sting or touch you, perhaps you do not know, as you should know, whether we be alive in the flesh or dead." To this, Duke Vladislav said: "This very hour you will see if this will be ascribed not to grace but to cowardice. My sword will do again here what it did so many times there." As quickly as he spoke, having snatched his shield, the duke leapt first some distance from the vanguard, thundered first against the opposite battle line, and surrounded by

158. Lk 4:29.

159. Wiprecht II of Groitzsch had two sons by his wife, Judith, the daughter of King Vratislav: Wiprecht III (d. 1116) and Henry (d. 1135). Given their mother's Czech origins, either might have also been known by the name Václav, but probably the elder, Wiprecht III, is meant here and in the next two chapters. I am grateful to Jonathan Lyon for his advice on this point.

160. Cf. Virgil *Aeneid* 2.378. In this instance there are no direct verbal borrowings but the inspiration is clear. In Fairclough's translation: "He spoke, and at once . . . knew that he had fallen into the midst of foes. He was dazed, and drawing back, checked his foot and voice. As one who has crushed a serpent unseen amid the rough briars, when stepping firmly on the ground, and in sudden terror shrinks back as it rises in wrath and puffs out its purple neck; so Androgeos, affrighted at the sight, was drawing away" (1:341).

enemies—like a bristly boar[161] hemmed in by a crowd of dogs—drove away these and threw down those until, completely covered in human blood, he came as a victor to his camp, now positioned at the base of Vyšehrad castle—having lost one *comes*, Vacena. There was a huge cry of joy in the camp, because they received the duke back safe from the battle.

But the son of Wiprecht—like a serpent whom a shepherd broke in half with his step and, lifting its head but having lost its tail, scarcely creeps[162]—the aforesaid boy, having lost some of his men and with others gravely wounded, very sad at heart, approached the steep ramparts[163] of Prague. The affair was like an omen: as many as were wounded, they all died. Why do we marvel, if on account of the single crime of Pelops's sons the sun covered up and overclouded its rays over the city of Argos,[164] when so many worse crimes were committed between these two neighboring burgs, Prague and Vyšehrad? Crueler than a civil war is it when a son challenges his father with a cymbal or a father his son to a duel. It is no different when someone challenges a brother-in-law to single combat, nor different when someone binds and polishes his brother like a captured opponent, nor when he slays his relative or kills his friend as an enemy—wherever a foul deed might be done or an abominable crime committed. O Jesus, good Lord, those things you suffer in man! How patiently you look forward to not having those whom you must punish according to their merits.

161. Ibid., 7.17.

162. Cf. ibid., 5.273, again a strong allusion with no direct quotation of key words: "Just as often, when caught on the highway, a serpent which a brazen wheel has crossed aslant, or with blow of a heavy stone a wayfarer has crushed and left half-dead, vainly tries to escape and trails its long coils; part defiant, his eyes ablaze and his hissing neck raised aloft; part, maimed by the wound, holding him back, as he twists in coils and twines himself upon his limbs ..."

163. Ibid., 12.745.

164. In the myth, Atreus and Thyestes, the sons of Pelops, were exiled for murdering their stepbrother in order to seize the throne of Olympia; this was part of a multigenerational curse on Pelops himself and involved subsequent crimes associated with the family of Atreus. It is not clear why Cosmas associates them with Argos, however, nor can I find the source for a specific story about the sun.

3.32. Meanwhile, Duke Vladislav had long since dispatched *Co-mites* Hermann and Sežima to King Henry, who was by chance celebrating the next Christmas in Bamberg. Promising him five hundred marks of silver, Vladislav humbly asked that Henry see fit—either by himself or through his messengers—to restore to him the duchy taken by his brother Bořivoj, at the instigation of Wiprecht. Although at that time the king was very angry with Wiprecht, nevertheless he burned more with love for the suggested payment.

Henry immediately assembled an army and entered Bohemia at the beginning of the year 1110, on the first day of January. Dispatching Margraves Diepold and Berengar, he ordered that Bořivoj and his brother Vladislav; Bishop Hermann; the son of Wiprecht; and the rest of the elders of Bohemia meet him in the bishop's court at Rokycany—a peace having been established between them. When they arrived, Bořivoj and the son of Wiprecht were seized without any hearing on the king's command. The bishop's case was proved to be just, the king's palm having been greased with gold. After this, with Duke Vladislav commanding it, among all the supporters of Bořivoj some were deprived of sight and property, others despoiled only of essential goods. The rest—those who were able to escape under cover of darkness—fled to Soběslav, the son of King Vrat-islav, in Poland. Among them, John, son of Čsta from the Vršovici lineage (of whom we spoke above [3.27]), was deprived of his sight and his nose at Vacek's order. Přivitan, who was considered senior in the burg of Prague, was likewise caught in this same sedition. A huge, mangy dog, drunk on yesterday's broth, was tied to his shoulders. Seized by the beard, Přivitan was dragged three times around the market, with the dog barking and shitting on his bearer, and the herald proclaiming: "This is the sort of honor the man will bear who breaks an oath given to Duke Vladislav." Then, with everyone in the market watching, his beard was cut on a tablet and he was sent away toward Poland, into exile.

3.33. Still, faithless men and sowers of discord[165] were not for

165. Cf. Prv 6:19.

this reason lacking—men who sowed such discord between brothers of the same mind, namely, Vladislav and Otto, that each feared the other's plots. For this reason Otto, invited by his brother, was afraid to come for Easter. After Easter, on the first day of May, at the third summons, Otto, defended by a garrison of his warriors, came to his brother Vladislav in the agreed-upon village, called Týnec-on-the-Mountains. There, having debated various matters all day, and having given and received oaths between them (as was observed [by me]), they were reconciled.

But since the same Otto had banned us from the market in the village of Sekyrkostel, which his father and mother had given to us, the servants of God and Saint Václav, to hold in perpetuity for the good of their souls, I was sent on behalf of the brothers before the duke and his *comites* to complain about Otto, so that he might not put out the lamp[166] of his parents which he ought instead to light. He said, "I am not putting out the lamp of my parents, but I do not want what I know was given specifically to you to be in the bishop's power. So now, I restore the aforesaid market not to the bishop or to any other person, but to the servants of God and Saint Václav." After the market had thus been restored to us before the duke and his *comites*, Otto returned to Moravia the next day.

3.34. On 13 July of the same year, a general synod was announced to all the princes of the land of the Czechs, at the court of Sadská, which is located in the midst of meadows. Also summoned to it, Otto came incautiously with only a few men, very much trusting in the oaths recently given and received between [him and Vladislav]. There [at Sadská], rising at dawn on the third day—all the business having already been decided—Otto ordered the quartermasters in his camp to prepare the necessities for returning home. He stood up at court to receive permission from his brother.[167] Why do I tarry with so many words? Why do I not say quickly what was done without delay? On the spot Otto, the most ferocious lion, was seized by Duke Vladislav, the gentlest lamb. When his advisors urged him to deprive Otto of sight, the duke said: "I do not want

166. See above, n. 123.
167. Actually his cousin; cf. above, n. 60.

in any way to be compared to the Polish Duke Bolesław, who summoned his brother Zbigniew with evil intentions, under an oath
of loyalty, and deprived him of his eyes on the third day.[168] I do
not want to enter into permanent discord with my brother. But I
want to chastise him so that, having been chastised, he will realize
and understand, and his successors will also learn, that the land of
Moravia and its rulers should always be under the power of the
prince of the Bohemians, as ordained by our grandfather, Břetislav
of pious memory, who first subjugated it to his rule."[169]

But what is stronger than a strong man? Behold, Otto, a strong
man among his armed retinue, danced. Bound with chains, he went
with a happy face and pleasant visage as if invited to a banquet, until he was thrust into prison in the burg of Vyšehrad. There, he is
reported to have said to the warriors watching him on their rounds:
"Friends with lying tongues are like bees: honey flows from their
mouths, but the tail on the other end stings. Believe me to have
been deceived by such a trick. Yet it is necessary to bear the blows
of changeable fortune. My brother did not do these things to me.
The evil man Vacek wanted it thus; this was done by Prostěj, the
judge. Whom I if I live—but I restrain myself."[170] Not long after
this, having rebuilt the castle at Křivoklát in the forest next to the
River Mže, Otto was handed over to be imprisoned there by armed
warriors for nearly three years.

3.35. In the same year, Duke Vladislav and the entire common
folk of the Czechs were celebrating the Feast of Saint Václav, their
patron, with pleasure and enjoyment, when a messenger approached
the duke and reported this: "You are feasting here in tranquility
and safety, but your brother Soběslav and Bolesław, duke of the
Poles, are plundering this land and seizing people like abundant
heaps of harvest. I alone scarcely escaped to tell you these things.[171]
Hasten to the road;[172] close now your storerooms and forsake your

---

168. It is not entirely clear, from this remark or from other sources, when Zbigniew's blinding occurred. *Deeds of the Princes of the Poles*, 274n1.

169. Cf. 1.40.

170. See 2.24 and n. 149 for this exact phrase.

171. Jb 1:19.   172. Valerius Flaccus *Argonautica* 7.265.

banquets. Mars calls you to battle. Tomorrow a thousand thousand armed enemies will be here."

Rising from the feast immediately and having quickly assembled an army, they met up on this side of the Cidlina, next to the region called Lučice. On the other side of the same stream, marching along without rapine or burning, the battalions of Poles proceeded until, arriving near the fortress of Oldříš, they approached the water of the Elbe River. From there they sent to Duke Vladislav with deception, saying: "We do not carry hostile lances[173] nor do we come to fight, but rather to make peace between you and your brother. If you do not want to assent to our warnings, tomorrow we will cross the river and afterward, the rest. Amen." Duke Vladislav answered this with a few words: "In this year, there will not, I think, be peace without much blood, because no one comes armed to a bond of peace. You will cross the river, and after 'the rest' there will be no 'amen.' You will cross the river but not go back unpunished. 'The rest' you mention, I will do. Do whatever 'the rest' you want." Immediately, wrongly believing the words and tricks of the enemy, Vladislav crossed the river with his men that night before sunrise and approached along the banks of same river from the opposite side. But the Poles, when they saw their tricks had worked, made their attack on the land, laying waste to it with fire and rapine. Burdened with enormous booty, they camped next to the bridges at Křivec. Because they were very weary from that night, our men were unable to cross back over quickly and stood stupefied.

3.36. Duke Vladislav understood himself to have been deceived through deception and perceived the spirits of some of his men to be disinclined toward fighting. Wrath, indignation, and pride in his prowess was kindled in the duke.[174] Powerful—like the trumpet[175]

173. There is a rhyming wordplay here that the English "hostile lances" effaces: "Non nos *hostilia* portamus *hastilia*."
174. Ps 2:13, combined with Virgil *Aeneid* 5.455; see also West's prose translation, 118: "pride in his prowess."
175. Is 58:1.

which rouses warriors to battle—his speech incited their sluggish minds thus: "O Czechs," he said, "once renowned in fame across land and sea, distinguished in virtues, exceptional in triumphs, now your tributaries, to whom you were an object of terror, insult you, still breathing, and lay waste your land. Do swords of linden hang on your thighs? Do the Poles alone have swords of iron? Why do we still live? O shame on us and our descendants forever! Behold your Ceres[176] reduced to ashes. Your homes produce smoke up to the clouds. Vulcan rages[177] over the whole surface of the land. And still your hearts, more icy than ice,[178] do not burn? Or if your heart melts,[179] what of your stomach, which now grows weak from hunger: why is it not inflamed with zeal for justice? Do feminine lamentation and ululation, which reaches the high stars[180] with hoarse cries, not move you? Who does not feel with a bitter heart the sobbing of the nursing women, or the groans of a pregnant woman or of a wife carried off by pagans? Who refrains from tears,[181] when he sees his crying babies killed like lambs or cast aside from their mother's breast?[182] Would it hurt less if this pain had not been inflicted by men less worthy? To be sure, if I have only three shields, I will not suffer uncertain fortune to go untested by battle today." Immediately the duke himself together with the whole army—every single one—stood on the bank and then, seeking not the shallow areas now but jumping in without order, swam across the water. Thus they chose to die for the fatherland.[183] Grief and the injuries inflicted gave them strength. They made haste to disrupt, as much as they could, the joyous triumph of the enemy, even at the cost of their lives.

176. See Book 1, n. 39.

177. See Book 2, n. 259.

178. This might be a paraphrased allusion to Ovid *Ex ponto* 3.4.33.

179. Ez 21:7.

180. Although phrases like "reaches to the stars" appear in many Latin texts, worded variously, the particular words here *(sydera tangit)* derive from Sedulius *Paschale Carmen* 4.56.

181. Virgil *Aeneid* 2.8.   182. Ibid., 6.428.

183. See Book 2, n. 200.

The next day, the oft-mentioned duke of Poland [tried to] cross the River Trutina. Because the river was not passable to them anywhere, Bolesław ordered some of his men, those with the booty and those who were weak, to go on ahead. With his horsemen ready to defend them, he himself stood fast, ready to resist, in a place that seemed to him suitable for battle. Perceiving all this, Dětříšek, son of Buza—whom we have often mentioned above [3.27 and 3.31]—withdrew to one place with the warriors who were at his side and said to them: "My brothers and fellow warriors, whoever has any little piece of trembling or fearful flesh in him, he needs to either cut it out first or desert our army. For the man who does not know how beautiful it is to die in arms[184] is worth less than seaweed."[185] When he saw that their spirits were eager for battle and that there were almost a hundred warriors—like a wolf who seeks to attack the flock secretly from his hiding place[186]— he suddenly attacked the enemy from the exposed side with great force. There, almost a thousand adversaries having been thrown to the ground (it is said), like a raging tiger the aforesaid warrior [attacked] the most closely pressed formations of the enemy.[187] Opposing them from right and left, Dětříšek mowed them down with a sharp sword as if they were ears of tender corn until, overwhelmed by an immense force of weapons, he fell on the huge pile of the slain. But the Czechs who fought on the opposite face of Mars,[188] alas surrendered their backs, having escaped in unaccustomed flight. Soběslav, with the Poles, achieved an unfortunate victory—unfortunate because it was [a war] worse than civil.[189] This slaughter took place on 8 October. The brothers Nožislav and Držikraj, sons of Lubomír, were killed, as were many others.

3.37. IIII. With Queen Svatava bustling between her sons and

184. Virgil *Aeneid* 2.317.
185. See Book 1, n. 270.
186. An allusion, perhaps, to Virgil *Aeneid* 2.355, though with no direct verbal borrowing outside the wolf comparison per se.
187. See Book 1, n. 138.
188. See Book 2, n. 201.
189. A favorite quotation from Lucan *Pharsalia* 1.1; cf. 2.45.

with Bishop Hermann mediating—and with even *Comes* Vacek favoring it, although contrary to his health—Duke Vladislav recalled his brother Soběslav from Poland and granted him the burg of Žatec with the whole province pertaining to it.

3.38. 1112. According to the decrees of the kings of old, at the will of King Henry IV [V], Duke Vladislav sent his nephew, Břetislav's like-named son, to Rome with an armed legion of three hundred shields. But since the king had already long before proceeded on, the aforesaid boy, crossing the Bavarian Alps with his men, found the king in the burg of Verona and celebrated Pentecost with him there.

In the month of August, the king entered Rome with a vast multitude of men of different nations and languages, ready to receive the imperial regalia according the custom of kings. But Pope Paschal[190] did not wish to fulfill the king's desire, judging Henry disreputable because he had once risen against his father. On the spot, the king ordered Paschal seized and, with a sword thrust at his throat, began to threaten death. The pope, fearing death, consented to his desire. On the third day, the two having made peace, the king was called and ordained "emperor" and "august" by the favorable acclamation of the whole Roman people and clergy. The next day the new emperor sent so many gifts to the pope that they were believed to satisfy human greed in proportion to his rank. These things thus completed, the emperor returned to Bavaria and our men returned uninjured to their homeland.

3.39. 1113. It was reported to Soběslav by certain men, who freely report groundless and uncertain things, that his brother Duke Vladislav wanted to capture him, with *Comes* Vacek suggesting and counseling it. He answered them: "Either I will die, or, before I will be captured, the man who set such things in motion will die." At that very hour a messenger arrived, summoning Soběslav to his brother's court—for which reason he believed the matter reported more likely to be true. Taking almost three hundred warriors, he

190. Paschal II (1099–1118), though the events described here took place in February 1111, rather differently than Cosmas claims. See Weinfurter, *Salian Century*, 171.

went to his brother's court with a few of them and ordered the rest, with their weapons, to remain at a distance not farther than one stade.[191] There, having greeted his brother and taken a meal, the duke went on ahead, bidding his brother to follow him to the burg of Vyšehrad. They were not far, just about ten stades distant from the burg. Then Soběslav sent for *Comes* Vacek and asked to speak with him while walking together on the road. Having done that and having exchanged very few words on the road, [Soběslav's retinue] pierced the heedless and innocent *Comes* Vacek through the midriff, from both sides and behind his back, with three death-dealing wounds[192]—on 18 June.

Soběslav returned to his men and immediately took to the road, wishing to cross into Poland through Sorbia, for he was very much afraid of his brother's presence. When he crossed the forest, Erkembert, castellan of Donin, a man full of the deceitful cunning of Sorbia,[193] met him. Feigning many things amicably, he promised Soběslav that he would obtain for him every justice through the emperor's grace, if he would come before him. With evil intent, he humbly invited Soběslav to come up to the fortress with a few men to eat together. (For at that time the aforesaid castle was under the emperor's power.) Soon, during the meal, an armed band having been brought in, Erkembert closed the door on his guest. After a few days, he sent him in chains toward Saxony, to a certain very strong castled named . . . ,[194] handing him over to his cleric, Ulrich, to be guarded. Of the companions in Soběslav's retinue, seeing their lord captured by deceit, some fled to Poland and some returned to Bohemia.

After one month, through Christ's mercy, Soběslav was released at night by the same cleric [Ulrich]. A rope was tied to a column between the lattice of the upper house, and thus he was let down by the wall in a basket.[195] The aforesaid cleric likewise escaped

191. See Book 1, n. 93.
192. See above, n. 146.
193. This remark presumably alludes to the story of During in 1.13.
194. The name of this castle is missing from all the manuscripts.
195. Echoing Acts 9:25 and 2 Cor 11:33, on being let down in a basket by the wall.

by means of the same rope, together with a certain warrior Conrad, son of Řivin. An accomplice to the deed, Conrad had also brought horses to below the wall that same night. Just as a little bird released from a cage flees and seeks the forest,[196] so, having escaped, those men headed for Poland in swift flight.

In December of the same year, Duke Vladislav released his brother Otto from chains and returned to him half the province of the whole of Moravia, with his burgs, i.e., the province he had previously held after the death of his brother Svatopluk.[197]

3.40. 1114. In the month of March, with Lord Otto commanding it, Prostěj and his brother-in-law Vacek, known as "the Gentle" (about whom we spoke above [3.35]),[198] were both deprived of sight.

In the same year, taking certain Poles with him, Soběslav approached the castle of Kłodzko and attempted, by pleas and promises, to convince the citizens to open the burg's gates. When they did not agree but instead resisted manfully, the aforesaid youth, inflamed by anger, set fire to the palace which was located next to the wall. With the wind pressing from the other side, the ramparts at the top of the tower, which by chance stood before the walls and near the wall, caught fire. Then the townsmen, very troubled, having no hope of salvation now, asked to be given a peaceful right hand in exchange for life, only unharmed and one at a time. Peace having been granted to them, they scarcely evaded the danger of death, as the whole burg was burned and utterly destroyed.

3.41. 1115. In January, Duke Bolesław of the Poles sent written letters of entreaty to his uncle Vladislav,[199] with these words: "If my entreaties have any value or are any compensation to you, and

196. An allusion to Boethius, *Consolation of Philosophy*, book 3, meter 2.18–26.

197. This is the territory centered at Olomouc, first conceded to Břetislav I's son, Otto, the father of this Otto. Note here that Cosmas conceives Moravia as a unity, divided simply into halves and, for the south, half again (thus Cosmas views them as quarters), when granted to a Přemyslid *dyarch* or *tetrarch* with its appurtenant burgs.

198. In 3.35 Prostěj is mentioned together with a man who must be this Vacek, and not the Vacek whom Soběslav's men just killed (in the previous chapter, 3.39).

199. Bolesław's mother, Judith (2.36), was Vladislav's older half-sister (2.20).

if they can bring about a state of indulgence for your brother Soběslav, I believe that the bond of our peace and friendship will be strong and enduring. For if I can persuade you on account of our enmity, surely you ought to make it—insofar as it is not fitting now for *me* to intercede further—so that the two of you, whom one mother carried in her womb under one heart, might be in accord? Indeed, when Saint Peter inquired whether he should forgive his brother seven times on the day of his sinning, the Lord said, 'Not only seven times, but even seventy times seven times.'[200] Therefore, let us be inspired by this example, so that we may forgive our brothers so many times that they may not be able to sin against us as many times." Compelled by these examples and entreaties, indeed moved by his inborn piety toward his brother, in March Duke Vladislav recalled Soběslav to his original favor and gave him the burg of Hradec and the whole adjacent province with four castles.

In July of the same year, Duke Vladislav and his brothers, Otto and Soběslav, met with Duke Bolesław of the Poles near the flow of the River Nysa, at a set assembly. Having given and received oaths from each other, they confirmed their bond of peace. The next day, they returned to their own homes joyful, laden with gifts mutually given to one other.

Meanwhile, with Oldřich, son of Duke Conrad, taken from our midst by unavoidable fate and his younger brother Lutold taken from this light sometime earlier, and with their sons still too young in age, Duke Vladislav gave that whole province (which Conrad, the father of the aforesaid brothers, had held) to his own brother Soběslav, with its burgs.

3.42. 1116. The Hungarian people are prodigious in energy, mighty in strength, and very powerful in military arms—sufficient to fight with a king of lands anywhere. After the death of their king, Coloman, their princes sent to Duke Vladislav to renew and confirm with the new king, named Stephen, their ancient peace and friend-

---

200. Mt 18:22.

ship.[201] Giving his assent to their will, the duke pledged that he would do things which pertained to peace.

Vladislav came to the River Olšava, which separates the realms of Hungary and Moravia. Immediately, the Hungarian people, innumerable as the sands of the sea or drops of rain,[202] covered the whole surface of the land in the field of Lučsko,[203] like locusts.[204] The duke made his camp on the other side of the aforesaid stream. But, as scripture says, "Woe to the land whose king is a child."[205] Their princes, through their inborn pride in themselves, strayed from the duke's peaceful words and sent replies more to stir up strife[206] than to bring the kiss of peace.[207] Whence the duke put off going to the assembly that day.

The Hungarians, taking this badly and suspecting that it might turn out differently, ordered three armed legions of foreigners, whom they had summoned, to leave the camp and stand in their defense on the opposite side of the stream. The duke, thinking them to be rushing forward into battle, ordered his men to take up arms and, more quickly than it could be said, they leapt across the boundary stream in front of them. Immediately a battle bloody and horrible—unexpected, unfortunate, and unpremeditated— was engaged. In it, the son of Stan (whom we mentioned above [2.35]), named Jiřík, castellan of Žatec, a most spirited warrior, died fighting bravely with other warriors from that same burg, on 13 May. And yet, with others turning their backs, even the duke himself was forced into flight.

But Otto and Soběslav, having four hardy contingents and also taking on strong troops from the Bohemians, circled the little mountain which happened to separate them. They unexpectedly attacked with great force[208] the Hungarians' camp, where the

---

201. Stephen II (1116–31); see Engel, *Realm of St. Stephen*, 49.

202. See Book 1, n. 28; also, Jb 36:27 ("drops of rain").

203. Cf. 3.9, above, for another battle between Czechs and Hungarians on this same field.

204. See Book 1, n. 29.   205. Eccl 10:16.

206. Prv 15:18.   207. Cf. 2.45, nn. 254–55.

208. 2 Mc 11:11.

king with his leaders and bishops was sitting, drinking and feasting sumptuously,[209] knowing nothing of the battle that had taken place. What more? If Archbishop Laurence[210] had not quickly run away with the king, not even he would have escaped the risk of death. Indeed, there was so great a number of Hungarians, noble and ignoble, present there, as were not present—they say—along the Lech River in the time of Saint Ulrich.[211] Returning from the slaughter, the legions of foreigners whom we mentioned, who prevailed even against our duke in war, when they saw their men put to flight and others thrown down in heaps—and their enemies dancing in their camp—went into shameful flight. Reckoning the hostile forces to be still following them when they saw them from a distance in the king's camp (their camp was now located in the fields beyond the bridge at Bělin), many more were drowned in the River Wag, fleeing out of fear. Our men having obtained the victory, they fixed their tents that night in [the Hungarians'] camp. The warriors plundered the Hungarian treasures, namely, the ostentatious abundance of gold and silver implements, while the commoners divided the rest of their goods for their own use.

3.43. 1117. On 3 January, a Friday, at the hour of vespers, there was a large earthquake—much larger still in parts of Lombardy. As we understand from rumor's report, many buildings fell down, many castles were destroyed, and many monasteries and shrines collapsed and crushed many people.

209. Lk 16:19.

210. Archbishop Laurentius of Esztergom (ca. 1105–18).

211. This is a reference to the famous Battle of Lechfeld in 955, in which Otto the Great vanquished the Hungarians and put an end to a protracted period of their raiding throughout western Europe. Note that Cosmas calls this battle to mind via a hagiographic source, the vita of St. Ulrich of Augsburg, rather than a historical one (though it is reported in the continuation of Regino's chronicle, which he had in hand [*Chronicon*, 168]). Cosmas might simply be appealing to his audience, clergy who knew Ulrich's vita from the regular celebration of his feast, which also explains the brief mention of Ulrich in 1.27. For the relevant excerpt form Ulrich's *vita*, see Charles Bowlus, *The Battle of Lechfeld and Its Aftermath, Augsburg 955* (Aldershot, UK: Ashgate, 2006), 176–78.

In the same year, on 23 January, Božetěcha, unseparated companion in all my affairs,[212] died.

Also in the same year, with our Lord Jesus Christ (in whose hands lie the hearts of kings)[213] eternally reigning and with him gently inspiring it, Duke Vladislav remembered his brother, Bořivoj. Looking down on Bořivoj's affliction[214] from his throne at the summit of the heavens,[215] the Lord now had mercy on his distress and misery.[216] Because it is impossible for a man not to have mercy on someone for whom God has mercy,[217] the aforesaid duke, impelled now by divine will and doing everything with the advice of Bishop Hermann, immediately sent for his brother Bořivoj and recalled him from exile—in the month of December. Making amends and submitting himself to his lordship, Vladislav set Bořivoj again on the princely throne. O the wondrous benevolence of the duke! But more to be marveled at: equanimity, which no secular dignity loves and no loftiness of honor clouds. A duke pleased to get power, and pleased to put it aside.[218] Whoever heard of such things being done?—say, I ask you. If only the Hungarian king, Coloman, had heard these things (if he had lived)—he who, fearing that his brother Álmos would reign after him, deprived him and his son of their penises and their sight.[219]

212. These two lines of poetry derive from Prosper of Aquitaine's "A Husband's Poem to His Wife" (*PL* 51:611), probably via Bede, who reproduces them as an example of Anacreontic meter in his *De arte metrica* (*PL* 90:173). Cosmas has replaced Prosper's *inremota* (unremoved) with *indimota* (unseparated).

213. Prv 21:1.

214. Dt 26:7.

215. Sedulius *Paschale Carmen* 1.31. Cosmas has borrowed the words and modified them grammatically to better fit his sentence, but they nevertheless resonate with Sedulius's meaning, to describe Christ enthroned with his Father.

216. Jb 10:15.

217. Cf. Mt 18:33.

218. The whole line is verbatim from Lucan *Pharsalia* 9.198, who even uses the word *dux* (which Joyce logically translates "leader" but which serves for Cosmas as "duke").

219. Coloman blinded both his brother and his nephew, Béla, in 1113. Engel, *Realm of St. Stephen*, 35.

Bořivoj, remembering the benefit he received, gave his brother a half-portion of his duchy, located beyond the Elbe River and extending to the north. And although Vladislav was his younger brother, Bořivoj did nothing without his counsel, obeying him in all things and preceding him with honor.

3.44. 1118. In September there was so much flooding; I don't think there has been as much since the Flood of the world.[220] This river of ours, the Vltava, suddenly burst headlong out of the riverbed. Alas! how many villages, how many houses in this suburb, how many cottages and churches it took away by its force. Although at other times it seldom happened that the flowing surge touched even the floor of the bridge, this time the flood rose higher than ten ells[221] over the bridge.

3.45. 1119. On 30 July, a Thursday, after it had already been a favorable day, a mighty wind from the southern plain, like Satan himself in a whirlwind, burst suddenly upon the duke's solarium in the burg of Vyšehrad and utterly destroyed the ancient, extremely strong wall there. From there—and this is really to be marveled at—with the other part, the front and back, remaining whole and undisturbed, only the middle of the palace was ripped out. More quickly than you can break a stem, the wind's force broke the upper and lower beams to pieces, as well as the house itself, and scattered them. This was such a powerful storm that whatever region it fell upon, it threw down by its force the forests of this land, newly planted trees, and whatever else stood in its way.

3.46. 1120. Now, my Muse, button your lip with your finger.[222] If, well taught, you have sense, take care not to say true things. To have sense like me, you should only say briefly: Bořivoj was again expelled from this land's lofty throne.[223] These things were done on 16 August.[224]

220. Noah's flood; cf. Gn 6–8.
221. A common measurement based on the length of a man's arm; equivalent to about twenty-four inches.
222. Juvenal *Satires* 1.160.
223. See Book 1, n. 345.
224. This entire chapter consists of four lines of verse.

3.47. 1121. The crops were much diminished on account of extreme dryness, which lasted for three uninterrupted months, namely, March, April, and May.

In the same year, Duke Vladislav rebuilt the fortress of Donin as well as the castle of Podivín, located in Moravia next to the River Svratka.

3.48. In the same year, certain Germans built a castle within the Czechs' boundaries, on a steep rock in the forest.[225] (The road to it leads through the village of Bela.) Hearing this, Duke Vladislav, taking three contingents of chosen warriors, occupied the castle, attacking suddenly and unexpectedly. There, in the first assault, two of the duke's warriors, Oldřich, son of Vacemil, and Olen, son of Borša, were wounded by arrows sent from the walls—not, however, to the point of death. Duke Vladislav would have ordered all those Germans captured in the castle hanged in that very forest without a doubt, if Count Albert[226] had not arrived and freed them by the sagacity innate to him and by many entreaties.

Winter of that same year was extremely windy and warm, and there was great flooding.

3.49. 1122. On 24 March there was an eclipse of the moon in the middle of the night on which the Jewish Passover fell.

In the same year, the priestly man Hermann, bright with the light of doctrine, submitted to fate on Sunday, 17 September, with day already dawning on the Feast of St. Lambert, bishop and martyr. While he lived he celebrated this feast most devotedly, because he was from the town of Utrecht and descended from a family from that same Lotharingia.[227] Occupying ninth place on the pontifical seat, he ruled this church for twenty-two years, six months, and seventeen days. He was remarkable, formidable to those who did not know him, easygoing with his household, incomparable in the quality of his character. A lamp shining in the world and

225. This unnamed castle is usually assumed to be Přimda, in the mountains on the Bohemian side of the Bohemian-Bavarian border.

226. This must be Count Albert of Bogen, mentioned above (3.3, n. 16).

227. St. Lambert, bishop of Maastricht (d. ca. 701). His major cult center was Liège, the site of his remains, though Cosmas seems to connect it here with Utrecht.

burning not under a bushel but placed on a chandelier,[228] he enlightened the hearts[229] of nonbelievers by the word of doctrine and by example.[230] Concerning his other virtuous deeds, although many things worthy of report shine forth, nevertheless we will leave them untouched—on account of men in present times, who do nothing good themselves and so refuse to believe the good deeds they hear of others.

Still, it should not seem discordant if we mention out of order things we ought to have mentioned earlier. The aforesaid bishop, when he perceived his illness to be growing stronger and saw a few of the members of his household standing around the bed, groaned and said, "My secret to myself, my secret to myself,"[231] and was silent. They stood stupefied and looked at each other's faces quietly. A little bit later the bishop opened his mouth and said: "Once, when I was healthy, I should have said standing in the pulpit what I am compelled to confess now, with my spirit already in its death throes. I confess that I, a sinner, did not contradict my fellow sinners concerning their sin. Not only did I honor the powerful agents of evil and transgressors, but in fact I even loved those whom I ought to have rebuked and excommunicated if they did not obey. After Břetislav the Younger—than whom there was no better duke, nor will there be—was laid to rest, evil flourished in this land,[232] pride has budded,[233] deceit, guile, and injustice grew, and I alone lamenting lamented that it was not permitted to me to die with the good duke.

Woe is me, because I was silent,[234] because I did not recall the rebellious people nor brandish the sword of anathema on Christ's behalf. I allowed me myself and the Christian people to be polluted by touching hands with an unholy people, just as it is written: 'He who touches the unclean, will be unclean'; and 'He who touches pitch will be defiled by it'; and 'What agreement does

228. Mt 5:15.
229. Sir 2:10.
230. See Book 2, n. 153.
231. Is 24:16.
232. Cf. Gn 6:13.
233. Ez 7:10.
234. Canaparius *Vita Adalberti* 6.

Christ have with Belial?'²³⁵ The Jews who after baptism relapsed into Judaism on account of our negligence, I call a rebellious people.²³⁶ For this reason I greatly fear that Christ might throw this before me and cast me down into hell. For in the dead of night,²³⁷ his voice was heard saying to me: 'You did not rise to face the enemy nor did you set up a wall for the house of Israel, to stand in battle on the day of the Lord.²³⁸ You have allowed the Lord's flock, ransomed not by gold or silver but by the precious blood of the true Christ,²³⁹ to be contaminated by one sick little sheep and to be banished from the heavenly kingdom.' Alas, poor me! The sort of man I wanted myself to be, how different I am from the man I once was.²⁴⁰ And I am now displeasing to myself because I see that I have done little good." So he spoke and immediately, as we mentioned above, his fleeing spirit disappeared into the empty air.²⁴¹

After him, Meinhard became the tenth bishop.

3.50. In that same year, in the month of March, *Comes* Vznata returned from both Jerusalem and Galicia;²⁴² he died on 16 October of the same year.

Also that year, honey and grapes abounded in the horn of plenty, and the grain grew enough, but there was no overflow in the kernels of the ear. A warm winter followed; for this reason, in the following summer, we missed the ice reserve.

3.51. 1123. In March, *Comes* Dluhomil traveled to Jerusalem together with Gumprecht, Gilbert, Henry (who was also called Zdík),²⁴³

235. Lv 22:5, Sir 13:1, and 2 Cor 6:15, respectively.

236. See Book 1, n. 221. The incident for which the dying bishop reproaches himself is described above, 3.5.

237. Virgil *Aeneid* 3.587.   238. Ez 13:5.

239. 1 Pt 5:2 and 1:18–19.

240. Citing again from Canaparius *Vita Adalberti* 6 (see n. 234, above). Here, however, Canaparius is himself alluding to Virgil *Aeneid* 2.274.

241. Sedulius *Paschale Carmen* 4.89, a line itself rooted in Virgil and Ovid.

242. A clear reference to Santiago de Compostela, a thriving pilgrimage center in the northeastern corner of the Iberian peninsula.

243. Soon to become bishop of Olomouc (1126–50); in contemporary sources he is variously called either Zdík, Henry, or Henry Zdík.

and others. Some of them returned in November and some died there. *Comes* Dluhomil, just about to return, died on 8 July. So too Bertold, a follower of my son, Henry, died on 6 August.

I am prevented by tears[244] and cannot express in writing what furor and what discord pushed brothers of one mind into a terrible rage, like twin bulls. For in March, Duke Vladislav, moved by immense rage, moved arms against his brother Soběslav and expelled him from Moravia with all of his men. The duke then returned to Conrad, son of Lutold, his inheritance. But a quarter of that territory—which Oldřich, the brother of this Lutold, had held as *tetrarch*[245]—he gave instead to Otto, Duke Svatopluk's brother.

Meanwhile Soběslav, fleeing from the face of his brother,[246] went to the emperor in the burg of Mainz. But his efforts accomplished little because without money,[247] in the presence of all kings, anybody's requests are in vain and the justice of laws is silenced. Just as a wolf, gaping longingly as he attacks a flock but chasing in vain, tucks tail and returns to the forest when he captures nothing—so too Soběslav, his cause stymied before the emperor, fled to Wiprecht and lived with him for seven months. Then in November, Soběslav crossed into Poland, where Duke Bolesław[248] received him honorably. The Hungarian king, Stephen, kindly received Soběslav's wife, the daughter of Duke Álmos, acknowledging her as his relative.[249]

In Lent, almost throughout the entire world, the powers of the air, like many stars, although they did not fall to earth, still seemed to fall.[250] In likeness to this, the Lord says in the Gospel: "I saw Satan falling from heaven like a flash of lightning."[251]

3.52. In that same year, there was the greatest plenty, both in

244. See Book 2, n. 238.

245. An unusual term used to indicate a ruler of a fourth portion, comparable to *dyarch;* see Book 2, n. 196.

246. See Book 3, n. 37.

247. Perhaps Plautus, *The Captives* 472, in *Plautus,* trans. Paul Nixon, 5 vols. (Cambridge, Mass.: Harvard University Press, 1950).

248. See above, n. 13.   249. A woman named Adelhaid.

250. Ovid *Metamorphoses* 2.321–22.   251. Lk 10:18.

autumn and in planted produce especially—except that, in many places, hail damaged it. Honey abounded in the fields, less so in forested places. Winter was exceedingly harsh and snowy.

Just as the year was ending, the last offshoot of Margrave Dedo having been rooted out by fate, Emperor Henry IV [V], considering the margravate of this Dedo lacking an heir, put it under the power of Wiprecht. But there was in Saxony a certain man named Conrad, born from the tribe of this same Dedo and to whose hand that margravate pertained by law. For this reason Duke Lothar and other Saxons, truly indignant, started a war against the emperor and in opposition to Wiprecht.[252]

3.53. At this time, Duke Vladislav and Otto, as the emperor had commanded them, crossed the forest with a combined army from both Bohemia and Moravia. They set up camp beyond the fortress of Gvozdec, opposite Duke Lothar. The archbishop of Mainz[253] and *Comes* Wiprecht stood on the near side of the River Mldava with a heavily armed throng. Positioned in the middle, between the two camps, the Saxons separated them and simultaneously prevented their adversaries from uniting.

The duke of Bohemia and Otto then sent a message to the Saxons, saying: "We did not take up arms against you out of arrogance. We came in aid of the archbishop of Mainz and *Comes* Wiprecht, by the order of the emperor. Yet since they, who ought to be here and to join the first battle, are not here, cede the place to us alone so that we might have the opportunity to go home. In

<hr/>

252. Count Dedo IV (d. 1124) of Wettin and Wiprecht II of Groitzsch (see Book 2, n. 230). At stake was the title of margrave and control of Meissen. The Conrad mentioned here was Dedo's brother, Conrad of Wettin (d. 1157), though Cosmas makes the relationship sound distinctly more distant. He was supported, against Wiprecht and Henry V, by Lothar of Supplinberg, duke of Saxony after 1106. Conrad of Wettin would become margrave of Meissen after Wiprecht's death later in 1124. Lothar would become king of the Germans and emperor after Henry's death in 1125 (see 3.61, n. 301). In the interim, however, there was a war in which the Czechs were involved, as Cosmas will describe. See Stefan Pätzold, *Die frühen Wettiner: Adelsfamilie und Hausüberlieferung bis 1221* (Cologne: Böhlau, 1997), 28–34.

253. Adalbert I of Saarbrücken, archbishop of Mainz (1110–37).

other words, it will seem that you have ceded and we have stood fast, and that we waited for them in the agreed-upon place." Duke Lothar responded to this, saying: "I am amazed that you, prudent men, do not discern by your wits the manifest deception by which you, brought into this without cause, have taken up arms against us innocents. Do you think any of the counsels of Archbishop Adalbert of Mainz are free of deception? Have you not yet experienced enough of his Attican prudence? Another Ulysses indeed,[254] Wiprecht, who was educated around the footstool of this same archbishop, is well known to you. Why did they not come themselves to greet us, we who would gladly have greeted them back? But it is safer to wait from afar than to join in war with a force, and to join one's own advantage to another's disadvantage. Certainly anyone can see, even through bleary eyes,[255] what they plot with their deception. They know and are well aware that, even if you are victorious, it will not be possible to conquer the Saxons without great damage to you; on the other hand, if we are able to prevail mightily, they will more easily be able invade Bohemia, widowed of her defenders. This is what the emperor wants; this is what the Archbishop of Mainz counsels. Your brother-in-law Wiprecht is always friendly with the Czechs. Your brother Soběslav, whom Wiprecht recently drove into Poland by a ruse, at your wish, will not be trusted by me further unless he quickly returns to that same Wiprecht. You should know that we are more ready to engage in battle than to cede this place to you." Having heard all this and wrongly trusting in these words composed with deception, the Czechs plundered the region around the burg of

254. These lines allude to book 2 of the *Aeneid*, where Laocoon warns the Trojans not to believe the Greeks have fled or to accept their gift of the horse: "Do you think any gifts of the Greeks are free from treachery? Is Ulysses known to be this sort of man?" (2.43–44). The connotation associated with Ulysses' name is here unfavorable; thus Wiprecht of Groitzsch is not being likened to an epic hero but to a deceiver and a trickster. The prudence described here as "Attican" (i.e., Athenian) is likewise certainly pejorative.

255. Horace *Satires* 1.3.25.

Meissen and returned home, with the sun tarrying in the sixth part of Sagittarius [24 November].

3.54. 1124. On 12 February, Hermann, brother of William, and Lutobor, son of Martin, traveled to Jerusalem.

On 2 February in that same year, Duke Bořivoj, an exile in Hungary, was released from the bonds of the flesh and departed to Christ, whom he worshipped with a pure mind and with whom he now rejoices in the great hall of heaven. After all the hardships of his life and of the world, he endured fifteen years spent as an exile; six of those years he suffered shut up in prison. Twice raised to the throne, why he was twice rejected it is not right for me to probe into, or for me to say such things. God, who creates all things and governs all creation, knows. Whoever has read this, let him say: "Duke Bořivoj now rests; he is in the land of the saints and the resting place of souls." On 14 March he was buried in the crypt of St. Martin, bishop and confessor, at the main Church of the Holy Martyrs Vitus, Václav, and Adalbert in the *metropolis* of Prague.[256]

3.55. During Lent of that same year, on 24 March, Bishop Meinhard accidentally discovered the bones of Podiven in the sacristy and buried them in the chapel under the tower (between the altar of St. Nicholas, bishop and confessor, and the tomb of Bishop Gebhard). Podiven was a follower and inseparable companion[257] of the holy martyr Václav, in his toil and trouble. For those wanting to know, his deeds are sufficiently explained in the vita of that same saint.[258] In his time, Severus, the sixth bishop of this see,

256. Here again Cosmas refers to Prague as a *metropolis*, both to indicate Prague Castle as the location of the cathedral church dedicated to Vitus, Václav, and Adalbert, and probably also to signal that Bořivoj was fittingly buried in the Czechs' political and ecclesiastical capital.

257. See Book 2, n. 55.

258. Podiven appears among the miracle stories at the end of the *Life and Passion of Saint Václav and His Grandmother Ludmila*, where he is indeed described as "a partaker and companion of all the deeds which the martyr first performed." Kristián also describes Podiven's burial in the cemetery of St. Vitus's church: "Thus Saint Václav, who is buried inside the church, and that warrior, who is buried outside of it, are separated

while expanding the chapel to make it larger, dug up the bones
of the aforementioned follower [Podiven] around the holy tomb
of the aforementioned patron [Saint Václav], because otherwise
the wall could not have been secured. Arranging the bones in a
sarcophagus, he put them in the chamber where ecclesiastical treasures are kept.²⁵⁹

On Easter day, 6 April, sending letters to all the princes and
bishops of his realm, Emperor Henry IV [V] commanded that
they assemble at his court in the burg of Bamberg on 4 May, having laid every other opportunity aside.

3.56. Meanwhile Soběslav, the brother of our duke, left Poland
with all his followers and took the road to Duke Lothar of Saxony,²⁶⁰ hoping to obtain counsel as well as aid from such a great
man. He was received by him honorably, with hospitality, and
he obtained the solace desired by his hope. The aforesaid Duke
Lothar, since he knew the prince of Bohemia to be at the royal
court, sent a messenger with his guest, saying to the emperor: "It
is fitting for royal power and imperial dignity mercifully to help
those suffering harm and royally to meet those doing harm with
the rigor of justice. You will give us and all peoples proof of such
grace and experience of princely judgment if, doing justice to
Soběslav, this innocent man suffering injury,²⁶¹ you reconcile him
to his brother."²⁶² Then the caesar, looking around at his whole
assembly and very indignant, said: "This margrave says enough before the emperor. He himself does us injury and begs that injuries
be avenged. If it is fitting for me, as he confesses, to avenge another's injuries, why should I not avenge mine first? Can there be
an injury greater than the fact that he himself, summoned to our
council, did not come? Therefore, whomever the zeal of justice

from each other only by a wall." Ludvíkovský, *Kristiánova legenda*, 84–88; Kantor, *Origins of Christianity*, 196–98.

259. This explains how Bishop Meinhard came to find them in the sacristy. Notice that he also buried them again in essentially the same place Severus found them.

260. See above, n. 252.

261. Ps 145:7: "who executes justice for them that suffer wrong."

262. Cf. Mt 5:24.

and this injury stings, let him now pledge an oath upon holy reliquaries that he will take up his arms and follow me into Saxony
after the Feast of St. James the Apostle [25 July]." All the princes
agreed, praised, and swore in favor of the caesar's proclamation of
war against the Saxons.

At this time, Wiprecht, the son-in-law of King Vratislav, died
(about whom we made sufficient mention above). Seeing this,
Soběslav—because fortune and the king's wealth helped his elder
brother more—turned in the direction of Wiprecht's son,[263]
his relative through his sister, whom he consoled about the death of his
father. From there, he sent *Comes* Stephen to the prince of Poland—
for through Stephen Soběslav made all his plans.

When Stephen was passing through the forest between Saxony
and Poland, he happened upon armed bands of robbers.[264] Standing at a distance, they said to him: "We spare and have mercy on
you, and we grant you your life. Go your way in peace. But leave
us your horses and everything you are carrying; for you few will
not be able to flee or resist the many of us." Undaunted, Stephen
said to them: "Give us a little space to take counsel." When they
granted it, the *comes* said: "O brothers, O companions in this final
fate, fear not the occasion of unexpected death. For who would
break his bread with us after we turned in disgraceful flight? After
a disgracefully continued life, who would grant us the necessities
of life? We do not know whether the barbarians will concede this
to us. Alas, we will regret too late and in vain that we did not die
manfully. Afflicted with diverse punishments—this one with his
nose cut off, another deprived of his eyes—they will make us a
byword and a taunt among all peoples."[265] His men unanimously
said: "Let us die, let us die; but let us see that we not die unavenged." When the pagans saw them to be fitted out with arms
more for battle than for flight, they came upon them suddenly.[266]

263. His name was Henry; see above, n. 159.
264. Cf. Lk 10:30.
265. A combination of Jer 24:9 and 3 Kgs 9:7.
266. Jos 10:9.

It was an unnatural battle between five small shields and the fifty oblong shields of stronger men. The priest among them, to whom they had entrusted their souls, fled holding a bow and quiver. One of the robbers, seeing this unarmed man fleeing, followed. But the priest, unable to escape, sent an arrow back and struck the horse in the middle of the forehead; the horse and its rider fell backward. In this way the priest alone escaped and announced in the burg of Glogów what had happened. The castellan of that burg, named Vojslav, rushing there with many armed men, found Stephen half-alive in the middle of the River Bobr, clinging to some bushes— for the barbarians, very angry when they saw many of their own men killed and others wounded, threw him into the aforesaid river. Vojslav took him and his companions, still half-alive, into his castle and there Stephen died on Sunday, 1 June.

Soběslav tarried with the son of Wiprecht during this time because, after the death of his father, the boy was cruelly pressed by enemies from all directions.

In July that same year, Duke Vladislav married his first-born daughter, named Svatava, with many feminine accoutrements and too much display of wealth, to the most celebrated man among the Bavarian nobles, named Frederick.[267]

3.57. In the same year, the virtue of Christ God and the wisdom of God, directing everything by his will, deigned to rescue this little land from the trap of Satan and his son, Jacob Apella.[268] Whatever his pitch-black right hand touches, it defiles.[269] Like a basilisk, the foul breath of his mouth kills those upon whom it blows.[270] Many

267. Frederick IV, cathedral advocate (Domvogt) of Regensburg (d. 1148) and member of a branch of the house of Bogen; as Cosmas notes, he enjoyed considerably more influence than this title suggests. Kubů, "Die Grafen von Bogen," 129.

268. Jacob Apella is almost certainly not the man's actual name. "Apella" recalls Horace, cited previously (Book 1, n. 81), presumably to emphasize his Jewishness. The name "Jacob" probably serves the same function, though of course it could also indeed be this person's proper name.

269. Cf. 3.49, where the same biblical verse (Sir 13:1) is used in reference to relapsed Jews.

270. A basilisk was a fanciful creature, king of the serpents, sometimes a kind of combination serpent and cock. It was said to be able to kill with a look or by its smell,

truthful men also bear witness about him: that Satan was often seen to cleave to his side in human form and to show his allegiance. For this reason [Jacob] elevated himself with such boldness—even madness—by Satan's arts that, overstepping his bounds, that most criminal man also exercised the office of vice lord after the duke. That was a great time of darkness for the Christian people. Turned apostate after baptism, at night [Jacob] destroyed the altar that had been built and consecrated in their synagogue. Taking the holy relics, he was not afraid to throw them in the sewer.

On 22 July, full of zeal for God and zealous for Christ, Duke Vladislav seized this sacrilegious criminal and ordered him held under close guard. Ah, how much of the mammon of iniquity[271] was offered from the house of that supplanter and received into the duke's treasury. Beyond this, the Jews, [Jacob's] partners in crime, paid the duke one hundred pounds of gold and three thousand of silver, so that the aforesaid bastard might not suffer capital punishment. Inspired by God's grace, the duke redeemed Christian slaves from all the Jews and commanded that no Christian serve them any longer. ("Amen, Amen," I say.) Whatever wrong had ever been done, with this praiseworthy deed Vladislav blotted it out completely and allied himself to the eternal name. O handmaid of Christ, always devoted, pious Mary Magdalen, the common folk offer their prayers to you, since they were rescued from the hostile enemy on your feast day.

On 11 August in the same year, there was an eclipse of the sun at the eleventh hour of the day, and a great pestilence of cows, sheep, and pigs followed. Many bees died, and there was a great shortage of honey. The autumn crops failed, and the spring ones as well, except only millet and peas.

In the same year, Duke Vladislav, a man most celebrated and venerable, celebrated Christmas and Epiphany in the village of Zti-bečná. Then, since he was ill, he had himself borne to the burg of Vyšehrad, where he remained until his death.

and to breathe fire. Cosmas probably takes his description from Isidore (*Etymologies* 12.4.6–9), though the basilisk also appears in other ancient and medieval texts.

271. Lk 16:9.

Entering the spring of that same winter, the most violent winds blew throughout the whole lunar cycle of the month of March.
3.58. 1125. Soběslav heard that his brother was severely ill. After taking advantageous counsel from his friends and with God's will now arranging it so, he returned from Saxony with his whole retinue. On 2 February, at night, he approached the burg of Prague from the forest around Břevnov monastery. The reason remained hidden as to why he had decided this was to be done in this matter. Nevertheless, a hero of such good disposition would not have brazenly entered this land, I think, if there had not been some among the *comites* by whose counsel he acted. That very night, turning his steps here and there, now through forests, now through villages, he secretly circled the land, bringing force to bear against no one, but always earnestly seeking his brother's favor.

All the Czechs of the first and second rank loved Soběslav and supported his party; only the duchess and a few men with her aided Otto. Since Otto had married her sister, the duchess strove in every way for him to obtain the throne after her husband.[272]

With Duke Vladislav's illness growing worse and worse, his body was greatly exhausted. In the midst of this the leaders of the land were alarmed and greatly troubled, like fish in turbulent water, uncertain, while their minds wavered.

Queen Svatava, the duke's mother, forewarned and instructed by Soběslav's friends, went to visit her son and said this to him: "Although I am your mother and a queen, I come to your knees humble and timid. On the trembling knees from which I bore you as a tender baby, I fall down before you now on your brother's behalf. I do not ask those things which could be denied by law, but those things which are both pleasing to God and acceptable to men. It pleases God (as he said: 'Honor your father and moth-

---

272. The duchess here is Richinza (d. 1125), daughter of the Swabian count, Henry I of Berg; she married Vladislav I in 1110. Her sister Sophie was the wife of Otto II of Olomouc. Salome, a third sister, married Duke Bolesław III of Poland. Immo Eberl, "Die Grafen von Berg, ihr Herrschaftsbereich und dessen adelige Familien," *Ulm und Oberschwaben* 44 (1982): 36–37.

er')[273] that you receive my old woman's entreaties gently and that you not, I beseech you, confound my face, wrinkled and covered with tears.[274] It is permitted for me, an old mother before her son, to bring about what the whole prostrate people[275] of Bohemia asks and demands. It is permitted for me, very old, to see you two pacified, you of equal make, born from my womb, and whom I see well brought up by God's grace. It falls to me, a little old woman about to die soon, not to die before God grants consolation to my incomparable grief. Justly indeed, I deserve that wild Erinyes reigns in this land and arms you brothers, once of one mind, now for battle.[276]

"Who does not know that an undershirt is nearer the body than a tunic?[277] Indeed nature, which made a relative closer by birth, makes it that he should be nearer to his own in every administration of affairs. Yet he, Otto, whom you make your brother, whom you now charge with the care of your offspring and your dear wife and to whom you commit them for protection, believe me, your mother, he will first be a snare, a pit, or a stumbling block to them.[278] But the other, Soběslav, whom you keep at a distance and reckon a kind of alien, since he is your true brother,[279] will be much more merciful to your family than the son of your uncle, to whom you are determined to give the throne of your father's duchy after you."

273. Ex 20:12.

274. 3 Kgs 2:16; cf. 2.45.

275. Cosmas here uses the Greek word *laon,* written in Latin letters.

276. Cf. above, n. 73. Erinyes is another name for the Eumenides or Furies (see Book 1, n. 66). In the passage from the *Aeneid* to which Cosmas alludes with this line, one of the Furies, Allecto, has just been summoned by Juno precisely to whip up hatred and move men to war.

277. Echoing Plautus *Three Bob Day* 1154, though with the terminology shifted to reflect the medieval understanding of these terms for clothing.

278. Jos 23:13; and cf. Book 2, n. 172.

279. Here Cosmas uses *germanus* in reference to Soběslav, and in contrast to *frater* for Otto, to emphasize Svatava's point about natural affinity and true brotherhood. It works in relation to the prevailing tendency to refer to all Přemyslids of the same generation as "brother" even when they may technically be cousins (cf. above, n. 60).

She was speaking and weeping and troubling her son with her wailing. When she saw him also weeping, she added this: "I do not grieve your fate, my son, unavoidable for a man. But I weep over your brother's life, more wretched than death. A fugitive, wanderer, and exile,[280] he now chooses to die happily rather than to live unhappily." Her son, tears pouring down his face,[281] said to her: "I will do, mother, I will do what you urge. I was not born from stone or from Charybdis,[282] so that I do not remember a brother of the womb."

Meanwhile Bishop Otto of the church of Bamberg, the talented warrior of Christ, having conquered and destroyed the idols of the Pomeranians,[283] on his return visited the duke, now failing in strength from sickness. To him the duke committed himself and his soul through holy confession. But the bishop vowed that indulgence could not be given or received until Vladislav had assured his brother true peace and lasting grace. Charging Bishop Meinhard with the care of his soul and the task to be performed, the aforesaid bishop immediately took to the road well loaded with gifts, as a consequence of princely generosity. (He hurried so that he might return to his see before Holy Thursday.) Someone was immediately sent for Soběslav—and now what was once contrived secretly was done openly among the people.

When Otto, the prince of Moravia, perceived these things to be, he who had always clung to the duke's side, fearing now lest he perhaps be captured, returned sad to Moravia.

Vladislav made peace with his brother [Soběslav] on 25 March, on Thursday in Holy Week. After the octave of Easter, on 12 April, a Sunday, which was then *Misericordia Domini* [Mercy of the Lord], the compassionate and merciful[284] Duke Vladislav departed to

280. See Book 1, n. 22.   281. See Book 2, n. 49.
282. Ovid *Metamorphoses* 8.121.
283. See above, 3.21 and n. 109. In 1125 Otto, later canonized and known as the "Apostle of Pomerania," was returning from one of his preaching campaigns to convert the Pomeranians to Christianity.
284. Sir 2:13.

Christ, not without the great lamentation[285] of his men. He now
surely received from the merciful Lord himself the mercy he had
always shown toward the poor in Christ's name.[286] He was buried
in the Church of the Holy Virgin Mary, which he himself built
in honor of Christ and his mother and sufficiently enriched with
every ecclesiastical treasure, and where he established a very honorable monastery of monks. (The name of the place is Kladruby.)

How great a duke he was, while breath still governed his
limbs,[287] can be known from what has already been written of his
deeds. The same holds for what kind of praise he might be worthy
of and how much esteem he should be revered with. Let this be
the book's end, where our duke's end is.[288]

3.59. It is true: I remember that in the beginning of the first
book I said this chronicle was produced in the times of Duke
Vladislav and Bishop Hermann. And they have now been transported by fate from this vale of tears[289] to a place perhaps delightful. But with material for a history still abundant, advise me now,
beautiful Muse,[290] my teacher: should I fix an anchor to the shore
here, or open the sails now, with the east winds raging on high?

For you, who will never grow old, do not cease to rouse me, an
old man, to juvenile endeavors. You are scarcely ignorant that in
old men like me the intellect is puerile and the spirit weak. O if
God would give back to me, now an octogenarian, the years that
are past,[291] when I once quite amused myself in the grassy fields
of Liège, under Franco, master of both grammar and dialectic! O
sweet Muse, so worthy of young men's love, always virtuous but
never old, why do you assail me, an old man? Why do you stir up

285. See Book 1, n. 259.   286. Cf. 1 Tm 1:16.
287. Virgil *Aeneid* 4.336.
288. This last paragraph consists of four lines of verse.
289. See Book 1, n. 291.
290. Cf. the last lines of Book 2, n. 285.
291. Virgil *Aeneid* 8.560, almost verbatim (replacing Jupiter with the Christian God
and inserting the reference to his own age). The original context is a similar lament
for youth, its abilities and triumphs.

my dull mind? Old age now bends my back,[292] wrinkled skin now disfigures my face, my weary chest breathes now like noisy feet, my hoarse voice now hisses like a goose, and sickly senility now weakens my faculties. To be sure, the soft part of the bread or a toasted morsel pleases me more than your sophisms, which at one time we sweetly sucked from your delicate breasts, softly reclining under your arm. O sophistic goring horn, to be sought afar by syllogistic [logic-wielding] men and already well known to us, leave off with old men but seek youths like yourself, sharp in intellect and clever in the art of arts [logic], who recently returned to the great table of Lady Philosophy, nourished with delicate foods after completely emptying the treasures of the new philosopher of France.[293]

The renowned virtue of Duke Soběslav awaits such orators, who should be able marvelously to gild with a golden pen his marvelous deeds. Whatever follies I am foolishly committing, I, an old man, humbly entrust to them to be smoothed to perfection.[294] With their leave and that of all readers, let me be permitted to put in writing something of the many deeds of the aforesaid duke. You who disparage me, an old man, since you yourself are wise, bring the treasures of your knowledge[295] into the light, and have this rough text as your material.

3.60. With our Lord Jesus Christ reigning, the triune and unitary omnipotent God, Duke Vladislav was removed from this light, as we mentioned above, and his brother Soběslav, younger in age but more mature than mature men in his wisdom, of a generous disposition, acceptable to the *cives*, dear to the common folk of both sexes and every age, was raised to the ancestral throne of the principate by hereditary right and with all the Czechs together favoring it, on 16 April.

292. Rom 11:10.

293. Presumably a reference to Peter Abelard (1079–1142), the famous, mostly Paris-based teacher and philosopher, particularly credited with the revival of logic (dialectic).

294. See Book 1, n. 9.

295. Col 2:3.

O you who in perpetual order govern the universe![296] Who might have hoped and who can believe that there might be peace in this year without great bloodshed? Especially since Lord Otto, impelled by the counsel of certain men, had bound himself by this oath: that he would not withdraw from the burg of Vyšehrad before he either suffered capital punishment, vanquished, or obtained the summit of the princely seat as a victor. But our Lord Jesus Christ, who brings the counsel of princes to nothing and rejects them,[297] mercifully arranged through the merits of the most holy martyr, Václav, what your charity knows well enough from what I said above.

And therefore the good duke now ceased to be displeased or angry with his brother Otto. He believed everything to be governed by God's reason and nothing to be possible without him. But since, as Solomon bears witness, anger rests in the bosom of a fool,[298] far be it from the most reverend Duke Soběslav that he should stain his extraordinary virtues through anger and displeasure, or defile his virtuous deeds through impatience. Truly, if anyone troubles to describe them one at a time, in his praise, the daylight and the page would desert him[299] before he could complete the work begun. Nevertheless, we make known to your charity one special thing as his memorial, an act for which he is surely to be preferred to almost everyone else: that a duke of such great power never wet his lips with mead, the plunderer of the mind. Surely it is no small virtue for any powerful man to bridle his mouth,[300] and not spurn natural drink as lees but [see] its enticements.

3.61. On 20 May of the same year, on Thursday in the most holy week of Pentecost, a great snow descended upon certain forested places. On the subsequent days it shuddered with a great cold and all kinds of fruits, especially those sown in autumn, as well as vineyards and trees, were greatly damaged, such that in

296. Boethius, *Consolation of Philosophy*, book 3, meter 9.1, verbatim.
297. Ps 32:10.   298. Eccl 7:10.
299. See Book 2, n. 105.   300. Jas 1:26.

many places orchards had been dug up from the roots and the smaller streams hardened with ice from the cold.

On Saturday the same week, 23 May, Emperor Henry IV [V] died. His and the imperial lineage failed there, partly from the sterility of the feminine sex, partly with every masculine royal descendent ended, cut off at a young age by withering fate.[301]

3.62. Meanwhile, as we step back from these heroic chronicles—peace having been established by the illustrious Duke Soběslav in his whole realm through God's grace—let us report how a certain priest extinguished the provocative flames in his chest through the burning of raw plants. He told me this himself, privately and familiarly, and asked through Christ and as a friend that I bring him forward with no name. I do so because I believe his life demonstrates faith through praiseworthy words.

He said that, after the Lord received him into the priesthood, he promised God with a devoted mind that he would no longer know any woman. But since it is very difficult to turn away completely from a habitual frame of mind, such a great temptation of the flesh assailed him—I don't know how many years afterward—that having almost forgotten the vow he pledged to God, he had nearly fallen into the devil's snare,[302] conquered by desire. What should he do? He had once read in the *Dialogue*,[303] how Saint Benedict had restrained the burning of his enemy flesh through the fire of nettles. When by celestial grace he suddenly looked upon and came to himself,[304] seeking but not finding a remote place for a similar act, he gathered a bundle of nettles stealthily, secretly sought out his cell, closed the little door on himself, and took off every stitch of his clothing. Ah, if anyone had seen this sane priest acting insanely, would he not have laughed, whether he wanted to or not, even if he had buried a dear parent that very day? Surely

301. Henry V indeed died, on 23 May 1125, without heirs. His successor would be Lothar of Supplinberg (d. 1137), duke of Saxony, mentioned above in 3.52, 53, and 56. See Weinfurther, *Salian Century*, 180; Haverkamp, *Medieval Germany*, 137–38.

302. 1 Tm 3:7.   303. Gregory *Dialogues* 2:2.

304. See Book 1, n. 157.

no furious master raged so much at his pupil, no angry lord at his servant, as this priest did at himself. Inflamed against himself and made senseless from anger, he raged with nettles at his genitals as well as his behind. From there he returned to his heart[305] and, raging cruelly at his innards, said: "You always torture me, you, most wicked heart! Now this way I will torture you. Evil thoughts—adulteries, fornications, and lusts—go out of you."[306] Making this satisfaction with his fury, the enraged priest lay dying for three days feeling great pain. Reckoning that he had not done enough for the cure of his soul, he gathered a bundle of nettles and hung them up in his room, so that he would always have them before his eyes. As often as he caught sight of them, whether hanging or cut down or flourishing along the road, his heart trembled and, internally reminded of evil, his evil thoughts vanished.

Let us turn the rage of this imitable priest toward the guarding of virtues. What he worked in the body, let us work in the mind. The Lord's eloquence is truth-speaking eloquence, when he says: "My father works until now, and I work."[307] Behold, while he burned externally by punishment, because he had burned with passion illicitly within, the priest extinguished it through God's grace. He conquered sin because he changed the fire.

COLOPHON. Let all the faithful of Christ know that the compiler of this chronicle, namely, Cosmas, the most reverend dean of the church of Prague, died on 12 October of the same year in which Soběslav was enthroned.

305. Cf. Is 46:8 ("Return, ye transgressors, to the heart").
306. Cf. Mt 15:19 on the heart as the source of all such evil; also, Book 2, n. 43.
307. Jn 5:17.

BIBLIOGRAPHY

Primary Sources

Ammianus Marcellinus. *Ammianus Marcellinus.* Translated by J. C. Rolfe. 3 vols. Cambridge, Mass.: Harvard University Press, 1937.

Augustine. *In Johannem Evangelium tractatus CXXIV.* Edited by Radbodus Willems. Corpus Christianorum 36. Turnhout: Brepols, 1954.

———. *Unfinished Commentary on the Epistle to the Romans.* In *Augustine on Romans.* Edited and translated by Paula Fredriksen Landes. Chico, Calif.: Scholars Press, 1982.

Boethius. *The Consolation of Philosophy.* In *Boethius,* trans. S. J. Tester, 130–435. Cambridge, Mass.: Harvard University Press, 1973.

Bruno of Querfurt. *S. Adalberti pragensis episcopi et martyris, vita altera.* Edited by Jadwiga Karwasińska. Monumenta Poloniae Historica, new series, vol. 4, fasc. 2. Warsaw: Państwowe wydawnictwo naukowe, 1969.

———. *Vita quinque fratrum eremitarum.* Edited by Jadwiga Karwasińska. Monumenta Poloniae Historica, new series, vol. 4, fasc. 3. Warsaw: Państwowe wydawnictwo naukowe, 1973.

Cicero. *On the Nature of the Gods.* Translated by P. G. Walsh. Oxford: Clarendon Press, 1997.

Codex diplomaticus et epistolaris regni bohemiae. Vol. 1. Edited by Gustav Friedrich. Prague: Sumptibus Comitiorum Regni Bohemiae, 1907.

Cosmas of Prague. *Cosmae pragensis chronica boemorum.* Edited by Bertold Bretholz. Monumenta Germaniae Historica, Scriptores rerum Germanicarum, new series, vol. 2. Berlin: Weidmann, 1923.

Crescente fide. Edited by J. Truhlář. Fontes rerum bohemicarum, 1:183–90. Prague: Nakladatelství Musea Království českého, 1973.

Disticha Catonis. Edited by Marcus Boas. Amsterdam: North-Holland, 1952.

Gesta principum polonorum/Deeds of the Princes of the Poles. Translated by Paul W. Knoll and Frank Schaer. Budapest: Central European University Press, 2003.

Graus, František. "*Necrologium bohemicum—Martyrologium pragense* a stopy nekosmovského pojetí českých dějin." *Československý časopis historický* 15 (1967): 789–810.

Gregory the Great. *Dialogues.* Translated by Odo John Zimmerman. Fathers of the Church 39. New York: Fathers of the Church, 1959.

Horace. *Odes and Epodes.* Translated by C. E. Bennett. Cambridge, Mass.: Harvard University Press, 1914.

————. *Satires and Epistles.* Translated by Smith Palmer Bovie. Chicago: University of Chicago Press, 1959.

————. *The Art of Poetry.* Translated by Burton Raffel, with James Hind and David Armstrong. Albany: State University of New York Press, 1974.

Isidore of Seville. *Etimologías.* Edited and translated by José Oroz Reta and Manuel-A. Marcos Casquero. 2 vols. Madrid: Editorial Católica, 1982.

Jerome. *Apologie contre Rufin.* Edited and translated by Pierre Lardet. Paris: Cerf, 1983.

————. *Praefatio Hieronymi in Ezram.* PL 28:1471–74.

Johannes Canaparius. *Vita antiquior (passio Sancti Adalberti martiris Christi).* Edited by G. H. Pertz. Monumenta Germaniae Historica, Scriptores, 4:581–95. Hanover: Hahn, 1841.

Justin. *Epitoma historiarum philippicarum Pompei Trogi.* Edited by Otto Seel. Stuttgart: Teubner, 1972.

Juvenal. *Satires.* In *Juvenal and Persius.* Edited and translated by Susan Morton Braund. Cambridge, Mass.: Harvard University Press, 2004.

Juvencus. *Libri evangeliorum quattuor.* Edited by Karl Marold. Leipzig: Teubner, 1886.

Kanovník Vyšehradský. Edited by Josef Emler. Fontes rerum bohemicarum, 2:203–37. Prague: Nakladatelství Musea Království českého, 1874.

Kantor, Marvin. *The Origins of Christianity in Bohemia.* Evanston: Northwestern University Press, 1990.

Kristiánova legenda. Edited by Jaroslav Ludvíkovský. Prague: Vyšehrad, 1978.

Leo Marsicanus. *Chronica monasterii casinensis.* Edited by W. Wattenbach. Monumenta Germaniae Historica, Scriptores, 7:551–727. Hanover: Hahn, 1846.

Livy. *Livy.* Translated by B. O. Foster. Vol. 1. New York: Putnam, 1919.

Lucan. *De bello civili.* Edited by D. R. Shackleton Bailey. Stuttgart: Teubner, 1988.

————. *Pharsalia.* Translated by Jane Wilson Joyce. Ithaca: Cornell University Press, 1993.

Mnich Sázavský. Edited by Josef Emler. Fontes rerum bohemicarum, 2:238–69. Prague: Nakladatelství Musea Království českého, 1874.

Ovid. *Metamorphoses.* Translated by Frank Justus Miller. 2 vols. Cambridge, Mass.: Harvard University Press, 1977.

————. *Tristia* and *Ex ponto.* Translated by Arthur Leslie Wheeler. 2d ed. Cambridge, Mass.: Harvard University Press, 1988.

Paul the Deacon. *The History of the Lombards.* Translated by William Dudley Foulke. Philadelphia: University of Pennsylvania Press, 1907.

Persius. *Satires.* In *Juvenal and Persius.* Edited and translated by Susan Morton Braund. Cambridge, Mass.: Harvard University Press, 2004.

Phaedrus. *The Fables.* Translated by P. F. Widdows. Austin: University of Texas Press, 1992.

Plautus. *Plautus.* Translated by Paul Nixon. 5 vols. Cambridge, Mass.: Harvard University Press, 1950.

Propertius. *Elegies.* Edited and translated by G. P. Goold. Cambridge, Mass.: Harvard University Press, 1990.

Prudentius. *Prudentius.* Edited and translated by H. J. Thomson. 2 vols. Cambridge, Mass.: Harvard University Press, 1949.

Quintus Curtius. *Quintus Curtius.* Edited and translated John C. Rolfe. 2 vols. Cambridge, Mass.: Harvard University Press, 1956.

Regino of Prüm. *Reginonis abbatis Prumiensis Chronicon cum continuatione Treverensis.* Edited by F. Kurze. Monumenta Germaniae Historica, Scriptores rerum Germanicarum in usum scholarum 50. Hanover: Hahn, 1890.

Sallust. *Sallust.* Edited and translated by J. C. Rolfe. Cambridge, Mass.: Harvard University Press, 1931.

Sedulius. *Opera omnia.* Edited by Johannes Huemer. Corpus Scriptorum Ecclesiasticorum Latinorum, vol. 10. Vienna: Gerold, 1885.

Silius Italicus. *Punica.* Translated by J. D. Duff. 2 vols. Cambridge, Mass.: Harvard University Press, 1934.

Staročeská kronika tak řečeného Dalimila. Edited by Jiří Daňhelka, Karel Hádek, Bohuslav Havránek, and Naděžda Kvítová. 3 vols. Prague: Academia, 1988.

Statius. *Statius.* Edited and translated by D. R. Shackleton Bailey. 3 vols. Cambridge, Mass.: Harvard University Press, 2003.

Terence. *Terence.* Edited and translated by John Barsby. 2 vols. Cambridge, Mass.: Harvard University Press, 2001.

Thietmar of Merseburg. *Ottonian Germany: The* Chronicon *of Thietmar of Merseburg.* Translated by David A. Warner. Manchester: Manchester University Press, 2001.

Die Urkunden Heinrichs IV. Vol. 2. Edited by D. von Gladiss. Monumenta Germaniae Historica, Diplomata 6. Weimar: Böhlau, 1959.

Valerius Flaccus. *Valerius Flaccus.* Translated by J. H. Mozley. Cambridge, Mass.: Harvard University Press, 1934.

Virgil. *The Aeneid.* Prose translation by David West. Harmondsworth, UK: Penguin, 1990.

———. *Virgil.* Translated by H. Rushton Fairclough. Revised by G. P. Goold. 2 vols. Cambridge, Mass.: Harvard University Press, 1999.

Die Vita sancti Heinrici regis et confessoris *und ihre Bearbeitung durch den Bamberger Diakon Adelbert.* Edited by Marcus Stumpf. Monumenta Germaniae Historica, Scriptores rerum Germanicarum in usum scholarum, vol. 69. Hanover: Hahn, 1999.

Secondary Sources

Albu, Emily. *The Normans in Their Histories: Propaganda, Myth and Subversion.* Woodbridge, UK: Boydell Press, 2001.

Althoff, Gerd. *Otto III.* Translated by Phyllis G. Jestice. University Park: Pennsylvania State University Press, 2003.

Bláhová, Marie. "The Function of the Saints in Early Bohemian Historical Writing." In *The Making of Christian Myths in the Periphery of Latin Christendom (c. 1000–1300),* ed. Lars Boje Mortensen, 83–119. Copenhagen: Museum Tusculanum Press, 2006.

Bowlus, Charles. *The Battle of Lechfeld and Its Aftermath, Augsburg 955.* Aldershot, UK: Ashgate, 2006.

Brandmüller, Walter, ed. *Handbuch der bayerischen Kirchengeschichte.* Vol. 1. St. Ottilien, Germany: EOS Verlag, 1998.

Bresslau, Harry. *Handbuch der Urkundenlehre für Deutschland und Italien.* Vol. 2. Berlin: De Gruyter, 1958.

Brunner, Karl. *907–1156: Herzogtümer und Marken, vom Ungarnsturm bis ins 12. Jahrhundert.* Vienna: Überreuter, 1994.

Bynum, Caroline Walker. *Docere verbo et exemplo: An Aspect of Twelfth-Century Spirituality.* Harvard Theological Studies 31. Missoula, Mont.: Scholars Press, 1979.

Conte, Gian Biagio. *Latin Literature: A History.* Translated by Joseph B. Solodow. Revised by Don Fowler and Glenn W. Most. Baltimore: Johns Hopkins University Press, 1994.

Davis, R. H. C. *The Normans and Their Myth.* London: Thames & Hudson, 1976.

Deliyannis, Deborah Mauskopf, ed. *Historiography in the Middle Ages.* Leiden: Brill, 2003.

Dendorfer, Jürgen. *Adelige Gruppenbildung und Königsherrschaft: Die Grafen von Sulzbach und ihr Beziehungsgeflecht im 12. Jahrhundert.* Munich: Kommission für Bayerische Landesgeschichte, 2004.

Eberl, Immo. "Die Grafen von Berg, ihr Herrschaftsbereich und dessen adelige Familien." *Ulm und Oberschwaben* 44 (1982): 29–171.

Engel, Pál. *The Realm of St. Stephen: A History of Medieval Hungary, 895–1526.* Translated by Tamás Pálosfalvi. Edited by Andrew Ayton. London: Tauris, 2001.

Geary, Patrick. *Women at the Beginning.* Princeton: Princeton University Press, 2006.

Gieysztor, Aleksander. "Medieval Poland." In Aleksander Gieysztor et al., *History of Poland,* 31–162. Translated by K. Cekalska. Warsaw: Państwowe Wydawníctwo Naukowe, 1968.

Glenn, Jason. *Politics and History in the Tenth Century: The Work and World of Richer of Reims.* Cambridge: Cambridge University Press, 2004.

Graus, František. "Kněžna Libuše—od podstavy báje k národnímu symbolu." *Československý časopis historický* 17 (1969): 817–44.

Haverkamp, Alfred. *Medieval Germany, 1056–1273.* Translated by Helga Braun and Richard Mortimer. Oxford: Oxford University Press, 1988.

Hrdina, Karel, trans. *Kosmova kronika česká.* Prague: Melantrich, 1950.

Jaeger, C. Stephen. *Envy of Angels: Cathedral Schools and Social Ideals in Medieval Europe, 950–1200.* Philadelphia: University of Pennsylvania Press, 2000.

Jurgensmeier, Friedhelm, ed. *Handbuch der Mainzer Kirchengeschichte.* Vol. 1. Speyer: Echter Verlag, 2000.

Kersken, Norbert. *Geschichtsschreibung im Europa der "Nationes" National-geschichtliche Gesamtdarstellung im Mittelalter.* Cologne: Böhlau, 1995.

Klaniczay, Gábor. *Holy Rulers and Blessed Princesses: Dynastic Cults in Medieval Central Europe.* Translated by Éva Pálmai. Cambridge: Cambridge University Press, 2000.

Kolář, Antonín. "Kosmovy vztahy k antice." *Sborník Filosofické fakulty university komenského v Bratislavě* 3, no. 28 (1924): 21–99.

Kubů, František. "Die Grafen von Bogen in Böhmen." In *Die Anfänge der Grafen von Bogen-Windberg: Studientagung zum 850; Todestag des Grafen Albert I, 17.–18. Januar 1997,* ed. Thomas Handgrätinger, 126–45. Windberg, Germany: Poppe-Verlag, 1999.

Landes, Richard. *Relics, Apocalypse, and the Deceits of History: Ademar of Chabannes, 989– 1049.* Cambridge, Mass.: Harvard University Press, 1995.

Lechner, Karl. *Die Babenberger: Markgrafen und Herzöge von Österreich, 976–1246.* Vienna: Böhlau, 1976.

Leyser, Karl J. *Rule and Conflict in an Early Medieval Society.* Oxford: Blackwell, 1979.

Mayo, Janet. *A History of Ecclesiastical Dress.* New York: Holmes and Meier, 1984.

McKitterick, Rosamond. *History and Memory in the Carolingian World.* Cambridge: Cambridge University Press, 2004.

Novotný, Václav. *České dějiny.* Vol 1. Prague: J. Laichter, 1912–13.

The Oxford Classical Dictionary. 3d ed. Edited by Simon Hornblower and Antony Spawforth. Oxford: Oxford University Press, 1996.

Palacky, Franz. *Geschichte von Böhmen: Grösstentheils nach Urkunden und Handschriften.* Vol. 1. Prague: In Commission bei Kronberger und Ríwnac, 1836.

Pätzold, Stefan. *Die frühen Wettiner: Adelsfamilie und Hausüberlieferung bis 1221.* Cologne: Böhlau, 1997.

Riché, Pierre. *The Carolingians: A Family Who Forged Europe.* Translated by Michael Idomir Allen. Philadelphia: University of Pennsylvania Press, 1993.

Rider, Jeff. *God's Scribe: The Historiographical Art of Galbert of Bruges.* Washington, D.C.: The Catholic University of America Press, 2001.

Robinson, I. S. *Henry IV.* Cambridge: Cambridge University Press, 1999.

Rupp, Gabriele. *Die Ekkehardiner, Markgrafen von Meißen, und ihre Beziehungen zum Reich und zu den Piasten.* Frankfurt: Peter Lang, 1996.

Shopkow, Leah. *History and Community: Norman Historians in the Eleventh and Twelfth Centuries.* Washington, D.C.: The Catholic University of America Press, 1997.

Smalley, Beryl. *Historians in the Middle Ages.* London: Thames and Hudson, 1974.

Třeštík, Dušan. "Kosmas a Regino." *Československý časopis historický* 8 (1960): 564–87.

———. *Kosmas.* Prague: Svobodné slovo, 1966.

———. *Kosmova Kronika: Studie k počátků m českého dějepisectví a politického myslení.* Prague: Academia, 1968.

———. *Mýty kmene čechů.* Prague: Lidové Noviny, 2003.

Tyroller, Franz. *Genealogie des altbayerischen Adels im Hochmittelalter.* Göttingen: Heinz Reise, 1962.

Uhlirz, Karl. *Die Jahrbücher des Deutschen Reiches under Otto II und Otto III.* Vol. I, *Otto II: 973–83.* Leipzig: Königliche Akademie der Wissenschaften, 1902.

Van Engen, John. *Rupert of Deutz.* Berkeley and Los Angeles: University of California Press, 1983.

Webber, Nick. *The Evolution of Norman Identity, 922–1154.* Woodbridge, UK: Boydell Press, 2005.

Weinfurter, Stefan. *Heinrich II (1002–1024): Herrscher am Ende der Zeiten.* Regensburg: Pustet, 1999.

————. *The Salian Century: Main Currents in an Age of Transition.* Translated by Barbara Bowlus. Philadelphia: University of Pennsylvania Press, 1999.

Wojciechowska, Maria, trans. *Kosmasa Kronika Czechów.* Warsaw: Państwowe Wydawnictwo Naukowe, 1968.

Wolfram, Herwig. *Konrad II, 990–1039: Kaiser dreier Reiche.* Munich: C. H. Beck, 2000.

Wolverton, Lisa. *Hastening Toward Prague: Power and Society in the Medieval Czech Lands.* Philadelphia: University of Pennsylvania Press, 2001.

INDEX

Barnabas, Polish martyr, 96–100
basilisk, 244–45
Bavaria, Bavarians, 124, 162, 185, 198n61,
214, 227, 235n225, 244. *See also* Arnulf;
Bertold; Rapoto II; Welf V
Bechyně, 39
Bela, village of, 235
Beleč, 155
Belial, 237
Bělin, 232
Bellona, 55–56, 126
Beneda, 166–68
Benedict VII, pope, 72n191, 160–61
Benedict IX, pope, 120n62
Benedict, Polish martyr, 96–100
Benedict, St. , 252; Rule of, 71, 73
Benno I, bishop of Meissen, 167
Berecynthia, 43
Berengar I, count of Sulzbach, 202, 221
Bertold, duke of the Bavarians, 70
Bertold, warrior, 12n24, 238
Bílina, burg, 128, province, 54; river, 45,
127
Bobr, river, 244
Bobřané, 162
Boemus, Bohemus, 36
Boethius, *Consolation of Philosophy*, 10n17,
32n14, 37n38, 38n46, 48n87, 88n266,
142n143, 210n126, 229n196, 251n296
Boii, 25, 36n34
Boleslav I, "the Cruel," duke of Bohe-
mia, xvi, xvii, 64–71, 77n213, 130
Boleslav II, duke of Bohemia, xvi, xvii,
71–73, 75, 77, 80–81, 83–87, 104
Boleslav III, duke of Bohemia, xvi, xvii,
85, 87–90, 105, 112n13
Boleslav, son of Vratislav II, xvi, 139, 171
Boleslav, burg. *See* Stará Boleslav; Mladá
Boleslav
Bolesław Chrobry, duke of Poland,
81n225, 83n237, 87n260, 88n264,
90n272, 92n282, 96n297, 104, 112n13,
120n60

Bolesław, son of Kazimierz of Poland,
111, 139
Bolesław III "Wrymouth," duke of
Poland, 3n2, 160, 184–85, 191, 199, 214,
223, 226, 229–30, 238, 246n272
Bořivoj I, duke of Bohemia, xvi, xvii, 33,
53, 63–64
Bořivoj II, duke of Bohemia, xvi, xvii,
8–9, 91, 139, 190–91, 193, 196–97, 199–
200, 202–10, 216–19, 221, 233–34, 241
Borša, 173, 235
Bořut, son of Božej, 212
Božej, son of Čáč, 187, 196–97, 204,
210–12
Božen, father of Smil, 143–44
Božena (Křesina), wife of Oldřich, 92,
129
Božetěcha, wife of Cosmas of Prague,
12, 233
Braniš, 166
Bratislava, 208n119. *See also* Pozsony
Bretholz, Bertold, 18, 144n150, 180n279
Břetislav I, duke of Bohemia, xvi, xvii,
6–7, 9, 33, 54n118, 92, 101–6, 109–13,
115–19, 121–22, 127–31, 133, 135, 139, 142,
173n256, 223, 229n197; decrees, 115n136
Břetislav II, duke of Bohemia, xvi, xvii,
7–8, 139, 164–65, 171–73, 175–77,
179–80, 182–96, 210, 236
Břetislav, son of Břetislav II, xvi, 195n53,
227
Břevnov, monastery at, 109, 246
Březnice, stream, 53
Brno, 171, 191
Bruno of Querfurt, *Vita Adalberti*, 50n96,
66n167, 81n225, 82n233, 83n237,
86n250, 143n148; *Vita quinque fratrum
eremitarum*, 96n297
Bruno, daughter of, 131
Brusnice, stream, 49, 132, 218
Buben, village, 201
Budivoj, son of Chren, 203
Bug, river, 162

The Chronicle of the Czechs was designed and typeset in Centaur by Kachergis Book Design of Pittsboro, North Carolina. It was printed on 60-pound EB Natural and bound by Edwards Brothers of Lillington, North Carolina.